MW00568707

Historic Unionville

A Village in the City

GEORGE DUNCAN

DUNDURN

TORONTO

Copyright © George Duncan, 2015

All rights reserved. No part of this publication may be reproduced, stored in a retrieval system, or transmitted in any form or by any means, electronic, mechanical, photocopying, recording, or otherwise (except for brief passages for purpose of review) without the prior permission of Dundurn Press. Permission to photocopy should be requested from Access Copyright.

Editor: Cheryl Hawley
Interior design: Laura Boyle
Cover design: Laura Boyle
Cover image credit: William Eckardt House, circa 1856, City of Markham
Printer: Webcom
Unless otherwise noted all photos were taken by the author.

Library and Archives Canada Cataloguing in Publication
Duncan, George, 1958-, author
Historic Unionville : a village in the city / George Duncan.

Includes bibliographical references and index. Issued in print and electronic formats. ISBN 978-1-4597-3163-9 (paperback).--ISBN 978-1-4597-3164-6 (pdf)--978-1-45973-165-3 (epub)

    1. Unionville (Markham, Ont.)--History. 2. Historic sites--Ontario--Markham. I. Title.

FC3099.U59D85 2015   971.3'547   C2015-900559-0
                                       C2015-900560-4

1 2 3 4 5   19 18 17 16 15

Conseil des Arts du Canada | Canada Council for the Arts | Canada | ONTARIO ARTS COUNCIL CONSEIL DES ARTS DE L'ONTARIO an Ontario government agency un organisme du gouvernement de l'Ontario

We acknowledge the support of the **Canada Council for the Arts** and the **Ontario Arts Council** for our publishing program. We also acknowledge the financial support of the **Government of Canada** through the **Canada Book Fund** and **Livres Canada Books**, and the **Government of Ontario** through the **Ontario Book Publishing Tax Credit** and the **Ontario Media Development Corporation**.

Care has been taken to trace the ownership of copyright material used in this book. The author and the publisher welcome any information enabling them to rectify any references or credits in subsequent editions.
—*J. Kirk Howard, President*

The publisher is not responsible for websites or their content unless they are owned by the publisher.

Printed and bound in Canada.

Visit us at
Dundurn.com | @dundurnpress
Facebook.com/dundurnpress | Pinterest.com/dundurnpress

Dundurn
3 Church Street, Suite 500
Toronto, Ontario, Canada
M5E 1M2

Historic Unionville

To the people who recognized that Unionville is a special place
worth preserving, before it was too late

Contents

Unionville's Golden Age

Unionville's Second Century

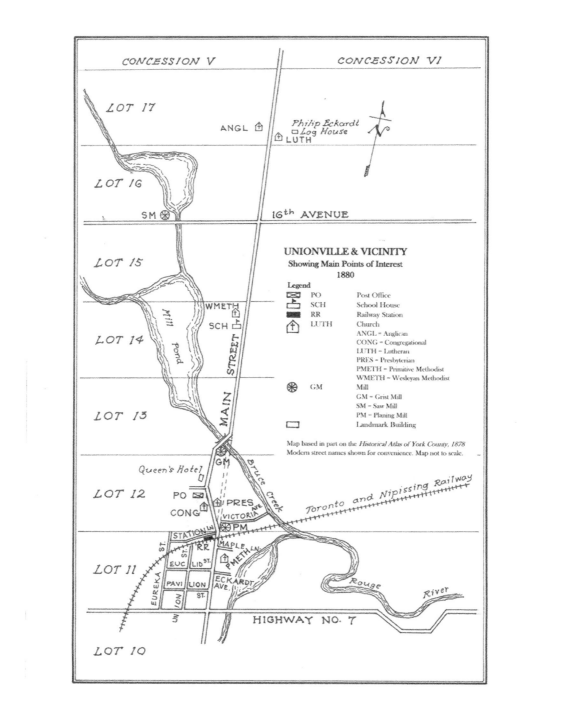

Acknowledgements

Historic Unionville began with the encouragement of Barry Penhale and Jane Gibson of Natural Heritage Books, with their suggestion that I author a book about the historical buildings of Markham, as I was well-placed for such an undertaking as Markham's senior heritage planner. A book about the historical buildings of Unionville seemed a natural choice for a topic that would capture the imagination of anyone interested in early Ontario architecture and the stories behind the buildings. As the project began to take shape, it quickly became apparent to me that a great deal of primary-source research was needed to confirm the existing historical accounts and, wherever possible, expand further on the facts and folklore behind Unionville's architectural treasures. To that end, the extraordinary helpful and knowledgeable archival staff of the Markham Museum, including at different times

Janet Reid, Corey Everrett, Katey Watson, and Mark Scheibmayr, provided access to the fragile and exceedingly valuable old records that provide a first-hand account of the community's past. Markham's official historian, Lorne R. Smith, a direct descendant of early settlers of Markham Township, kindly agreed to provide a foreword for the book and also carefully read through the draft typescript to point out matters requiring clarification or correction. At times when the thread of history was lost, Lorne, with his far-reaching knowledge of the community and local authorities, made enquiries on my behalf and helped me to piece together some forgotten fragments of Unionville's fascinating past. Doug Denby, a local authority on Unionville's development, shared his valuable insights into fire insurance maps that chronicle changes within the commercial centre of the village. My colleagues at the City of Markham, Regan Hutcheson, manager of heritage planning, and Peter Wokral, heritage planner, were patient sounding boards for a number of research conundrums I encountered as I tried to sort out the sometimes complex histories of some well-known sites. Thanks and appreciation is also due to my wife, Linda, for her role in the same regard.

The vast files of the City of Markham's Heritage Section, dating from the mid-1970s when the Heritage Markham municipal heritage advisory committee was formed, were generously made available to me to provide the foundation for all of the building histories contained in this book. It is truly amazing how much information lies pressed within the scores of file folders that are maintained for each historic property. It would be difficult to acknowledge and thank all of the researchers, student, professional, and amateur, who have contributed to the contents of those files without leaving out a name, as numerous as they are. To all those fellow seekers of local history, thank you, and to the staff of Dundurn, thank you as well for allowing my project to capture your imaginations and for shepherding me so graciously through the publication process.

Foreword

I grew up just northeast of the village of Unionville. From my earliest recollections from the 1940s, Unionville was the service centre for our farm. We bought our groceries at the Brown and Connell general stores. We bought our hardware from Perkins Hardware. We bought our Cockshutt tractor and implements from Wilbur Latimer. I got my first haircut from Mr. Findlay at the Queen's Hotel. We skated at the Crosby Arena. We visited Stiver Bros. Feed Mill to have our grain ground and to buy our chicken feed, coal, and garden seeds. Our baby chicks came into the train station. Bethesda Lutheran Church on Union Street was our church. This church, in different buildings over the years, has been serving the Unionville community since 1794 when my ancestor, Francis Schmidt, came here with William Berczy and was a member of the first congregation.

One of my earliest recollections of Unionville was my first haircut at the hotel. I cried the entire time — here was this stranger cutting off my hair! My previous experience with hair-cutting had been my father, who used the cattle clippers. This time I was having it "professionally" cut. Later I came to realize that this barbershop was a very interesting place, with lots of candy bars, magazines, comic books, knickknacks, and little things that children like to look at. Next door was the pool hall where only the "big boys" went for entertainment.

What is now Jake's Pub was the home of Mrs. C.H. Stiver, who lived with her two unmarried daughters, Helen and Dorothy. In the weeks leading up to Christmas, the children from Bethesda Lutheran Church Sunday school would gather at Mrs. Stiver's on a Saturday afternoon to practise for the Christmas Pageant. I remember the house being very dark and foreboding, with dark panelling, heavy drapes over the windows, and not many lights.

Where Il Postino Restaurant is today was the location of the Stiver Bros. office. Helen Stiver was the bookkeeper to whom we would give the cheque and receive a receipt, which we took home and put in a shoe-box for the income-tax accountant. We also purchased our spring garden seeds from Stiver Bros., from drawers in a cabinet. They would weigh out and put in a brown paper bag your requested amount of peas, beans, sweet corn, pumpkins, cucumbers, etc. There would also be a jute bag containing a couple of kinds of seed potatoes.

On our farm we raised two kinds of chickens: layers and meat birds. I am not sure where we ordered them from, but in April each year about 300 day-old chicks would arrive on the train at the Unionville station. We knew the day they were to arrive so we would drive down to the village to pick them up. The freight room would be alive with the *cheep, cheep, cheep* of hundreds of chicks in cardboard boxes, each about twenty-four inches by twenty-four inches, waiting there for the local farmers. Of course they had to be kept warm all of the way home. Each box was sectioned into four with twenty-five chicks in each. They had to be taken home quickly and put into our warm brooder house and given feed and water. It was always amazing how few casualties there were after this long journey. Our second batch of meat birds would come in mid-summer to be ready for slaughter for Thanksgiving and Christmas.

Being at the mill and station when the steam train arrived was a real treat. I was fascinated with the huffing and puffing and escaping steam from that "live" piece of technology. The engineer was always friendly and would wave to me, a little guy watching the action. The ultimate experience was the whistle as the engineer started to move the train with a burst of steam that spun the drive wheels — steel on steel.

George Duncan has brought back these and so many other memories through his thorough descriptions of not only the buildings I used to visit but also the people who lived in and did business in them. By going back to the time of the earliest settlement using buildings and sites as markers of the past, he gives meaning to the progression of the community from its pioneer stage to a thriving village in rural Markham Township.

This publication provides an entire new historical picture of the village of Unionville, capturing the people and their interaction with each other and the community they called home over a 200-year period. Using his knowledge of the architecture of older buildings, Mr. Duncan is able to demonstrate the evolution of the built village and the people who provided the building materials and skills for its early construction. I am overwhelmed by the entrepreneurial spirit of a number of the early inhabitants of the village, particularly Frederick, William, and James Eckardt, in subdividing their properties into lots, George Robinson and Josiah Hall as ambitious builders, and the Eakin brothers and Stiver families in creating businesses to serve the community. Again, this has brought new meaning to me about the history of our village of Unionville.

It is doubtful if Markham will ever again see the spirit of entrepreneurship as once existed in the early days of this historic village. Thankfully, George Duncan has captured this vanished world in great detail, person by person, building by building. What a joy it is to be made aware of the stories of the familiar old buildings we have come to know on the streets of this intriguing place. To the author, a job well done. I hope everyone will enjoy this new publication as much as I have.

Lorne R. Smith
Official Historian, City of Markham

Introduction
Unionville — A Village in the City

Unionville is a place apart from the subdivisions and commercial strips of the modern city. It's a place you might need to search for if you don't have the exact directions. Kennedy Road, once the main street of the village, takes a generous detour to the east, swinging around the historic district of the prestigious neighbourhood that stretches far beyond the original boundaries of the nineteenth-century village.[1] On Highway 7 a series of strip malls and a converted gas station provide little indication of what lies a short distance to the north, on Main Street. If it wasn't for the sign at the street corner that proclaims "Historic Unionville," you'd probably drive right on by.

The history of Unionville is remarkably similar to the history of many other Ontario villages and towns. It began with early settlement by families of European and American origin, who with unimaginable labour cleared the land of trees and boulders for agriculture.

A midsummer afternoon on Victoria Avenue.

This pioneer stage occurred hand in hand with the establishment of saw- and gristmills adjacent to a river that provided a power source to work the machinery of the mills. The development of local resources led to the emergence of a village of tradesmen, businesses, and workers clustered around those industries. Prosperity came about with the arrival of the railway, only to be followed by a period of decline when industry and population migrated to the city. The eventual rebirth of the community thanks to suburban growth is the most recent phase of a familiar pattern that has played out here as well as in countless other places around the province.[2]

Unionville is said to have been named for the Union Mills, built circa 1840 by Ira White.

Markham Museum Archival Collection

What makes Unionville so different among other old Ontario communities is its survival in the midst of the tremendous changes that have taken place in the modern era following the Second World War. Unlike many old villages and towns that have been absorbed or even obliterated by large-scale urban and suburban development, Unionville has preserved the majority of its historic buildings and retained much of its character as a distinct village.

For a while, Unionville was a tired little village in rural Markham Township. Most of its industries had disappeared along with the horse and carriage, and its businesses were hit and miss. The development of a subdivision to the west of the village in the 1960s brought traffic and the need for better roads. In the short term, Unionville's days as a sleepy suburb combined with the lack of economic growth placed the rich heritage of older building stock in a holding pattern.[3] There was little incentive to renovate or redevelop the properties on Main Street, as the commercial focus was on Highway 7. Then, around the time of Canada's Centennial, people from Toronto and other areas began buying some of the old Victorian homes along Main Street and restoring them to their former glory. The growing interest in what was then commonly referred to as "Canadiana" led to the opening of a good number of antique shops in some of the old stores and homes, and Unionville became known as the self-proclaimed antique capital of Ontario.[4]

Unionville has miraculously remained an oasis of restored century homes and shops clustered around its unique meandering main street that began as a lane leading to the Union Mills. Its collection of historical buildings spanning over two centuries, representing

Markham Museum Archival Collection

Many of the buildings seen in this picturesque early view of Unionville's distinctive, winding Main Street still stand today.

most of the major stylistic influences that shaped Ontario's architecture in that same period, is a carefully tended treasure. The valleylands to the east provide a green backdrop to the commercial area while acting as a natural barrier to development that has contributed to the preservation of some of the more modest heritage buildings on Main Street. But Unionville is not a museum village or frozen in time — it's a living community that has preserved the best of the past while adapting to the present.

The preservation of Unionville did not happen by accident. Suburban development exerted a great deal of pressure for road improvements. York County planned to widen Kennedy Road to a four-lane thoroughfare in the 1960s, and it was quickly recognized by the local residents that their quaint main street, with its picturesque old shops and shady trees, would be changed forever.[5]

It has been said that nothing stands in the way of roads, but in this case that assumption proved wrong. With the historic value of Unionville highlighted to the municipal administration through the efforts of the Unionville Conservation and Development Association, a Kennedy Road bypass was proposed and put in place. The annual Unionville Festival, which began in 1970 and continues to this day on the first Saturday in June, showcased Unionville to the greater Markham community and beyond, and in time the village became a popular day-trip destination for people in the Greater Toronto Area.[6] Restaurants joined the antique and gift shops, and later more restaurants

City of Markham photograph

The Unionville House restaurant and tea house was a project of the community-based Unionville Conservation and Development Association in the 1970s.

appeared alongside stores selling high-end fashions, coffee, ice cream, and artisan candy. The mix of commercial enterprises continues to evolve on Main Street Unionville.

In 1997, after many years of meetings and proposals for the implementation of a formal structure to ensure Unionville's preservation, the Unionville Heritage Conservation District was put into place by Markham Council.[7] The protection and restoration of the heritage buildings, and the inevitable changes to buildings and properties that must occur to keep them in active use, are guided by a district plan that acts as a kind of recipe book to ensure the area's flavour remains intact and vibrant.

Today, new pressures and challenges are being brought to Unionville's preservation. Unionville's appeal has generated high property values and expensive commercial rents, which sometimes are at odds with the modest scale of the older buildings. There is a price to be paid for "gentrification," and that is the temptation to overdevelop and alter the village-like scale of buildings that had a humble beginning. A three-room mill worker's cottage once worth a couple of hundred dollars is now a property worth well over a million! How times have changed.[8]

The history of Unionville is best told through the buildings that remain from the earliest period of settlement through to the present day. Each site embodies the stories of the community, remembered in a mixture of fact and folklore that colours our view of the people, places, and events of the past.[9]

The Buildings of Unionville

Unionville is a showcase of Ontario vernacular architecture from the earliest time of settlement, through the Victorian era, and into the twentieth century and beyond.[10] Vernacular architecture, simply put, is the architecture of ordinary people — buildings that reflect local conditions at their time of construction. Vernacular buildings are not generally the work of architects; rather they represent a collaboration between the builder and the owner. They are built from locally available materials and scaled to suit the means available to the person paying for them. They blend the personal taste of the builder and owner with the influence of pattern books and existing buildings locally and abroad. Often they combine more than one architectural style, sometimes uncomfortably and sometimes with great artistic merit, as in the case of Salem Eckardt's beautiful board-and-batten house of circa 1856, at 197 Main Street.

Markham Museum Archival Collection

The builder of the old wheelwright shop at 166 Main Street dressed up a utilitarian structure with a touch of Neoclassical refinement.

Most of oldest buildings in the village reflect the Georgian architectural tradition that came to Canada from Britain and the United States. Notwithstanding the Germanic cultural background of the majority of Unionville's earliest residents, houses constructed in the community's early days were mainly designed in this conservative British-American mode of building, which stressed symmetry, simplicity, and a careful system of proportion. Variations on the basic Georgian formula, including the Neoclassic and Classic Revival, provided further inspiration to Unionville's pre-Confederation builders, particularly guiding the design of front entrances.

Another British-influenced style used for some of Unionville's first residences was the Ontario Regency Cottage, a house form that is best characterized by its one-storey height and low-pitched hipped roof. The Frederick Eckardt House at 206 Main Street, circa 1829, is a fine example of this style, and features Venetian windows and perhaps the best Neoclassical entryway in Markham.

Houses following the balanced design of the Georgian tradition were still being built well into the 1870s and 1880s, mostly for modest workers' cottages. They differed from the earlier houses of this style by having a steeper roof pitch and windows with fewer panes. For more ambitious and stylish dwellings, by the 1860s the picturesque designs of the Gothic Revival, with L-shaped plans, ornamented gables, and round or pointed-arched feature windows, became locally popular, perhaps following the example set by Salem and William Eckardt in their fine residences of the 1850s at 197 and 124 Main Street respectively.

The 1870s through the 1880s was Unionville's "gingerbread" era, when bargeboards, brackets, and other wooden ornaments dressed up many of the homes in the village and when some of the most iconic buildings were constructed. The Gothic Revival wasn't the only style employed for Unionville's late Victorian buildings. The Second Empire style, characterized by its mansard roof and dormers, was used for the Queen's Hotel of 1871 and for several residences. A fine Italianate villa with segmentally headed windows, hipped roof, and bracketed eaves was constructed in 1873 for the owner of the village planing mill.

As Victorian Ontario transitioned into the twentieth century, a movement toward the simplification of architecture was underway. The patterned brick, board and batten, and fretwork of the 1870s and 1880s gave way to new houses of plain red brick, dressed up with the clean lines of Edwardian Classical design for porch columns and cornices, and influenced by the Arts and Crafts movement and Prairie style in the design of windows and doors. Windows became larger, and often had no pane divisions at all. Irregular floor plans, well-suited to the picturesque outlines of the Gothic Revival, were replaced with compact, functional "foursquare" plans, and the one-and-a-half-storey height that prevailed from the earliest time period to the 1890s was discarded in favour of full two- and two-and-a-half-storey heights. Larger, more prestigious, houses such as the home of Charles Howard Stiver, 1907, retain vestiges of late Victorian house forms, with elements of the Queen Anne Revival reflected in its irregular plan, steep hipped roof, and patterned-shingled gables.

To a student of the architecture of old Ontario, Unionville is a three-dimensional guidebook of building styles, construction techniques, and cultural influences. The preservation of such a wide range of heritage buildings in a single community is truly remarkable.

Unionville's Legacy of Historical Research

This book builds on the excellent work of generations of historians, both amateur and professional, who many years ago recognized the cultural heritage value of Unionville and assembled an impressive legacy of research on the community and its architectural treasures. An excellent overview of Unionville's history can be found in the books *Markham, 1793–1900* and *Markham Remembered*, both published by the Markham District Historical Society. A walking tour of old Unionville, published by the Unionville Historical Society in 1988, describes the history of most of the older buildings in the commercial and residential areas of the village. Further knowledge of these sites is contained in the Building Inventory that forms a companion to the *Unionville Heritage Conservation District Plan* of 1997.

The foundation of *Historic Unionville* is this legacy of historical research, but the historical accounts in this book are not mere compilations of existing secondary sources. In each case, primary sources have been revisited and building histories have been re-examined by digging deeper into early records and adding and clarifying details. Sometimes accepted stories of some of Unionville's historical buildings have needed to be questioned and updated with new information, resulting in the reinterpretation of a few of the existing published accounts. Even so, there are some things that we may never know for certain, such as the year when Gottlieb Eckardt's brick wheelwright shop at 166 Main Street was actually built. There are at least three dates that have appeared in print for this landmark structure.

Deed abstracts and deeds, census records, township directories, early maps, and township assessment rolls represent the core of primary research sources used as the basis for the building histories in *Historic Unionville*. A limited number of available contemporary accounts and reminiscences of long-time residents have provided valuable social history to flesh out the hard facts of the official records. Some puzzles have been figured out by better understanding family relationships and their connection with buildings and properties.

Historic Unionville differs from previous publications about Unionville in that sites outside of the village proper, also important to the overall story, have been included. Some modern-era buildings have also been included to illustrate the ongoing nature of history and to highlight some important themes that are as much a part of Unionville's character as those of a century or more in the past. In every case, the buildings that have been selected to appear in this book are signposts to stories of people and places, as well as sites of architectural beauty and interest.

The Eckardt log house photographed over one hundred years ago, in its earlier, two-storey form.

Markham Museum Archival Collection

Pre-Confederation Unionville

The early history of Unionville is in many ways the story of one leading family from William Berczy's group of German-speaking settlers, the Eckardts. About 1808 Philip Eckardt established himself on a hilltop farm north of the present-day village. Many of the buildings that remain from the time of Unionville's formative period were originally owned by the sons of Philip Eckardt and Ann Elizabeth Koepke. The Upper Canada Rebellion of 1837 was a time of uncertainty in the community, but not long after the construction of a sawmill and a gristmill on the banks of a tributary of the Rouge River helped a village to emerge around these first signs of development.

Philip and Ann Elizabeth Eckardt Log House, 60 Aksel Rinck Drive, circa 1800

Lorne Smith

Philip Eckardt Log House.

Where historic buildings are concerned, people are always interested in knowing about the oldest one, the first house that serves to mark the beginning of the community. When the Eckardt log house was built, the first European settlers were getting themselves established in a new land that would be "home" for their families for generations. The Aboriginal peoples who once populated this area in palisade-enclosed villages of bark-covered long houses, who also relied on the same fertile land for agriculture, had moved northward several hundred years before the Eckardt family arrived in Markham Township, among a group of sixty-seven or so German-speaking families led by William Berczy in 1794.[1]

Initially, this group of immigrant families had hoped to settle in New York State, in a location known as the Genesee Tract.[2] When they learned that they would be tenants, not owners, of their land, these determined people approached John Graves Simcoe, lieutenant-governor of Upper Canada, to locate to British North America instead. A large number of concession blocks, each containing five 200-acre lots, were set aside for the Berczy group, and by the mid-1790s lots were allocated to individual families and the process of clearing the land of trees and stones was begun.

Lot 17 in the 6th Concession of Markham Township, the property upon which the Philip and Ann Eckardt log house stands, was first owned by Frederick Ulrich Emelius Westphalen, having been assigned to him in 1794.[3] In William Berczy's settlement records of 1803, Westphalen was noted as residing on this lot.[4] In that same year he received the Crown patent, which meant that he had completed at least the minimum requirements for being awarded the land grant, namely clearing five acres of bush, building a dwelling house of no less than sixteen by twenty feet in size, and opening the road allowance in front of the property.

Given that the construction of a modest house was a requirement for receiving title to the land, and noting that the existing house is a mere twenty-six feet square, it is quite possible that the log house generally associated with Philip Eckardt was actually built by Frederick Westphalen during his period of residency on the land.

Nevertheless, local tradition generally attributes this unique and unusual little dwelling to Philip Eckardt, who purchased the property in 1808, relocating from another lot within the Berczy settlement.

The Eckardt farm, located on a rise of land north of the older, built-up area of Unionville, is an important historical focus for the commemoration of the Berczy settlers and their contribution as the acknowledged founders of Markham. The significance of this place is such that it is sometimes called "Settlers' Hill."[5] The farm lane was located on the north side of a cemetery where many of the original Berczy settlers, as well as their descendants, have been laid to rest. In 1910 the Lutheran church that once stood next to the cemetery was dismantled and relocated into the heart of the village of Unionville for the convenience of its members.

Philip Eckardt farmed here from 1808 until his death in 1845. He was an important member of the Berczy group, contributing his diverse skills as a millwright, carpenter, surveyor, and mechanic. He became known as an important cattle breeder and lumber merchant.[6] The timber frame barn that once was the companion of the little log house, likely built by Philip Eckardt, was a tribute to his abilities as a carpenter and builder. Its golden-hued timbers, mellowed with age, were precisely shaped with axe and adze. In 2012 the barn was carefully documented and dismantled for future rebuilding in the community of Sunderland, where farming still remains the dominant land use.

For an early structure like this to survive, the descendants of Philip and Ann Elizabeth Eckardt, and later families who owned the land, must have attributed some historic, or at least sentimental, value to this modest old dwelling. The family believed that Lieutenant-Governor

John Graves Simcoe and moderate reformer William Warren Baldwin were among those who visited Philip Eckardt's hewn log residence. In fact, Albert J.H. Eckardt, Philip Eckardt's great-grandson, believed that Simcoe made several visits here to settle disputes among the Berczy group. He also credited his ancestor with being the builder of a number of important buildings and structures, including the sawmill and gristmill at German Mills, and a wharf and several log houses in the early Town of York. The home of John Graves Simcoe, and the log house known as the Scadding Cabin — moved to the Canadian National Exhibition grounds by the York Pioneer and Historical Society in 1879 — were among the significant buildings that A.J.H. Eckardt attributed to Philip Eckardt.[7]

Where on other fertile Markham Township farms the early log houses were replaced as soon as practical with more up-to-date farmhouses of frame, brick, or stone, this "first house" was left standing on its original site, not restored as a museum piece but retained as a residence. In 1948, when William Bartlett became the owner, there was some possibility that the old home's time had finally run out. A deputation of concerned citizens appeared before Markham Township Council that year to express their opinion that this historic landmark deserved to be preserved. In response, Mr. Bartlett offered the log house to anyone who would offer in trade sufficient lumber to construct a new farmhouse to serve the needs of his family.[8]

As it turned out, there was enough lumber in the later kitchen wing that had been added to the log house in the late nineteenth century to form most of the framing of a modest, new one-and-a-half-storey residence for the Bartlett family. The original building was not relocated to another site and instead was renovated for use by tenants. The logs were protected under modern claddings that disguised the structure's antiquity, and in many ways turned it into a rather ordinary-looking small house. The early six panelled doors and small, squarish original windows, with eight over eight tiny panes, were retained in the renovations, probably out of a concern for economy rather than historical authenticity.

After the Bartletts, the Beckett family, who had owned the adjoining farm to the south since 1919, purchased the property in 1950. They preserved the log house during their ownership, which lasted until 2011 when both farms were sold for the development of a new community called "Upper Unionville." This most historic of old Unionville buildings remains on its original site in the context of this large subdivision, surrounded on two sides by a park that preserves some of its predevelopment context, including a few of the mature trees and the relationship of the house to the nearby Lutheran cemetery.

The Philip and Ann Eckardt log house is a unique example of Germanic Colonial rural architecture transported to Canada via the Berczy settlers, possibly influenced by Pennsylvania Germans who were also early settlers in Markham, arriving shortly after 1800. The unusual roof design, incorporating a pent roof on the north side, appears to be derived from the vernacular domestic architecture of the Pennsylvania German culture.[9] A similar cultural influence is seen in the plank-form log construction of the walls, which uses relatively thin sections of large-diameter logs, hewn flat and joined at the corners with meticulously crafted dovetail joints. The wide overhang of the eaves is of sufficient depth to act as a porch around three sides of the building.

The architectural history of the log house presents a puzzling story. The conventional belief runs like this: the building began as a one-storey log house with a loft above. As the family grew and more living space was required, the log house was raised up on a new ground-floor level. A two-storey porch protected the north, east, and west walls. Later, a one-and-a-half-storey kitchen wing was added on the south side. In the 1940s the house was restored to its original appearance, with the removal of the later ground floor and the kitchen wing.

It is curious that such effort would be employed to add space to an existing log house by raising it in the air and building a frame structure beneath it. Archival photographs suggest that the south end of the supposedly later ground floor was cut off, and the south end of the roof of the log house ends abruptly, as if a continuation of the building had been removed. Archaeological investigations done in preparation for the transformation of the land into a community of new homes indeed revealed that prior to the late-nineteenth-century kitchen wing the house extended to the south and contained a fireplace on its end wall.[10] Was the ground floor the first stage of building, and the log portion added on top? It's a question worth considering.

The interior of the house, recently stripped of modern-era walls and ceilings, has been revealed to have been plastered directly on the inside surface of the logs. The hewn log walls were extensively chipped with a hatchet to act as keying for a plaster coating that once brightened the interior. The main room was trimmed with wainscotting, with only the ghosting of its former existence remaining impressed upon the wall surface. Since there are no cut-outs in the log walls to indicate the earlier existence of a fireplace, but there are patches in the middle of the floor, it is likely that the original fireplace and chimney were built in the centre of the house, rather than on one of the gable-end walls.

Bethesda Lutheran Cemetery, 9423 Kennedy Road, Established 1820

A blue provincial plaque that tells the story of the Berczy settlers stands near the entrance of the Bethesda Lutheran Cemetery, north of the village of Unionville. In the early days of the community, before the village began to take shape, signs of settlement were spread out along the 6th Concession Road. Farmhouses, early industries, and the church that served the largely Lutheran population of German-speaking people were spaced widely apart. For a time, it looked like the core of the village might have been centred at Hunter's Corner at Kennedy Road and 16th Avenue, where by the second quarter of the nineteenth century there were two churches, a general store, a tavern, and a sawmill. History, however, took a different turn and today the Bethesda Lutheran Cemetery seems detached from old Unionville because of how the focus of the village moved south by the 1850s.

It is fitting that Philip Eckardt, considered by historians to be the founder of Unionville, deeded a portion of his land for a Lutheran church and cemetery. He chose a picturesque site on the same hill upon which his home was built, within easy view of the homestead's west-facing windows. The earliest marked burial, dated 1803, suggests that the community had the idea of reserving this place for a burial ground long before 1820, when Philip Eckardt formally transferred ownership.[11] The first church built on this site, named St. Philip's, was constructed in that same year. Heinrich Pingel was the supervisor of construction, with many of the Berczy families contributing to the cost of the building. Some Pennsylvania German Mennonite families from the neighbourhood also provided financial support for this early place of worship.

St. Philip's was first served by the Reverend Johann Dieter Petersen, who came from Pennsylvania at the invitation of the Lutheran Church communities of York County, which included congregations in Unionville and Buttonville, in Markham Township, and Sherwood in Vaughan Township to the west.[12] The Reverend Petersen was the first full-time Lutheran clergyman in the area. Services were conducted in the German language during this formative time. After a split occurred in the congregation in 1837, due to heated political differences, after some time had passed the Lutheran church was renamed Bethesda, after the healing pool in Jerusalem described in the New Testament Gospel of John, where Jesus performed the miracle of making an infirm man whole again after thirty-eight years of being disabled.[13]

In the nineteenth century, before the advent of commercial, non-denominational cemeteries, people either buried their dead in a family plot on the farm, or in a cemetery associated with their church. Church cemeteries were an important part of the religious life of the early settlers, both as a source of comfort and of convenience, as the mortal remains of the departed faithful were never far from the continuing tradition of worship of those they left behind.

Numerous cemeteries associated with churches were established in Markham Township, as they were all across Ontario, serving a diverse range of faith groups. As churches consolidated or closed due to changing population patterns, the cemeteries of these churches were sometimes left as the only sign of a once vibrant congregation. The old grave markers, where they remain legible, provide a valuable source of genealogical information on the early families in their area. In the case of the Bethesda Lutheran Cemetery, the congregation did not fade away but continues to remain active after over two centuries. Their second church building, erected in 1862, never suffered the indignity of closure and abandonment; rather, the structure was dismantled and relocated into the heart of the village in 1910.[14]

The Bethesda Lutheran Cemetery is a place of quiet contemplation, enclosed within a low metal fence and shaded by venerable old maple and oak trees. It silently proclaims the historical associations of the site in the midst of the dramatic changes occurring in the landscape that surrounds it. Where only a few short years ago was a colourful patchwork quilt of fields cultivated by the Beckett family, new houses and streets have been constructed in the development of the Upper Unionville subdivision. Careful community design has ensured that the cemetery is buffered from some of the effects of these changes by a border of parkland. The cemetery remains in active use as a burying ground, aided by a gift of additional land on its northern side, provided by the Beckett family.

The oldest grave markers can be distinguished from the newer ones by their designs and materials. The majority of nineteenth-century markers were made from thin slabs of white marble. The softness of the stone has allowed decades of weathering to gradually wear away the inscriptions that were intended to endure indefinitely into the future. Fortunately, genealogists have taken the time to transcribe the names and dates of the deceased in recognition of the fragile nature of these simple monuments to lives lived so long ago. Some of the markers contain only words, but others are adorned with carved decoration with religious meaning or symbols of comfort or even of sorrow, including the imagery of a descending dove, a hand pointed Heavenward, clasping hands, an open Bible, a weeping willow, and others.

Newer grave markers have been made from more durable pink, grey, or black granite. Unlike their older neighbours, the more recent markers have deeply incised inscriptions and, for the most part, lack the artistic flourishes that add so much interest to the pre-1900 monuments, except for a few that have laser-etched images with subjects such as farmsteads and cottages. What has not changed in all of the time that has passed since the cemetery was established are the surnames carved in stone, commemorating the founding families of the Unionville area as well as their descendants, many of whom still reside in the general vicinity of their ancestral homes.

Eckardt-Stiver Cottage, 206 Main Street, circa 1829

Philip Eckardt's home farm was on the hill that gently rises above the village of Unionville, north of today's 16th Avenue. He must have been a successful and enterprising individual, because by the mid to late 1820s he purchased additional farm properties upon which several of his sons became established. One of these was the east half of Lot 12, Concession 5, a one-hundred-acre property that today encompasses most of the commercial centre of the village. William Berczy intended that this lot be reserved for the residence of a medical doctor to be invited to settle there. Instead, Watson Playter received the Crown patent for the lot in 1811. The property was then sold to Elizabeth Rogers in 1821. It would be many years before Dr. Thomas Philip Eckardt would establish a practice here after attaining two medical degrees.

In 1829 Philip Eckardt's son Frederick purchased the lot that his father had bought from Edward Perry of Philadelphia, the heir of Elizabeth Rogers, in 1825. Near the northeast corner of the property a one-storey adobe-brick cottage was built, most likely by Frederick Eckardt about the time of his purchase. Some sources attribute the cottage to Philip Eckardt and date it to 1825, but it seems more likely that it was constructed for his son circa 1829.

Adobe-brick, or mud-brick, construction was never common in Markham Township, but a number of houses were built in this way in the early nineteenth century. Mid-nineteenth century census records provide an idea of their distribution throughout the township before many were replaced with more up-to-date dwellings of brick or frame. Adobe brick was made in large blocks in wooden forms using a mixture of clay and straw, then left to dry in the hot sun. Given the heavy clay that underlies the fertile topsoil of Markham, ample resources were locally available for the production of adobe brick.

In the classic textbook on historic building technology in old Ontario, *Building with Wood and Other Aspects of Nineteenth-Century Building in Central Canada* by John I. Rempel, the author makes note of another prominent local example of this type of construction.[15] Rempel described the first stage of the building of the Heintzman House in Thornhill, believed to have been erected by Colonel Cruikshank about 1816, as the earliest example of adobe-brick construction in Ontario. The use of this building technology in Ontario seems to have been concentrated in York County. To protect the mud brick from the weather, houses built in this way were clad in various materials, including stucco, clapboard, or fired-clay brick.

The early history of occupancy of the Eckardt-Stiver cottage is difficult to trace. Frederick Eckardt's period of residency here seems to have been quite limited, despite the high quality of the building. By the time of Walton's directory of 1837, he was living on the west half of Lot 16, Concession 6, a Clergy Reserve property just south of the Eckardt homestead. During the Upper Canada Rebellion of that year, Frederick Eckardt, a supporter of William Lyon Mackenzie, was briefly held by the authorities for questioning, then released without charges.[16]

By 1842 Frederick Eckardt had received the Crown patent for the hundred-acre lot he had been leasing; however, the township directory for 1846 to 1847 places him back in Unionville on the adobe-brick cottage property. His stay there was brief. For most of the remainder of his life, Frederick Eckardt lived on the north farm in a one-storey brick house, though for a while in the 1860s he lived on the family homestead while his son, Tobias, worked his north Unionville farm.

The 1851 census tells us that the adobe-brick cottage in the village was tenanted by Ambrose Pennock, a labourer, who was also noted as living there in the 1861 census. In Mitchell & Co.'s directory of 1866 his occupation is given as "constable." Frederick Eckardt married Diana Pennock, so it seems probable that Ambrose Pennock was a relative by marriage. The Pennocks were neighbours of the Eckardt family, living near Hunter's Corner. It may be that the front of the cottage was clad in local clay brick during the interval between the 1851 and 1861 census, because in 1851 the building is described as a one-storey mud house, but in 1861 it is noted as a one-storey brick house.

Frederick Eckardt's nephew Philip D. Eckardt purchased the cottage in 1862. He was a son of Gottlieb

Eckardt, the owner of the wheelwright and carriage shop that still stands at 166 Main Street. Philip D. Eckardt was unmarried and lived in the household of his brother William Eckardt. According to the 1861 census, he was a farmer. In the 1871 census his occupation had changed to carriage maker. Philip D. Eckardt didn't live in the adobe-brick cottage, which continued as the rented home of Ambrose Pennock into the mid-1860s.

A story long associated with this property states that Dr. Thomas Philip Eckardt, Philip Eckardt Jr.'s son, had his residence and practice here for a period of time.[17] He grew up on the family farm south of Unionville, and at the time of the 1851 census he was nineteen years of age and living with his parents. Thomas P. Eckardt became a medical doctor after the 1851 census was taken. He moved away to pursue his medical education in the U.S. and then Toronto, but returned to Unionville in the mid-1860s. Current research suggests that Dr. Eckardt lived in the adobe-brick cottage after his marriage to Abigail Robinson in April of 1866, renting from Philip D. Eckardt. In 1872 the couple moved into a new, two-storey brick house built for them a short distance to the south, now addressed 198 Main Street.

In 1874 Daniel Burkholder, a member of a Pennsylvania German Mennonite family, purchased the Eckardt property through William Eckardt, acting on behalf of his brother Philip D. Eckardt, who had moved to California. Daniel Burkholder worked locally as a labourer and was married to Agnes Jenkins, who was the daughter of Benjamin and Maria Jenkins and the granddaughter of the Reverend William Jenkins, said to have been the first Presbyterian clergyman in Upper Canada. The Reverend Jenkins's farm was located near the crossroads community of

Cashel, north of Unionville. Jenkins preached at St. Andrew's Presbyterian Church in the community of Bendale, Scarborough Township, and Richmond Hill Presbyterian Church in the village of Richmond Hill. He was one of the few non-Anglican clergymen in Upper Canada with the authority to conduct marriages in the early nineteenth century.[18]

In 1880 Daniel Burkholder sold "Fern Cottage" to his father-in-law, Benjamin Jenkins, who immediately sold it back to his married daughter, Agnes Burkholder. Perhaps Daniel Burkholder was experiencing some financial or legal difficulty that necessitated the transfer of ownership to allow the family to stay in their home. The Burkholders had two children, Jenkins and Marein. The cottage eventually passed to Jenkins and Marein from their mother's estate.

Marein Burkholder married Charles Howard Stiver, a Unionville entrepreneur and township clerk. Their family home was next door, at 202 Main Street. In 1924 Jenkins Burkholder sold his share in the property to his sister, Marein Stiver, who was widowed by that time. Marein Stiver gave the house to her son, Ewart Jenkins Stiver, and his wife, Winifred Cassie, who were married in 1919 after Ewart J. Stiver returned from active service in the First World War. The couple probably lived here prior to the formal transfer of ownership between Jenkins Burkholder and Marein Stiver. The family made minimal changes to the historic cottage, nearly a century old by that time, preserving the building's significant original architectural details, inside and outside.

After the death of Ewart Jenkins Stiver, in 1979, the family converted the cottage into an antique and country-decor store known as the "Stiver House." The business thrived, and in the mid-1980s the building was expanded at the back with a two-storey, board-and-batten addition. In more recent times, a commercial art gallery was located in the Stiver House, a fitting neighbour to the nearby Varley Art Gallery at the top of the street.

The Eckardt-Stiver cottage is an excellent example of an Ontario Regency Cottage.[19] This is a house style most often associated with families of British origin, so it is remarkable that a family with a Germanic background would build in this form. This style was popular throughout the British Empire's colonial outposts in the early nineteenth century, and is thought to have originated in the hot climate of India. The one-storey form, with a hipped roof with a wide overhang, high ceilings, and generously sized windows, was well-suited to places with warm weather. Early settlers in Upper Canada found the summers uncomfortably hot and humid at times and designed their houses with features to help them cope with that, a reason why most Ontario Regency Cottages had shady verandahs on one to three sides. In the case of the Eckardt-Stiver Cottage, there is no evidence to suggest verandahs ever existed on this building.

The pilastered front doorcase, with its finely detailed mouldings and deep, panelled reveals, shows a Neoclassical influence characteristic of the 1820s to 1830s period in Upper Canada. Other examples of entryways as fine as this one can be seen in Niagara-on-the-Lake, but in Markham this is one of the few remaining, and may well be the best preserved. The three-part Venetian windows flanking the front door are a further indication of the refinement of the design and the skill of the builder. Inside, pine mouldings around doors and windows, and high baseboards after the style of American architect Asher Benjamin in his 1830 pattern book, are as architecturally significant and rare as they are beautiful.

Wheelwright and Carriage Shop, 166 Main Street, circa 1835

In old Ontario, in the days before the reign of the automobile, the carriage maker's shop was an essential service found in almost every village of any appreciable size. Here a diverse range of horse-drawn vehicles, from sturdy farm wagons to fine carriages and sleighs, would be made and repaired. Often the carriage maker's shop would include a blacksmith's forge, where the metal parts of the vehicles were manufactured or mended, and metal tires were installed on wooden wheels. The making of spoked wagon wheels was an art in itself, and a specialized feature of a shop such as this one. Without a doubt the wheelwright, a carefully trained tradesman, was an important person in the community. This wheelwright and carriage shop is the last of its kind still standing in Unionville as a reminder of the era of the horse-drawn vehicle.

According to local tradition, Gottlieb Eckardt built this wheelwright and carriage shop in the mid-1830s, though some sources place the date at circa 1840 or 1845.[20] Of brick construction and two storeys high, in its day this must have been one of the most substantially built premises of its kind in the township. The upper level is an indication that the building was designed for carriage building, with the main floor used for the construction of vehicles, and the upper level reserved for finishing work.

The main floor, where the forge was located, was entered through a set of double doors. With few windows to let in natural light, the glow of the forge must have been a focal point of the otherwise dim interior. On the level above, double doors provided an entry point for vehicles or parts of vehicles hoisted upstairs by block and tackle for painting and striping. The presence of additional windows on the second level provided more natural light and ventilation for the finishing work.

Gottlieb Eckardt, one of the sons of Philip Eckardt, lived on a farm at the northeast corner of what would eventually come to be called Main Street and Highway 7, a property purchased by his father in 1827. Today, this is the location of the east half of Unionville's residential quarter, bordering the shallow valley of the Rouge River. There, on the banks of the meandering river, Gottlieb Eckardt operated a sawmill, said to have been established at an early date by Philip Eckardt. The wheelwright and carriage shop was not located on Gottlieb Eckardt's property, but on that of his brother Frederick Eckardt, on the west side of Main Street. In the early days of Unionville's development, the shop marked the southerly limit of the emerging business district of the village.

Gottlieb Eckardt and some of his brothers were active supporters of William Lyon Mackenzie and his agenda for government reform. According to a family history written down in 1910 by Albert J.H. Eckardt, whose great-grandfather was Philip Eckardt, the Eckardt brothers delighted in taunting some of the staunchly Tory-minded people in the area as well as the authorities by placing American flags high up in the branches of tall elm trees north of the bridge over Bruce Creek. The American flags were supposed to have been quite an affront to those of Loyalist sentiment, and difficult to safely remove from their position in the uppermost tree branches. Government supporters had to resort to shooting the flags down from the ground while a crowd of local Reformers would jeer at them, so the story goes.

Although history does not tell us if Gottlieb Eckardt was present at Montgomery's Tavern that fateful December during the Upper Canada Rebellion of 1837, he must have been involved enough to be pursued by government forces. After the failed rebellion, Gottlieb Eckardt and his brothers travelled down the Rouge River valley to the shore of Lake Ontario, where they planned to escape to the United States by boat. Instead, the fugitives were captured and taken into custody before they could get away.[21]

Most of the Eckardt brothers were held for only a few days and were released after questioning by the authorities. Unfortunately for Gottlieb Eckardt, he was detained in jail over the winter of 1837 to 1838. He was tried and found guilty of high treason. Unlike Samuel Lount and Peter Matthews, Gottlieb Eckardt escaped execution, but was sentenced to be transported to Van Diemen's Land, since renamed Tasmania, an island now part of Australia. Before that happened, Peter

Milne Sr., magistrate at Markham Village, secured a pardon for Gottlieb Eckardt and he was released. It is said that he died before his time, due to the effect the winter incarceration had on his health.

Hewlett or Hulet, one of the sons of Gottlieb Eckardt, learned the trade at his father's side and carried on the business after his father died in 1852. The 1851 census confirms twenty-three-year-old Hewlett Eckardt's occupation as "carriage maker." The wheelwright and carriage shop and its associated property were sold by Frederick Eckardt to William Eckardt, another of Gottlieb Eckardt's sons. In 1862 John Stephenson, a blacksmith, became Hewlett Eckardt's partner in the shop. Mitchell & Co.'s directory of 1866 lists John Stephenson as a "waggon and carriage maker and general blacksmith." Hewlett Eckardt, by this time, had left Unionville for the United States and the operation of the shop was assumed by his business partner. Although John Stephenson was the owner of the business, he was a tenant on the property. When the 1871 census was taken, his occupation was given simply as "blacksmith," which is consistent with the later history of this building as being chiefly the location of a blacksmith shop.

John Stephenson went on to expand his business interests in the village with the construction of the Queen's Hotel in 1871, a little to the north of the blacksmith shop. The blacksmith shop property passed through a number of owners, with different tenant blacksmiths at the forge over the years. In 1875 John Stephenson purchased the shop he had once worked in from Alexander Thomson for $325, and rented to George C. Caldwell, a blacksmith from Markham Village, who soon had his own shop on the east side of Main Street. The shop was then sold to John Webber as part of the sale of the Queen's Hotel. Some of the later blacksmiths at this location included Arnold Martin, Alfred McPherson, Alfred Marks, and Lorne Smith.[22]

Although constructed as a utilitarian structure, the wheelwright and carriage shop was designed with a measure of refinement that shows the skill and sensibility of the builder. Its gable-fronted, symmetrical facade has doors and windows arranged in a carefully ordered pattern. Once decorated with eave returns and a fanlight over the upper-level doors, the wheelwright and carriage shop reflected the Neoclassical style in use for domestic, commercial, and institutional architecture from the time between the War of 1812 and about 1840. Turning the gable end to the street was a typical design feature for workshops and other business premises in village, town, and city settings. It was also characteristic of Neoclassical style, reminiscent of the Greek temples that were its inspiration. The sturdy brick walls of Unionville's wheelwright and carriage shop were constructed of locally produced brick, with its distinctive range of colours that vary between yellow to orange to salmon pink.

During Unionville's period as the antique capital of Ontario, the wheelwright and carriage shop housed an antique store. In more recent times, the building was converted to a fine-dining restaurant. In the process, an addition was made to the rear of the building in a complementary style, but at the same time some of the original features that remained from its days as an industrial building were removed. The loading doors on the upper level, where carriages were once raised and lowered, were made into plate-glass windows, and the multi-paned windows with bubbly early glass that added to the building's appearance of antiquity were replaced with modern windows.

Worker's Cottage, 260 Main Street, circa 1845

There is no building that better illustrates the differences between Unionville's past and present than this tiny worker's cottage. Where today some of the area's largest and most expensive homes are located, some approaching 5,000 square feet in size, were once the humble dwellings of tradesmen and workers employed in local industries.[23]

The northern portion of old Unionville, past the bridge over Bruce Creek, a residential district backing onto the picturesque greenspace of Toogood Pond, has undergone a dramatic transformation from the time when Ira White, a millwright from New York State who came to Unionville at the invitation of Peter Reesor, purchased a hundred-acre tract of land at the upper end of a settlement that later became the village of Unionville. This property, the east half of Township Lot 13, Concession 5, was valuable in the enterprising eyes of a millwright as an ideal location to harness the water power of Bruce Creek, a tributary of the Rouge River, for the construction of a sawmill and grist or flour mill.

In 1839 Ira White built a sawmill on an adjoining property, and in 1840 a gristmill on his own lot. The mills were named the "Union Mills," which was likely done in honour of the historic union of Upper and Lower Canada in 1841. When the emerging village established its first post office in 1851, the name Unionville was chosen, and the local tradition is that the mills lent their name to the community.[24] In those early days, the winding lane that led to Ira White's mill complex was called Union Street.[25]

The establishment of a milling industry provided an impetus for the formation of a village composed of mill workers, coopers, blacksmiths, and other trades and businesses. Beginning in the 1840s, Ira White began selling off small parcels of his hundred-acre lot, fronting on the west side of the 6th Concession Road, now known as Main Street. On these lots backing on the millpond, the small frame cottages of the mill workers and others of modest means were constructed. The cottage at 260 Main Street is one of these, and is the last intact example of its kind still standing in north Unionville. Although a few other heritage buildings still can be found in the area, they are later in date than the numerous frame houses from the early mill era that no longer exist.

This worker's cottage, built in a simple vernacular expression of the Ontario Regency Cottage style, is a one-storey building with a low-pitched, hipped roof. As originally constructed, it would have contained a main room as the primary living space, with one or two bedrooms off it. The kitchen was contained in a small rear wing that no longer exists. The roof, with wide overhanging eaves, is typical of the style. The symmetrical front, with a centre door flanked by six-over-six windows, has been restored after being altered through the addition of a pair of bay windows in the 1980s. The roughcast stucco replicates the original exterior finish that had long ago been replaced with vertical wood siding.

The underlying construction, revealed during restoration work, is of particular interest as an example of plank-on-plank or sawmill plank construction.[26] This mid-nineteenth-century building technology employed large quantities of inexpensive rough-sawn lumber, unquestionably a material easily available in the vicinity of a sawmill. The planks were laid flat, stacked, and nailed together, with each layer slightly offset to allow for interior and exterior plastering without the need for the application of wood-lath strips.

Measuring only sixteen by twenty feet, the cottage is the same size as the minimum house required by the early government of Upper Canada in order for an applicant to qualify for a land grant.[27] A house of this size offered only the most modest of accommodation for a family. In the case of 260 Main Street, there was no living space upstairs, due to the low pitch of the roof. The presence of a shelf chimney is a clue that this early dwelling was heated by a wood stove rather than a fireplace. When the interior was gutted of its modern wall finishes, it was revealed that the main room was decorated with a touch of elegance in the form of a chair-rail moulding.

When a new house was proposed for this desirable property in the early 2000s, the problem of how to preserve such a tiny building as part of the construction of a 4,000-square-foot executive home had to be faced in order to respond to the heritage district's policies. In the end, the solution was to convert the cottage to a free-standing garage, with the large garage doors in the back, virtually invisible from the street. The street view of the cottage was restored to its 1840s appearance as the foreground of a two-storey brick house rendered in a neotraditional architectural style.

Philip Jr. and Susannah Eckardt Farmhouse, 60 Meadowbrook Lane, circa 1845

Not many people are aware that at the end of Meadowbrook Lane, tucked in behind a cluster of 1990s townhouses, is one of Unionville's old farmhouses. The street is east of Main Street, on the south side of Highway 7, outside of the designated heritage district and therefore not well-known to visitors of Unionville. The house remains on its original fieldstone foundation and is the "still point" in an environment that has greatly changed since the property was first occupied by Philip Eckardt Jr., the Canadian-born son of Philip and Ann Elizabeth Eckardt of the log house on Settlers' Hill.

The house sits on a small remnant of the 200 acres of Lot 10, Concession 6, that was part of the hundreds of acres of land granted to William Berczy by the Crown. Philip Eckardt Sr. purchased this lot in 1827. In that same year, the western one hundred acres were deeded to his son Philip who established a farm here. According to Walton's directory of 1837, Philip Eckardt

Jr. was living on the property at that time. His brother George lived on the eastern hundred acres.

In some historical accounts, a construction date of 1823 is given for the house at 60 Meadowbrook Lane. This date was calculated when a large old maple tree that stood near the house was cut down and the number of growth rings were counted.[28] Although the house displays some early features, its solid-brick construction would have been quite unusual at a time when most other families were housed in dwellings of log or wood-frame construction. It is more likely that the present house is the second to have been built here. The brick probably would have been made on the property from local clay, before the establishment of a brickworks in the community, which didn't take place until the mid-1850s.

The first detailed records for the property are found in the 1851 census. At that time Philip Eckardt was listed as a farmer, living in a one-and-a-half-storey brick house with his wife, Susannah, and their three children, Sarah Ann, Thomas Philip, and Edward. Unlike most of the Berczy settler families, this family was not Lutheran, but members of the Congregationalist Church. Philip Eckardt's commitment to the church was such that he served as a deacon and provided housing for the travelling student minister when he was preaching in Unionville.

Philip and Susannah Eckardt's son Thomas Philip Eckardt became a physician and, according to Mitchell & Co.'s directory of 1866, had his home and possibly also his practice here prior to a move into the heart of the village following his marriage to Abigail Robinson. The farm remained in the ownership of the Eckardt family until 1883, when Edward Eckardt, the youngest son, sold to local merchant John Davison.

Since the house was listed in the census as a brick structure, we can confidently say that it was built before 1851. Although its exterior finish is currently stucco, archival photographs show that it was originally red brick with contrasting buff-brick quoining and arches over the doors and windows.[29] This style of patterned brickwork first made its appearance in Ontario in the 1840s and continued in popularity until the 1890s. The stucco finish was added in the 1950s when the Greenhough family, owners from 1949 to the late 1980s, updated the old farmhouse.

For the most part, the style of the Philip Eckardt Jr. Farmhouse reflects the one-and-a-half-storey, symmetrical, patterned-brick farmhouses typical of mid-nineteenth-century Ontario, quite conservative in its Georgian-Classical Revival architectural influence. The front doorcase, the most striking feature, has a panelled door, a flat-headed transom light, and multi-paned sidelights — a simple but inviting main entrance characteristic of the vernacular Classical Revival. The seven-panelled front door is an unusual departure from the six-panelled "cross and bible" door that was the standard model at the time of construction. When first built, this house would have had multi-paned windows, most likely in the six-over-six glazing pattern that was common during the mid-nineteenth century. In the 1870s, the Eckardt Farmhouse was updated with a bay window on its south-facing gable end and, a little later, new windows with larger panes in a two-over-two-pane arrangement.

A noteworthy feature of the Eckardt Farmhouse is the tight eave overhang of the low-pitched gable roof, a detail seen more commonly on buildings predating this one by thirty years or more. Particularly puzzling are the gable end windows of the second storey, spaced widely apart toward the building corners. Inside, the reason for the window placement is revealed to be four shallow chimney breasts placed toward the centre of the wall. Above the roofline, the four chimneys that would have extended from the chimney breasts have long ago disappeared. These may have served wood-burning stoves rather than fireplaces on the main floor, given that in some cases there are windows directly below them.[30]

Meadowbrook Lane follows the route of the old farm lane, leading south from Highway 7. As it has done for over a century and a half, the house still overlooks the Rouge River that meanders past its front door.

Union Mills House, 209 Main Street, circa 1846

The name "Unionville" is said to have originated with Union Mills, a complex including a sawmill and gristmill established on the banks of Bruce Creek in the late 1830s to 1840. It is believed that the mills were named in recognition of the historic union of Upper and Lower Canada in 1841, an important step in Canada's journey to nationhood. Unionville's distinctive curving Main Street, which skirts the western edge of the river valley, was the winding route to the gristmill, preferable to the surveyed road allowance, which runs through the river's flood plain and historically was wet and impassible for much of the year.

This one-and-a-half-storey frame house, with its low-pitched centre gable, is locally known as the Union Mills House. The mill itself was located next door to the north, about where today's Carlton Road runs east from Main Street toward the river. This building is often mistaken for the Union Mills Mill Owner's House, which later suffered the indignity of being converted to an automotive garage. That house, built by Ira White, once stood at the head of Main Street, which is the present location of the Varley Art Gallery. This other mill house, at 209 Main Street, may have been the residence of the head miller, who was responsible for the day-to-day operation of the business on behalf of the owner. In the 1920s the Parkinson family lived here, with Harold Parkinson's automotive repair garage in the former residence of Ira White nearby, to the north.

Ira White was an ambitious millwright from the State of New York. He came to Upper Canada in 1819, initially building mills in the Galt area of southwestern Ontario but eventually choosing to come to Markham Township.[31] The Union Mills were not Ira White's first enterprise in Markham. He got his start in the eastern part of the township, constructing mills for the Stouffer and Reesor families.

Walton's directory of 1837 places Ira White in the community of Cedar Grove. In 1825 he had purchased from Peter Reesor a one-hundred-acre lot through which the Rouge River runs, which was ideal for a mill site. On this Cedar Grove property on the east side of Reesor Road, north of 14th Avenue, the White's Hill Mill was built at an early date. Later, this mill was operated by Ira White's son Benjamin.[32] Ira White was a Reformer in politics, and due to his sympathies with the cause of William Lyon Mackenzie he was arrested, questioned, and then released by the authorities at the time of the Rebellion of 1837.[33]

The gristmill at Unionville was built in 1839 or 1840 at the point where the Bruce Creek, a tributary of the Rouge River, crosses present-day Main Street. White also constructed a sawmill near the same location, likely before the gristmill.[34] Rowsell's township directory of 1851, and the 1851 census, place Ira White and his family in Unionville at that time. Ira White was a significant member of his community, a long-time magistrate, and a founding member of the local Congregationalist Church. By the time of the 1861 census, the Whites had left Unionville and Markham Township to seek other mill-building opportunities in southwestern Ontario.

Benjamin White of the White's Hill Mill next assumed the management of the Union Mills for his father, and then Ira White's son-in-law Hugh Powell Crosby took over. Mitchell & Co.'s directory of 1866 lists H.P. Crosby as the proprietor of the Union Mills. About the year 1885, John Stephenson took over the operation of the mill. He was a different John Stephenson from the blacksmith and builder of the Queen's Hotel. His brother Herbert Stephenson next ran the mill on behalf of its owner, Mrs. C.S. Carlton of Toronto, who had owned it since 1895. After a storm washed out the mill dam in 1929, the old gristmill became a chop mill for livestock feed. In 1934 the building was destroyed by fire, removing a major landmark from the village.

The Union Mills House has the long, low profile and shallow depth that are often hallmarks of a very early dwelling. The mid-1840s date of construction coincides with Ira White's purchase of the mill property from Elizabeth Size in 1846.[35] This modestly scaled house displays a classic Georgian sense of balance, with its front doorway centred between two windows. The design of the doorway, with narrow sidelights but without a transom light, echoes the more elaborate Neoclassical treatment of the front doorcase of the Frederick Eckardt House at 206 Main Street. It is possible that later alterations have stripped a more elaborate decorative door surround from the Union Mills House. The front gable, more commonly seen on post-1860 houses, is probably a later addition.

When Unionville was the antique capital of Ontario, this was the long-time location of the Jug and Basin Antique Shop. This property was one of the first to add a large addition to accommodate the growing demand for commercial space in old Unionville. In 1983 a front verandah was added and a two-storey structure in a heritage-sympathetic style was built at the rear of the original building.

First Congregational Church, 149 Main Street, 1847

Although this building looks like it was once a house, 149 Main Street began its history as a church built in the 1840s. The northern part of the present structure was originally constructed as a Congregational Church on a village lot purchased from Frederick Eckardt in 1847. The Congregationalists were evangelical Christians who first organized in Stouffville in 1842. The group

had affiliates in Markham Village and Unionville, and in its formative years shared a minister between the meeting places. Unionville's Congregationalists first met in a member's home in the vicinity, beginning in 1844. The minister used to spend the night at Philip Eckardt's Jr.'s farmhouse, south of the village.[36] Some of the founding members of the Unionville Congregational Church included Ira White, Philip Eckardt Jr., Mark Braithwaite, and members of the Eakin, Stiver, and Summerfeldt families.

When first built, the church had its gable end facing the street. A long drive shed was attached to the rear of the church, accessed from the concession road rather than Main Street. Fire insurance maps of the 1890s show that a tower was centred on the front of the church at that time, but this tower may have been a later addition, perhaps constructed by Unionville's Presbyterian congregation after they acquired the building in the 1880s.

In 1879 the Congregational Church congregation must have been prospering, because they constructed a larger brick church across the street from their modest first place of worship at that time. The frame church was sold to the local Presbyterian congregation, who had been meeting in the home of Isabella Mustard, now addressed 155 Main Street, while they waited to establish a church of their own. Unfortunately, the fortunes of the Congregationalists changed for the worse not long after their ambitious building project, and their membership began to dwindle. The Congregationalists disbanded and sold their brick church to the Presbyterians, who changed their place of worship from the frame church to the larger one in 1894.

The church trustees sold the frame church, except for the drive shed, to Reuben A. Stiver, a local entrepreneur, in 1896. The tower was removed and the church building was repositioned on the property so that the longest side was parallel with the street. With the addition of a second floor, a generous front verandah supported on treillage posts, and residential-style windows and doors, the former church was converted to a dwelling for Reuben Stiver's mother, Ann Bell Stiver, the widow of Robert H. Stiver. Ann Stiver shared the house with her sister Isabella Mustard, also a widow, after she moved from her house at 155 Main Street.[37] Nothing on the exterior remained to hint at the structure's original use. Its form became that of a one-and-a-half-storey clapboarded house in the conservative Georgian architectural tradition. Inside, however, one clue to the building's past as a place of worship remained visible on the second floor. An ornate piece of woodwork that would have decorated the upper portion of the wall as a cornice, where it met the slope of the ceiling, could still be seen up until the recent remodelling of the interior.

After serving as a residence into the late 1970s, the former Congregational Church became an art gallery, then a bakery-cafe, and, most recently, a fine-dining restaurant. In the mid-1980s, a large two-storey addition was constructed on the south end of the original building, significantly altering its character. Much of the 1890s interior remained intact through the various uses of the property until alterations that opened up the space to serve the needs of the urban-style restaurant resulted in the removal of interior walls, doors, and trim.

St. Philip's Old Rectory, 9418 Kennedy Road, circa 1850

Directly opposite the historic Bethesda Lutheran Cemetery stands an old house, set well back from the traffic of Kennedy Road, that is a touchstone to a tumultuous time in Unionville's history. In the years leading up to the rebellion led by William Lyon Mackenzie, the community

was divided between the supporters of Mackenzie and his politics of reform, and the established government of the day. Many members of the Eckardt family and their neighbours were strong supporters of the Reformers, and some of them may have participated in the march of rebels down Yonge Street in early December, 1837.[38]

The Reverend Vincentius or Vincent P. Mayerhoffer, who presided over St. Philip's Lutheran Church from 1829 to 1837, was a vocal supporter of the Tory-dominated government of Upper Canada.[39] His support of the established order was not surprising, given the fact that he was examined for his orders in the Church of England, today the Anglican Church, at the residence of Lieutenant-Governor Sir John Colborne. His political stance placed the Reverend Mayerhoffer at odds with the views of many of his parishioners.

As feelings against the government grew throughout the population of York County, and locally within Unionville, emotions ran high. The community became strongly divided. Frustrated by the Reverend Mayerhoffer's lack of sympathy for their cause, the Reformers among the St. Philip's congregation decided to take decisive action to drive him from their place of worship. In 1837 a group of parishioners barred the reverend's entry into the church to conduct an afternoon service. Although he tried to regain access to the church with the aid of his contacts within the Church of England and the government, the congregation successfully expelled him through court action.[40]

Not all of the members of St. Philip's Lutheran Church were opponents of the Reverend Mayerhoffer. Most of those favouring Anglican worship left their home church to found a new church and cemetery on the opposite side of the road, and took the name "St. Philip's" along with them.[41] This location, on Vincent Mayerhoffer's own land, seems to have been purposely selected as a tangible expression of the opposing viewpoints of the members of the two church groups. Reverend Mayerhoffer had purchased the seventy acres upon which he resided in 1832, a short time after he came to St. Philip's. By 1835 he had dedicated his property back to the Crown and, by extension, to the Church of England. Old maps mark the land as "Glebe" as early as 1853 to 1854.

In 1839 a frame church in the early Gothic Revival style was constructed on the new site.[42] Nothing is known about the Reverend Mayerhoffer's residence, but it may have been of log construction if it was the first dwelling built on the property. Two years or so after the Reverend Mayerhoffer and his family moved out of the area, eventually settling in Whitby, the congregation of St. Philip's constructed a new Rectory to house the incumbent rector, the Reverend George Hill, appointed in 1848. The Rectory also housed the clergy for another church in the same diocese, Grace Anglican in Markham Village.

The Rectory was designed in the conservative Georgian architectural tradition, with a front door with sidelights centred between two windows. It was built in frame, clapboarded, and one-and-a-half storeys in height. The roof was constructed with an unusually deep overhang, unique in the area. It seems likely that the Rectory previously occupied by the Reverend Mayerhoffer was deemed unworthy of the new church and its distinguished new rector.

The Reverend Hill served the congregation until 1876, when he passed away. He was followed by a succession of others and their families as residents of the Rectory, until 1913, when the last of the Anglican clergy to reside there was the Reverend G.B. Johnson.

Just as the Lutheran congregation was drawn down to the village in the early 1900s, in 1913 the St. Philip's Anglican Church building was also dismantled and relocated where the population was more concentrated. The Old Rectory was sold off to become a private residence, along with an appropriate parcel of land. The cemetery remained as the most enduring marker of St. Philip's original site, until 1986 when a new church was constructed next to the cemetery grounds, in recognition of the growth of the congregation.

The Old St. Philip's Rectory has been updated over the years with modern doors, windows, and siding; however, the essential character of the building still remains intact with the changes being of the cosmetic kind, rather than structural. The house is secluded and surrounded with greenery that makes it easy to miss if one doesn't know where to look for it.

First Post Office and Store, 188 Main Street, circa 1850, North Section 1870s

When Unionville was granted its first post office in 1851 the community was already a recognizable village. Interspersed among the farms along the 6th Line that divided the 5th and 6th Concessions, businesses, industries, churches, and a schoolhouse had gradually emerged. John Braithwaite's general store and the churches of the Lutherans and Anglicans marked the northern end of Unionville, known as Hunter's Corner, while Gottlieb Eckardt's wheelwright and carriage shop and the Congregational Church marked the southern end. In between were the sawmill and gristmill built by Ira White, and hotels and workshops, mainly north of the Bruce Creek crossing of Main Street.

Andrew Eckardt, one of the sons of Philip Eckardt and Ann Elizabeth Koepke, was appointed as Unionville's first postmaster, a position he held until 1864. According to the reminiscences of an Eckardt descendant, Andrew Eckardt was also Unionville's first merchant.[43] He purchased a half-acre village lot from his brother Frederick Eckardt in 1845, and may have already been established as a merchant in this location by the time he was appointed postmaster in 1851.[44] In the early 1850s his home was in the south half of this building, which is the oldest part of this combined store and residence. Andrew Eckardt didn't reside at this location for long. For most of his life in Unionville he lived on a farm on Lot 13, Concession 6, according to census records and township directories. This would have placed him north of the bridge over the creek. His principle career was farming. Perhaps the day-to-day operation of the post office was later managed by someone he employed to do the job.

Andrew Eckardt and his wife, Charlotte Hunter Eckardt, retired from farming to a house in the village by the time of the 1881 census, probably the small frame cottage at 187 Main Street now known as the "Unionville House." By then Andrew Eckardt was working as a carpenter, and the store and post office property had been sold to the couple's daughter, Eliza, in 1863, about the date of her marriage. Eliza Eckardt married George Eakin, who was clerk of Markham Township from 1860 to 1873 and the co-owner of the Unionville Carriage Factory with his brother William. George Eakin ran the general store at 188 Main Street and was postmaster from 1864 to 1875.[45] In 1874 he became the clerk of York County, a more prestigious position, and relocated his family to Toronto. His business card read, "George Eakin, Issuer of Marriage Licenses, Estate and Insurance Agent, and County Clerk, Court House, Adelaide Street."[46] George Eakin's mother-in-law, Charlotte Eckardt, lived with the Eakins in their Toronto home near Moss Park after the death of her husband.

In 1874 George and Eliza Eakin sold the house and store to George M. Davison, a farmer who lived at the north end of the village, closer to 16th Avenue. His son John Davison ran a general store here, and inherited the property in 1877.[47] In 1885 he became Unionville's fourth postmaster, taking over for Mark Braithwaite, who ran a store and post office down the street at a building now addressed 154 Main Street. John Davison continued in this position until 1913, when his son George A.M. "Art" Davison became the operator of the family business and served as postmaster from 1913 to 1935. After Art Davison's death, his wife, Matilda, assumed the role of postmaster, and continued until 1949. Unionville's post office remained at this location until 1961, when a new, modern post office opened next door at 186 Main Street, which has since been enlarged, remodelled, and converted to a restaurant.

Art Davison was perhaps Unionville's most ambitious businessman.[48] He left a significant mark on the community. In addition to his store and post office, he served as Markham's Township clerk and treasurer from 1918 to 1934, and opened a Ford Motor Company dealership and repair shop across the street from the store in 1913. He served as a trustee for the Police Village of Unionville, and was the chair of the finance committee of the Markham Fair Board, as well as president of the fair for two terms. The family had an interest in horses and were well-known in horse breeding and show circles. After Art Davison retired from his position as township clerk and treasurer, a small office remained in part of the Davison Store where the next township clerk, Charles Hoover, had his office and maintained the papers and records of the municipality until the former Chant house at 147 Main Street became Markham Township's offices in 1944.

The building at 188 Main Street, as it stands today, represents two distinct periods of development. The south portion, more house-like in character than commercial, started as a clapboarded, one or one-and-a-half-storey frame building when first constructed in the mid-nineteenth century. The facade has a Georgian sense of balance, with a centre door flanked by two windows in the classic double-square proportions of the time. Originally, the windows would have been divided into many small panes, but late-nineteenth-century renovations updated them to their present two-over-two-paned design. Fortunately,

conversion to retail use never resulted in the enlargement of the original openings to showcase window proportions.

The front entrance is a noteworthy early feature, exhibiting a refined Neoclassical design, with corner blocks and symmetrical pilasters. At one time the doorcase was capped with a finely proportioned cornice. This treatment is reminiscent of the interior mouldings found in Frederick Eckardt's adobe-brick cottage farther up the street, and suggests that the building may predate the establishment of the post office, perhaps by a decade or more. The door within this early entrance surround is a remarkable piece of folk art. It dates from the late nineteenth century and its glazed and panelled design is typical of the 1880s, except for the carved fan and maple leaf motifs seen in the lower panelled section. The door is a true piece of Canadiana.

The upper part of the front of the building has a mansard roof in the Second Empire style, with a bracketed cornice and a trio of gable dormer windows facing the street. The patterned shingle treatment of the mansard roof is based on archival photographs. Historically, it was painted in alternating bands of colour to resemble a more costly slate roof. The second storey is likely coincident with the construction of the store at the north end of the building. The store may have replaced a smaller, older store attachment to the original building around the time when the Davison family acquired the property. The architecture of the store, with its boomtown front and tall window proportions, is a strong indication that the north part of the building is a late Victorian addition. It was once sided in board and batten.

Hunter-Reed Cottage and Store, 193 Main Street, circa 1850, Store 1880s

One of the smallest and least ornamented buildings on Unionville's Main Street is the key to a remarkable story that has somehow been forgotten in the history books. In 1848 Hannah Hunter purchased village lot number 5, on the east side of Main Street, from Frederick Eckardt. She was the daughter of John Stamm, burgomaster of Copenhagen, Denmark, in 1792.[49] The Stamm family left Denmark the same year that Hannah was born, and emigrated to the United States. It is surprising that John Stamm would leave the country of his birth, given his status there, for the uncertainty of becoming established in a new land. What was it that compelled him to relinquish such a high station in a major city? The few fragments that remain of the story are not enough to let us know.

The Stamms were part of William Berczy's group of settlers that came to Markham in 1794. Hannah Hunter's obituary, dated 1881, provides some interesting commentary on Markham Township's pioneering period:

> The family with others, settled in what is now known as the German district of the township of Markham. Their lands, through Berczy, were deeded direct from the Crown ... Markham township, at the present time the home of many of the richest and best farmers of this country, was, prior to the entry of the Berczy pioneers, a wilderness, giving shelter alike to the bear and the deer.[50]

Hannah Stamm married John Hunter Sr. in 1811, and lived on a farm north of Unionville, on the east half of Lot 19, Concession 5. By 1823 she was left a widow with three children. Unlike many other relatively young widows of her time, Hannah Hunter did not remarry. She continued to live on the family farm until about the time she bought the Unionville property, perhaps with the aim of having a small house built there for her retirement from farm life.

At the time of the 1851 census, Hannah Hunter lived in the household of her daughter Hannah Reed and her husband, Dr. Nelson R. Reed. Dr. Reed was born in the United States, and may have been Unionville's first resident doctor. Township assessment rolls place Dr. Reed in the village of Unionville, at this location, as early as 1852. The spelling of the family's surname varies between documents, sometimes written as Reed, Read, or Reid. Hannah Reed's sister Charlotte was married to Andrew Eckardt, the local postmaster and storekeeper.

Nelson and Hannah Reed's married life was brief. Dr. Reed died in 1857, and Dr. Charles Justice stepped into his place as Unionville's local M.D. The couple had no children. Hannah Hunter and Hannah Reed, now both widows, shared the small board-and-batten cottage at 193 Main Street, surviving on Hannah Reed's income earned as a dressmaker, perhaps assisted by her mother. Like her mother, she did not remarry, either by choice or because no suitable opportunity presented itself. The dressmaking business carried on here into the early 1880s. Hannah Hunter died in 1881, at the age of ninety-nine years according to her grave marker in the Bethesda Lutheran Cemetery. At the time of her death it was said that "The old settlers of those days have during the past decade been quietly passing away, full of years and honor. By the death of Mrs., Hunter the chain between the past and the present of Markham Township has been broken."[51]

Hannah Reed remained in Unionville following her mother's death, and sold the tiny cottage to Colin Webster, a butcher, in 1887. Now on her own and getting older herself, she moved in with a neighbouring family. Colin Webster, the next resident of 193 Main Street, likely added the small frame store to the north end of the residence from where he operated his business.

The use of this building as a butcher shop was a longstanding one, beginning with Colin Webster in the late 1880s and continuing from 1921 under the proprietorship of George Dukes and Oliver Anderson, and later Harold Dukes.[52] The butcher shop remained at this location into the 1960s.

The Hunter-Reed cottage and store is a rare example of a virtually intact village-scale business premises and attached residence. In spite of all of the changes that have taken place in Unionville since its renaissance in the 1970s through the 1980s, this almost miniature building has retained its original character and size. While other historical structures, both former houses and commercial buildings, have been greatly expanded with large additions to enhance their modern-day uses, this one has not changed very much, other than updating the details of the doors and windows.

The former residential portion has classic Georgian symmetry in the placement of its centre door and flanking windows. An archival photograph shows that the windows were originally glazed with multi-paned sash in a twelve-over-eight configuration, and the front door was six panelled, with no glass. Similar to other early Unionville houses in this style, the siding was, and remains, board and batten. The low-pitched gable roof has returned eaves, typical of the period of construction.

The shop, being a later addition, was clad in vertical tongue and groove siding, which has in recent years been covered over with new board and batten to match the rest of the building, except for the north wall, where the original treatment remains visible. The shop is distinguished with a "boomtown front" that wraps around the south wall and conceals the low-pitched gable roof. The shop is small and therefore in scale with the earlier cottage. It once had a shed-roofed porch sheltering the shop front.

Hewlett Eckardt House, 158 Main Street, circa 1853

In his youth, Hewlett Eckardt worked alongside his father, Gottlieb Eckardt, in the brick wheelwright and carriage shop that still stands at 166 Main Street. The

family also ran a sawmill in the river valley on the east side of Main Street, a little north of today's Highway 7. No traces of the sawmill remain, and it is not certain when it was first established, but township maps of 1853 to 1854 and 1860 illustrate its approximate location on the west half of Lot 11, Concession 6.

Gottlieb Eckardt died in 1852. In his will he left a village lot to his son Hewlett, together with a quantity of uncompleted wheelwright work and the proceeds it would generate.[53] He also willed him a quantity of lumber from the family sawmill, sufficient to build a one-storey house twenty-four by twenty-four feet square in dimension. A house of this size would have been smaller than the Eckardt's log homestead.

The house at 158 Main Street, thought to have been built about 1853, surpassed the size of the modestly scaled house provided for in Gottlieb Eckardt's will. Instead of working within those narrow limitations, Hewlett Eckardt built a one-and-a-half-storey village house, with a rectangular plan that was of the quality and size befitting a business owner of the day. The clapboarded frame house was set back from the road, with a generous front yard creating a green buffer from the activity of Main Street. It was designed in the Georgian architectural tradition, with a formal centre entrance complete with sidelights, and flanked by two windows with a six-over-six glazing pattern. The medium-pitched gable roof and deep eave returns were the standard for houses built during this time period. The full-width verandah now on the front of the house is an early twentieth-century addition.

In the mid-1860s Hewlett Eckardt left Unionville to seek his fortune in California. His business passed to his blacksmith partner, John Stephenson. The portion of the property containing the house was sold to Margery Keller in 1865. In 1870 James W. Fenwick purchased the former Eckardt property and built a frame store on the vacant part of the land to the south. This store, much expanded and remodelled, still stands at 156 Main Street. Bradstreet's directory of 1871 listed the business as "J.W. Fenwick and Co. General Store." The house at 158 Main Street was his residence.

The property was sold to Josiah Hall, a local builder, in 1883. Henry Brown, a farmer turned general merchant from Victoria Square, leased the house and store from Josiah Hall in 1884. When the property was sold to Robert Stiver in 1888, Henry Brown relocated his family and business to Stouffville, but returned to Unionville only a couple of years later. After Henry Brown died due to illness not long after coming back to Unionville, his capable wife, Eliza, carried on the business. Her success as a merchant enabled her to purchase the store and home they once leased from Ann Stiver, Robert Stiver's widow, in 1892.[54]

Henry and Eliza Brown's son Arthur later ran the store. In 1920 a two-storey brick bank building was constructed in the deep front yard of the family home to house a branch of the Standard Bank of Canada, which became absorbed into the Canadian Imperial Bank of Commerce. The bank building, rendered in the Edwardian Classical style and built of buff brick accented with Indiana limestone, was similar in design to the Standard Bank's branches across the province. Looking at the site today, it is difficult to imagine how such a substantial structure could have occupied such a small space. When the bank was held up in an armed robbery in 1930, it caused quite a sensation in the otherwise quiet village. In 1986 the old bank was demolished, opening up to full view once again the former home of Hewlett Eckardt, after decades of being hidden away.

McKinnon-Eakin House, 145 Main Street, Mid-Nineteenth Century

The McKinnon-Eakin House stands apart from Unionville's Main Street, not only for its location on the original alignment of the concession road but for its formal Georgian style. Locally this one-and-a-half-storey, board-and-batten house is noteworthy for the part of its history when the village lock-up was located within the building.

Published histories of this house link it to Neil McKinnon, a native of the Isle of Mull, Argyllshire, who left Scotland in 1812, along with other members of his family, as part of Lord Selkirk's group of settlers. The McKinnon family was among the founders of the Kildonan Settlement at the junction of the Assiniboine River and Red River, in a territory that was once known as Rupert's Land, now part of Manitoba. Their fledgling community was located in the heart of today's Winnipeg. After suffering three years of hardship and danger from North West Company raiders and their Aboriginal allies, the McKinnons left Lord Selkirk's settlement along with the other families and journeyed to Upper Canada in search of a more secure and promising place to become established in British North America.[55]

Neil McKinnon and his family found their way to Markham Township by 1817. Their home is said to have been on Lot 26, Concession 5, near the crossroads hamlet of Cashel, north of Unionville. This rented property was later purchased by Allan McKinnon, one of his sons, and later again was owned by another son, Angus McKinnon.

Neil McKinnon's brother Hugh McKinnon, who had stayed in Scotland rather than participating in Lord Selkirk's risky enterprise, was influenced by the family to come to Upper Canada, and arrived in Markham in 1820 after a brief stay in the town of York. Luckily, he never had to endure the hardships faced by his more adventurous brother. Hugh McKinnon became established on Lot 9, Concession 6, a farm property just south of Unionville, where his neighbour was Philip Eckardt Jr.

Neil McKinnon died in 1829, so the Neil McKinnon of Unionville who was a tenant of King's College, which later became the University of Toronto, on Lot 12, Concession 6, is not the Neil McKinnon of Cashel. Both Neil McKinnon and his brother Hugh McKinnon had many children in their respective families, and given names were repeated a number of times. At present not enough is known of the McKinnon genealogy to say for sure how the Neil McKinnon of Unionville fits into the family tree. His early presence on the Unionville property is noted in Walton's directory of 1837. He was also involved with millwright Ira White in 1839, in the construction of a sawmill on the banks of Bruce Creek. Although it has been speculated that the house at 145 Main Street was built in either circa 1835 or circa 1845 by Neil McKinnon while he was a tenant on the land, census records as early as 1851 suggest otherwise. By that time, Neil McKinnon had died and Alexander McKinnon, possibly his son, and some of his siblings lived here. Alexander McKinnon operated the sawmill constructed by Ira White in 1839, and resided in a one-storey log house, not a one-and-a-half-storey frame house.[56]

William Eakin bought the property containing the White-McKinnon sawmill, as well as the surrounding hundred acres of farmland, a former Crown reserve from King's College in 1854. He was a son of Irish immigrant Samuel Eakin and his Canadian-born wife, Elizabeth Pingle, who farmed north of Unionville. He lived for a while in the McKinnon log house but when firmly established built a new frame house for himself

and his family. In 1857 William Eakin acquired Village Lots 12 and 14 from Frederick Eckardt, directly in front of his home on the east side of the concession road. On the southernmost lot, now addressed 147A Main Street, William Eakin and his brother George constructed a carriage works that was known as the Unionville Carriage Factory, which operated through the 1860s. William and George had previous experience in the trade, having worked as carriage makers at Cashel.

The Unionville Carriage Factory manufactured and sold "Light & Heavy Duty Waggons, Gigs, Sulkies, Buck-boards, & c." In a *York Herald* newspaper ad from 1861 under George Eakin's name, a poem proclaims, "Come one, come all, and buy of me,/For I have buggies, as you will see,/That are neat, that are strong, and without doubt/Are much superior to any turned out!/My terms are easy, my price is small —/Pray do not forget to give me a call." The Eakins' carriage-making enterprise gradually transitioned into the manufacturing of agricultural implements.[57]

At the time of the 1861 census William Eakin, his wife, Margaret Hunter, and their children lived in the house at 145 Main Street along with George Eakin, who at that time was listed as a widower. George Eakin had been appointed as clerk and treasurer of Markham Township in 1860. William Eakin's occupation was given as "farmer," while his brother was listed as "carriage maker," his main occupation in addition to his role with the township. It may have been in this period when the windows of 145 Main Street were barred to protect the funds contained in the municipal safe located in George Eakin's office, and the small village lock-up was installed on the premises for the temporary holding of minor offenders.[58] After George Eakin married Eliza Eckardt, the daughter of Andrew Eckardt and Charlotte Hunter, he moved out of his brother's house about 1863 to a house and store owned by his new wife at 188 Main Street. There, George Eakin operated the general store established by his father-in-law circa 1850, and assumed the role of Unionville's second postmaster in 1864. His wife was a milliner, an artisan who made hats for women.

The Unionville Carriage Factory operated until about 1871. In 1873 William Eakin built a sash-and-door factory next to the Toronto and Nipissing Railway line that bordered his property. This red board-and-batten industrial building, more commonly known as the Unionville Planing Mill, was a landmark at the south end of the village for over a century, until it was destroyed by fire just when Unionville was experiencing its renaissance as an historic-themed tourist destination. After the fire a new building, also called the Planing Mill but a retail complex not a centre of woodwork production, was built on the site.

The Planing Mill was a success, but industry was not the only interest that captured the imagination of William Eakin. He also had political aspirations. In 1873 he was elected reeve of Markham Township. He was returned to office in the election of 1879 and held the position until 1883, when he decided to leave the safe haven of his Unionville home to become a pioneer in the Canadian west.[59] By that time, William Eakin had sold his original home at 145 Main Street to his brother George, as an investment property, and his business and second home to Robert Harrington. The property was sold out of the family in 1879. Later owners were the Clements and Procunier families.

The McKinnon-Eakin House is a well-preserved example of a Georgian tradition, one-and-a-half-storey village dwelling. The formality of its architecture contrasts with the decorative exuberance of its younger neighbours, one of which is an Ontario Gothic Revival farmhouse moved to this location in 1995 to save it from demolition on its original site.

The house has a balanced front elevation with a centre doorcase that features a four panelled door, a multi-paned transom light, and a dignified Classic Revival surround with robust pilasters supporting a nicely proportioned entablature. The windows have six-over-six sash, framed with moulded surrounds. The ground floor windows are larger in proportion to those lighting the upstairs, a common characteristic of early Ontario domestic architecture. The fine but restrained detailing of the decorative treatment of the front door and window surrounds is an indication of the care that went into the building's construction. The low pitch of the roof, and the remnants of eave returns, are in keeping with the mid-nineteenth-century origin of the McKinnon-Eakin House.

Unionville House, 187 Main Street, Mid-Nineteenth Century

This small tradesman's cottage is supposed to have been built by Andrew Eckardt, Unionville's first postmaster. Andrew Eckardt, one of the sons of Philip Eckardt and Ann Elizabeth Koepke, lived on a farm to the north of the bridge over Bruce Creek, a property he purchased in 1831. The village lot where the Unionville House stands was bought from Andrew Eckardt's brother Frederick Eckardt in 1852. Since the cottage was not his residence, it was likely constructed as an income property. Andrew Eckardt also owned another property on Main Street, which he purchased from Frederick Eckardt in 1845, and where Unionville's first post office is believed to have been located. Today that property is addressed 188 Main Street.

According to local tradition, the cottage once housed a shoemaker, but his name and what time period he was located there are not known.[60] Between 1864 and 1875 the property was owned by Andrew and Charlotte Eckardt's son-in-law George Eakin, who was married to their daughter Elizabeth. The years when George Eakin served as Unionville's postmaster, after taking over the position from Andrew Eckardt, coincide exactly with the period when George Eakin was postmaster. This raises the question of how the cottage was used, if the general store and post office at 188 Main Street, with its attached residence, was where the Eakin family lived. Could the post office have been located in the little cottage rather than in the Eakin general store?

George Eakin sold the cottage and property to his mother-in-law, Charlotte Eckardt, in 1875. The sale price was a mere $50, the same price that Andrew Eckardt sold it for in 1864. A fire insurance map of 1891 shows that a small one-and-a-half-storey shop was once located on the north side of the cottage, linked to the rear lean-to by a short passage. It may have been part of the original structure, or was added when the property went into commercial use. The shop, positioned where the present-day ice cream stand is, had a covered porch that stretched along the front. After Andrew Eckardt retired from farming he and his wife moved into the village, and for a time lived in this small cottage. He wasn't quite ready to retire from work altogether, because in the 1881 census his occupation is given as "carpenter." It's not hard to imagine Andrew Eckardt, now an older gentleman of seventy years of age, doing odd jobs close to home to keep from being idle.

Henry Brown is the best documented of all of the tenants to occupy the Unionville House. His first career was as farmer, on a rented farm north of the crossroads hamlet of Victoria Square. When farming proved too challenging, he and his wife, Elizabeth "Eliza" Flavelle Brown, decided to try their hands at the mercantile business. In 1884 they moved to Unionville and operated out of a store owned by Josiah Hall, now addressed 156 Main Street. After only a few years, the Brown's business was successful enough to enable them to consider buying the store from its owner, but another interested party, Robert H. Stiver, outbid them. In 1888 the family relocated to Stouffville and purchased David Stouffer's grocery store there instead.

In 1890 Henry and Eliza Brown decided to return to Unionville, and rented the cottage and shop from Charlotte Eckardt.[61] The Browns also bought out a local bakery near the crossroads of present-day Highway 7 and Main Street. Henry Brown employed a baker, while he took care of bread deliveries. Sadly, Henry Brown died only two short years later, leaving the store and the bakery in the hands of his widow, Eliza, who capably carried on there for another year before moving across the street to their original Unionville location.

By the early 1900s, Dr. Charles R. McKay had his medical consulting office here. By that time, the link between the cottage and shop at 187 Main Street had disappeared. Eventually, the shop was removed as well, but the tiny cottage remained little altered from its original appearance through all the time and changes. Unionville's last blacksmith, Fred Minton, lived here in the 1940s, next door to his shop located in the basement at the rear of 189 Main Street.

In the late 1970s, as part of Unionville's rebirth as a tourist destination, the little clapboarded cottage was restored and transformed by the Unionville Conservation and Development Association into the Unionville House Restaurant and Tearoom. In more recent years, a variety of other restaurants have been located here.

The Unionville House is a well-preserved example of a tradesman's cottage designed in a vernacular version of the Georgian architectural tradition. Its general proportions and low profile suggest a mid-nineteenth-century time of construction. The asymmetrical arrangement of the front door and its flanking windows is an indication that the builder was more concerned with the practical layout of the limited interior space rather than achieving a perfectly symmetrical facade in the classic Georgian sense. The saltbox form of the cottage, with the rear slope of the gable roof extending to form a lean-to at the back, is a distinctive feature borrowed from an old tradition of house expansion rooted in seventeenth-century New England.

William Eckardt House, 124 Main Street, circa 1856

The William Eckardt House is one of Unionville's most significant and most-often photographed early homes. Its crisp, white lines contrast with the expansive green lawn and mature trees that provide a deep foreground for this architectural treasure. The house was built circa 1856 on the east hundred acres of Lot 11, Concession 5, purchased from King's College, later known as the University of Toronto, that same year. Some sources say that William Eckardt's house was built in 1852, four years before the formal purchase of the land.[62]

William Eckardt was the son of Gottlieb Eckardt, operator of the Eckardt sawmill on the Rouge River and the brick wheelwright and carriage shop on Main Street. While still living in his parents' house on Lot 11, Concession 6, William Eckardt operated a pump-making factory in association with the sawmill.

Water pumps in use on Ontario farms in those days were made of wood rather than metal.

The ambitious William Eckardt, farmer and justice of the peace, built a fine brick house on his newly purchased property and contributed to the development of Unionville by subdividing the eastern portion of his land for village-sized building lots and backstreets the same year he acquired the acreage.[63] The western part remained farmland. The fact that he envisioned the potential for development so early in Unionville's history is remarkable. In 1856 a railway passing through the area had not even been contemplated.

At the time of the 1861 census, William Eckardt, sadly, was a widower. His younger brother, Philip D. Eckardt, lived in the brick farmhouse and probably helped run the farm. Ten years later, William Eckardt had remarried. His second wife was Sarah Harrington. They wasted no time in raising a large family, with five children between the ages of nine and one month by 1871.

In spite of William Eckardt's ambitious plan to create a residential neighbourhood in the southwest quarter of Unionville, the sale of lots and the construction of houses were slow to take off. The picture changed dramatically in the late 1860s, when planning was underway for the Toronto and Nipissing Railway. Although at first it looked like the railway would bypass Unionville altogether, through the influence of Hugh Powell Crosby, local MPP and former member of the railway's provisional board of directors, the route was modified to pass through the south end of the village, right through William Eckardt's land.[64] With the opportunity to at last cash in on his investment and planning, it is no wonder that William Eckardt was a railway

booster, but the large curving track had both positive and negative impacts on his property. The railway line effectively cut the Eckardt subdivision into two separate parts, sparking development on the east side of the tracks but stifling it on the west side.

William Eckardt's interest in real estate speculation compelled him to leave Unionville in 1876 for the larger business opportunities offered by the expansion of Toronto and its suburbs. By the time of the 1881 census, he was firmly rooted in Yorkville, with an office on Yonge Street. His beautiful home on Main Street, Unionville, and the mature residential neighbourhood surrounding it, are his legacy to the community of his birth. One of William Eckardt's sons, Albert J.H. Eckardt, became the very successful owner of a funeral furnishings company in Toronto called the Eckardt Casket Company, but later renamed the National Casket Company after becoming re-established after the great Toronto fire of 1904. Eckardt's business was a larger factory operation that also produced hearses and wagons. In the early 1900s the company letterhead stated that this was the "Largest Funeral Supply House in Canada." A.J.H. Eckardt's interest in the history of his family compelled him to write a number of remarkable historical accounts of the life and times of his ancestors that are preserved among the papers associated with Bethesda Lutheran Church.

This house is one of the first in the area to have been constructed of clay brick. Only the Philip Eckardt Jr. House is older. The brick is thought to have been made locally at the nearby Snowball brickworks. Snowball brick, named after the family that manufactured it, has a distinctive mottled colour, varying from shades of buff to salmon. John Snowball had formerly been located in the hamlet of Buttonville, some distance to the west of Unionville. He moved his home and business nearer to Unionville and Markham Village in the mid-1850s, likely attracted by the growing communities that would have a higher demand for brick than the more remote and less prosperous mill village of Buttonville.

The William Eckardt House has been featured in a number of books and articles on old Ontario houses. It was once home to Howard Pain, a noted collector and authority on early Canadian furniture. What a fitting place to house an important collection of early Ontario furniture.[65]

The William Eckardt House is a true vernacular building, combining elements of a number of architectural styles popular at its time of construction into a pleasing composition that works in spite of its eclectic nature. The one-and-a-half-storey house follows the form of a Classic Ontario farmhouse, with a steep centre gable and a Georgian sense of balance in its symmetrical facade. The gable contains a tall Gothic Revival window with delicate interlacing tracery. According to local tradition, this window was a later addition to the house, salvaged from the Bethesda Lutheran Church when it was relocated from its original site and rebuilt at 20 Union Street in 1910. The front doorcase has a flat-headed transom light and sidelights with rectilinear, Ontario Regency-style glazing, and a single-panel door in the Classic Revival mode. Flanking the front entrance is a pair of tall French doors, again with rectilinear glazing that reflects an Ontario Regency aesthetic.

The character of the William Eckardt House, as it has been for decades, is markedly different from its earlier appearance. Originally, the brick was unpainted, with a red-brick body trimmed with buff-brick quoining and window arches. The eaves were once decorated with curvilinear Gothic Revival bargeboards, and

across the front was a tent-roofed verandah accented with fretsawn brackets. In a number of ways, the detailing of the William Eckardt House echoes that of the Salem Eckardt house at 197 Main Street, believed to have been constructed about the same time. Both are unique expressions of the Gothic Revival, enlivened with elements borrowed from other architectural styles.

Eckardt-McKay House, 197 Main Street, circa 1856

This picturesque board-and-batten residence was constructed on Village Lot 4 on the east side of Main Street, a property purchased by Salem Eckardt from his brother Frederick in 1856. Most histories of this remarkable house attribute it to Andrew Eckardt, Salem Eckardt's older brother, and assign it an earlier time of construction, which varies from circa 1850 to as early as circa 1835. Andrew Eckardt, whose varied career included farmer, storekeeper, postmaster, and carpenter, may have done the actual construction, but he was not likely the original resident.[66] Historical records place him elsewhere in the area, close by 197 Main Street, but not upon this village lot.

Salem Eckardt, the apparent original owner and occupant of this house, is best remembered as Unionville's long-time auctioneer and the person who planted the sugar maples that once shaded Main Street until the aged trees were unceremoniously cut down to make way for a road widening that thankfully never happened.[67] Although there is a local tradition that Salem Eckardt added the decorative flourishes that make this house so distinctive, including the steep Gothic Revival gable and the sculptured bargeboards, there is no clear indication from an examination of the structure that it has been altered to any great extent, suggesting that these features were part of the original design.

At the time of the 1851 census, Salem Eckardt was living on the Eckardt homestead on Lot 17, Concession 6, north of Unionville. His father, Philip Eckardt, had passed away in 1845, leaving the running of the homestead farm up to his youngest son. By the time of the 1861 census, Salem Eckardt had moved into the village. His residency here is also confirmed by Mitchell & Co.'s directory of 1866, which lists his occupation as "general agent." It may be that Salem Eckardt built his fine home in the mid-1850s, while he lived with his wife, Catherine Kleiser, and their children in the old hewn-log house on the hill. Architectural similarities between this house and William Eckardt's brick house of circa 1856 suggest the possibility that both houses were constructed by the same builder at about the same time.

According to an unpublished account of the history of Unionville, and in particular the Eckardt family, A.J.H. Eckardt wrote that in 1840 Salem Eckardt organized a brass band. The village band travelled in a large "band wagon" pulled by four horses to participate in various events and competitions, winning the prize for province at Cobourg in a year not identified in the story.

The Eckardt House was purchased in the late 1950s by Kathleen Gormley McKay, a descendant of three early Markham families, the Eckardts, Milnes, and Gormleys. Kathy and her husband, Donald McKay, hosted Fred Varley, a Canadian art celebrity, during the latter years of his life and career. His studio was within the fieldstone walls of the basement, with windows overlooking the Rouge River valley at the rear of the house. Kathy McKay later generously donated the collection of Canadian paintings that she and her husband had assembled to the citizens of Markham. The core of the McKay collection was a number of important works by Fred Varley, and today these paintings are housed in the Frederick Horsman Varley Art Gallery of Markham at the top of Main Street. The McKays' former home, which they carefully restored in the 1960s, is owned by the city of Markham and functions as an art centre in association with the Varley Art Gallery, exhibiting the work of local artists.[68]

The Eckardt-McKay House itself is another Canadian celebrity, an outstanding example of Ontario vernacular architecture best described as "Carpenter Gothic." This house has an honoured place in a classic book on Ontario's early domestic architecture, *The Ancestral Roof*, 1963, by Marion MacRae and Anthony Adamson.[69] For years the front yard of the house was enclosed with a low, ornate cast-iron fence and garden gate, probably added by the McKays, which was unfortunately removed due to safety concerns in a recent renewal of the landscaping on the property.

In form, the house is a simple rectangle in plan, with a one-and-a-half-storey height and a medium-pitched gable roof. The board-and-batten siding has moulded battens of a quality suitable for a house, not the plain one-by-two battens reserved for outbuildings. The house was built into a natural slope that allowed a ground level entrance at street level, as well as a ground level entrance and large windows for the basement kitchen that once was located there.

The front facade has the common Georgian symmetry of its mid-nineteenth-century period of construction, and six-over-six paned windows equipped with operable, louvered wooden shutters. Where the house gets really interesting is on the upper floor, with a broad front gable and its smaller, steeper companion gable to its left, containing an angular Gothic Revival window. The eaves are lavishly adorned with highly sculptural bargeboards made in the era before planing mills turned out the two-dimensional, machine-made kind more commonly seen on Victorian buildings.

The front porch is a remnant of a once-larger verandah. Its delicate posts have a Neo-Egyptian quality to their design, while the front doorcase and window surrounds evoke the Classic Revival style. The sunroom on the south end of the house, likely a later addition, has grouped, pointed-arched windows following the Gothic Revival style. It may have been constructed from windows salvaged from another building, and reworked to fit the Eckardt-McKay House.

The Crown Inn, 249 Main Street, circa 1860

An early reference to a hotel or tavern in the vicinity of Unionville is found in the *Colonial Advocate* newspaper from February of 1834. A political meeting of Reform-minded citizens had gathered at Mr. Hunter's tavern on the 6th Line of Markham Township in support of their elected representative, Mr. William Lyon Mackenzie.[70] They were unhappy that the government of Upper Canada had expelled Mackenzie from the Legislative Assembly due to his criticism of the partisan policies and actions of the political elite. Rebellion was in the air. A list of Markham's Reformers, who signed a statement in support of William Lyon Mackenzie, shows that many of Unionville's leading families were sympathetic to the Reform cause. The names on the list represent a diverse range of cultural and religious backgrounds.

Hunter's Tavern was located on the northwest corner of what is today Kennedy Road and 16th Avenue. George Hunter, the proprietor, was an Irish immigrant and a member of the family who lent their name to the crossroads, known for a time as Hunter's Corner. Although George Hunter received a renewal of his tavern licence from the local magistrate in 1841, his career as a tavern keeper was not a long one. In the annals of history he is primarily remembered as a blacksmith.

Hotels and taverns were important community amenities in nineteenth-century Ontario. They provided food, drink, and lodging for travellers, as well as a gathering place for locals. They functioned much like today's neighbourhood pubs or coffee shops, where people socialized and met to discuss everything from the state of the year's crops to politics. Nearly every community of any size had at least one hotel or tavern on the main street, often at a crossroads. In 1852 Markham Township Council passed a by-law to regulate taverns within its boundaries. Those receiving a tavern licence were required "to have in such house and constantly keep for his or her customers six clean and comfortable beds and bedding, one sitting room, exclusive of bars: good stabling with sufficient provender for 12 horses; also a convenient driving house and shed. No intoxicating liquor to be sold or given on Sunday."[71]

Unionville's oldest remaining hotel, most often referred to as the Crown Inn, is thought to have been built about 1860 on the east side of Main Street, north of the bridge over Bruce Creek. The hotel was a one-and-a-half-storey frame building constructed on the property of William Size. Size owned the building and property, but didn't live there. Instead, he rented to a series of hotel keepers, or tenants, as they were called at the time. When the hotel was built, William Size was a widower and resided with his parents, Anthony and Nancy Size, in a hotel they kept on the opposite side of the street, called the Union House. It is curious that William Size would build a hotel in the same vicinity as his parents' establishment, in effect becoming their competitor.

One of the first hotel keepers at William Size's hotel was Avery Bishop, the great-grandfather of the World War One flying ace William Avery "Billy" Bishop, whose seventy-two successful missions made him Canada's top pilot in aerial combat during that era.[72] Toronto's island airport is named for this celebrated Canadian war hero, who was the recipient of many awards, including the Victoria Cross.[73] In the early 1860s, when Billy Bishop's ancestor Avery Bishop was the proprietor of this hotel, it was known as the American Hotel.

From 1865 to 1867 the hotel was called the Centre House, with Joseph Ferris as the proprietor. The Centre House was one of the hotels listed in Mitchell & Co.'s directory of 1866. In 1868 the name was changed to the Crown Inn, which is the one most often associated with William Size's hotel. During the early 1870s, William Spring was the hotel keeper. Through the years 1873 to 1879 William Size himself may have been the proprietor, possibly changing the name of the establishment to the Royal Hotel in 1875. Some accounts suggest the name "Crown Inn" remained in use until 1879. Perhaps as an indication of the growing strength of the temperance movement, in its final years as a hotel the building was named the Temperance House. John Devlin, a harness maker, was a tenant here from 1880 to 1883.

William Size and his family left Unionville to farm in the area of Parry Sound in the mid-1880s. He continued to own his property in Unionville, renting it out to residential tenants until it was offered for public auction in 1900, due to the taxes falling into arrears. Sara Rainey was the buyer. By 1904 she had married Hiram Powers, a builder and grain dealer from Elizabethville, north of Port Hope. According to local tradition, the Powers family converted the old hotel into a private residence, although it had not functioned as a hotel since the early 1880s and therefore had already been used as a dwelling.

The current form of the building, and its architectural details, suggest that Hiram Powers either undertook significant renovations or rebuilt the Crown Inn in the early 1900s.[74] Since early census records tell us that the hotel was a one-and-a-half-storey building, and the house as it stands is a full two storeys high, Powers must have raised the walls and built a new roof to provide a full second storey. At the same time, the windows would have been changed to the larger paned windows popular during the period of the remodelling, and a spacious wraparound verandah added. The prominent corner tower was included as part of the renovations, for the pleasure of Hiram and Sara Powers's daughter, so the story goes. One element said to have been left in place from the building's days as a hotel was the bar, a serving window with a small room behind it that can still be seen in the kitchen.[75]

The Crown Inn is without a doubt a vernacular building with design elements from a number of different architectural styles, the most dominant being the Italianate. After the renovations or rebuilding of circa 1904, the building had a cubic form with a nearly flat roof concealed behind a bracketed, flat-topped parapet on the three sides visible from the street.[76] In later years, a hipped roof more suited to the Canadian climate was added. The tower, with its mansard roof and dormers, is a feature associated with the Second Empire style. By the early 1900s, both of these architectural styles had fallen out of fashion, particularly the Second Empire, so their use on this building is unusual for its time.

Hiram Powers may have decided to use some out-of-date features for his renovated home out of a feeling of nostalgia for other places he had lived. In contrast, he used window details that were current at the time, such as the popular cottage window that combined a large, wide single sheet of glass with a flat-headed transom light. Inside, he installed pressed-metal ceilings and cornice mouldings in the principal ground floor rooms. These panels were manufactured in numerous patterns as an inexpensive imitation of ornate plaster work, and were mainly in vogue for use in commercial and public buildings from the 1890s to the 1910s. The elaboration didn't stop with the ceilings. Hiram Powers also applied pressed-metal panels to the walls, creating unique, highly decorated rooms that have no equal elsewhere in the community. Even the simple wooden casings around interior doors and windows were embellished with decorative work impressed into the surface, much like the carving used on pressback chairs popular around the same time period.

After the Powers family moved on, the former Crown Inn passed through the hands of a succession of owners. During this process some of the features added in the 1904 remodelling disappeared as the exterior was updated and simplified, including the removal of a small balcony and the decorative brackets on the wraparound verandah. In more recent times, the verandah details have been restored, and the house expanded with an addition at the back that preserves the character of this historic building.

Braithwaite House and Store, 154 Main Street, circa 1867

This combined house and store is an exceptionally authentic example of how business was done in the days before commuting to work became the norm. In nineteenth-century Ontario villages and small towns it was common for the owner of a business to reside on the premises, or in a house nearby. Where space permitted, a building plan developed where the shop was the prominent feature, projecting forward toward the street, and the residential quarters were at the rear, set back from the street to provide space for a front garden. Archival photographs of buildings like this often show the garden space enclosed with a picket or paling fence to separate the private realm of the shop owner and his family from the public realm of the storefront.

The Braithwaite House is the last dwelling on Unionville's Main Street to remain in residential use.

Its front and side yards are private green spaces that provide a pleasant contrast with the hard-surfaced surroundings of many of the other former houses that have lost their residential landscape character. Towering lilacs that line the sidewalk are a reminder of a once-greener village.

Mark M. Braithwaite originally lived on the family farm north of the village, at the southeast corner of Kennedy Road and 16th Avenue. He was married to Elizabeth Eckardt, the daughter of wheelwright and sawmill operator Gottlieb Eckardt. His first career was a wagon-maker's apprentice, employed in the shop of William Wilkinson. Mark Braithwaite's father, John Braithwaite, had a store at the crossroads as early as 1842. This store is marked on Tremaine's map of York County, dated 1860.[77] At the time of the 1861 census, Mark Braithwaite's occupation was listed as "merchant and farmer," working in the store near the family farm, established by his father.

In 1863 Mark Braithwaite purchased a sizable portion of Frederick Eckardt's property on the east half of Lot 12, Concession 5, in the heart of Unionville. Most of the property was farmland that formed the backdrop to the commercial establishments on Main Street. In a few years he would build a combined house and store on the Main Street frontage, that today looks much the same as it does in an old photograph of the 1890s. In Mitchell & Co.'s directory of 1866, Mark Braithwaite's diverse business is described as "dealer in dry goods, groceries, hardware, boots and shoes & c., also issuer of marriage licenses, and insurance, north union store."[78] The last part of that description seems to suggest that his location at that time was still in the store at the crossroads north of the village, rather than on his newly purchased property.

Although Mark Braithwaite had purchased the Eckardt property in 1863, he probably didn't build his house and store right away. Between the date of Mitchell and Co.'s directory and the 1871 census he had relocated his family and business into the heart of the village of Unionville, close to the activity generated by the newly arrived Toronto and Nipissing Railway. From 1875 to 1885 Mark Braithwaite was Unionville's postmaster, in addition to the many services he offered at his store.[79] After Mark Braithwaite's time, the old store served other businesses, including a showroom for Edwin Dixon's taxidermist shop, before he moved to the front of Christopher Chant's cabinet shop across the street. For a while the store was the location of the public library, which seemed to move from location to location over the years, occupying vacant commercial space when it was available. Local people still call this the Trunk Store after Vernon and Carol (Braithwaite) Trunk, later owners of the property.

The store portion of the building approaches museum quality in terms of its state of preservation. The storefront is a rare survivor of a Confederation-era village shop, with its glazed and panelled double doors recessed into the facade, large four-paned showcase windows, and simple Classic Revival surround. Its gable-fronted form is typical of businesses occupying commercial frontages, but it also allowed for a wide front garden for the attached residence behind it. In the 1990s structural issues required extensive restoration work, to stabilize the building. The repairs were carefully done, ensuring that the significant original details remained intact. The store would not look out of place in a museum village, and because of its authentic nineteenth-century appearance, the building has appeared in movies, commercials, and television programs.

The residential quarters are in the form of a Classic Ontario farmhouse, with a one-and-a-half-storey form, a Georgian sense of balance in the placement of the entryway and windows, and a steep centre gable containing a pointed-arched window and delicate curvilinear bargeboards. Board-and-batten siding, louvered shutters on the six-over-six windows, and a tent-roofed verandah decorated with fretwork brackets complete this ideal picture of "Ontario Gothic," not too different from the look of the house Grant Wood's famous oil painting, *American Gothic*.

The Queen's Hotel expresses the mood of optimism and promise that accompanied the arrival of the Toronto and Nipissing Railway in 1871.

Markham Museum Archival Collection

Unionville's Golden Age

Unionville prospered in the years following Confederation. The building of the Toronto and Nipissing Railway through the south part of the village attracted business and population away from the area around the Union Mills and the area to the north of the bridge over the Bruce Creek. This was a time of expansion and investment, when the planing mill produced the diverse wooden components needed to feed the building boom, including the gingerbread trim that decorated many of the new houses in and around the village. The legacies of local builders Josiah Hall and George Robinson include many of Unionville's best examples of late Victorian architecture.

Fenwick-Brown General Store, 156 Main Street, circa 1870

One of Unionville's largest and most distinctive commercial buildings had a modest beginning. When Hewlett Eckardt, the owner of the wheelwright and carriage shop that still stands south of the Queen's Hotel, decided to leave Unionville for the greener pastures of California, he sold the large property containing his house and a quantity of vacant land to Margery Keller. In 1870 Margery Keller sold to James W. Fenwick, one of the grandsons of the enterprising Captain James Fenwick of the rural community of Cashel. The captain was the owner of an inn, distillery, and store at the crossroads of Kennedy Road and Elgin Mills Road East. James W. Fenwick's father, Archibald Fenwick, was a successful farmer, a well-to-do land owner, and former member of Markham Township Council, so James W. Fenwick must have had enough knowledge and experience in the world of business to enable him to strike out on his own.[1] Perhaps he received financial support from his distinguished family. With these resources behind him, James W. Fenwick built the first phase of the store on this property, which is the two-storey centre section of the existing building, around 1870.[2]

Bradstreet's business directory of 1871 provides the following listing for the store: "J.W. Fenwick and Co. General Store." James W. Fenwick was assisted by his younger brother, Benjamin, in running the store. Their partnership lasted about five years. By the time of the 1881 census, Benjamin Fenwick remained in Unionville as a merchant, while his older brother had moved to Vaughan Township, where he worked as a bookkeeper for Patterson Brothers, manufacturers of agricultural implements. In 1885 James W. Fenwick embarked on yet another career change and relocated to Toronto, where he founded the Parkdale Furnace Company.

Benjamin Fenwick didn't continue in the store he had shared with his brother. Instead, he moved his business farther up to the street to a rented store owned by his father-in-law, Salem Eckardt, now addressed 182 Main Street. By the time of the 1891 census, Benjamin Fenwick had changed careers. He was listed as a farmer residing in the household of Salem and Catherine Eckardt.

Josiah Hall, a local brick mason and builder in 1870s Unionville, bought the property from James W. Fenwick in 1883. Hall rented out the store to Henry Brown and Eliza Flavelle Brown, who operated a general store there and hoped to buy the property once they became well established. Unfortunately for the Browns, when the property was offered for sale in 1888 they were out-bid by Robert Stiver, which compelled them to relocate to Stouffville for a period of time to run their business in another location. Robert Stiver rented the store to John Devlin, a harness maker.[3]

The Brown family came back to Unionville about 1890–91, and operated a general store out of a small shop attached to a one-storey cottage at 187 Main Street, rented from Mrs. Charlotte Eckardt of Toronto, the wife of Andrew Eckardt. Many years later, this frame cottage became known as the Unionville House Restaurant. The Browns also purchased a local bakery at about the same time. Henry Brown managed a bread delivery route, employing a Mr. Shouldice and members of his family to do the baking. Tragedy struck the family in 1891 when Henry Brown contracted typhoid and died.

Elizabeth Brown carried on the family business, and by 1892 was able to buy the Unionville store where they first operated from Ann Stiver, Robert Stiver's widow. Mrs. Brown built a new bakery in a separate building located behind the general store, employing a series of bakers until her son Arthur Brown, who was in charge of the store's grocery department, was ready to run that part of the business. He was assisted by his brother John. Meanwhile, Elizabeth Brown specialized in millinery and dry goods.

Arthur Brown definitely had inherited the entrepreneurial spirit from his parents, continuing to expand the family's enterprise. In 1904 he opened a photography studio on the second floor of the store, then added an ice cream parlour. After Elizabeth Brown died in 1908 Arthur

Brown and his brother carried on with the store and other ventures, including the construction of a two-storey, brick bank building next to the store about 1920, in the front yard of the house at 158 Main Street. This new building housed a branch of the Standard Bank of Canada, which later became part of the Canadian Imperial Bank of Commerce. The bank was demolished in the 1980s.[4]

The Browns sold the store in 1944, but later repurchased it in 1966 and rented the building to the Unionville Public Library. During Unionville's time as the "Antique Capital of Ontario," an antique store run by Ruth Ingram was located there. It was one of the last vestiges of the thriving antique businesses to remain as Unionville's Antique Capital status faded away.

The building has undergone many changes since it was first constructed circa 1870. Originally the store was a simple, two-storey, board-and-batten building with a "boomtown" front. The storefront was sheltered by a front porch, dressed up with fretsawn brackets. Over the porch was a small-paned window that is thought to have been widened to its present size when Arthur Brown opened his photography studio. As the business continued to prosper, the front of the building was updated with the application of pressed-metal siding in a textured brick pattern. A pressed-metal cornice with ball-shaped finials was added to enhance the store's updated look. This would have taken place in the 1910s, when pressed metal was in popular use for exterior siding and tin ceilings. The storefront was modernized with a leaded-glass transom sash at the same time. In more recent times, a one-storey wing was added to the south side of the building. After the demolition of the old bank, a matching wing was added to the north side of the original building to balance the facade. In its current

form, the Fenwick-Brown General Store has appeared in a number of television commercials as a good representation of a country store of the early 1900s.

Raymer Cheese Factory, 233 Main Street, circa 1870

Some Ontario counties share a rich history of cheese production. In the nineteenth century a number of rural communities had cheese factories as part of their agricultural economy. John Noble Raymer, a member of a Pennsylvania German Mennonite family that had come to Markham Township in 1809, is believed to have established one of the first cheese factories in the province.

Some farmers made their own cheese before the emergence of cheese factories. The Pennsylvania Germans made sour curd cheese, or *schmier kase*, using sour milk after it had thickened. The milk was heated and the solids would be placed in a cloth bag to drain. The cheese was seasoned with salt and butter then rolled into a ball shape and left to cure. This cheese was sometimes placed in crocks to ripen in a warm place until it acquired a distinctive strong taste and a particularly pungent smell. The distinctive cheeses made by the Pennsylvania Germans became popular among people of diverse cultural groups who lived in the same areas.[5]

John Raymer lived on a farm east of the crossroads hamlet of Box Grove, in the southeast part of Markham. The nearby community was called Cedar Grove, a rural neighbourhood that was mainly populated by Pennsylvania German Mennonite families that had been Markham's second wave of settlers after the Berczy group. John Raymer was married to Christina Reesor, whose family had come to Markham in 1804. Peter Reesor had first visited this area in the 1790s to determine its suitability as a potential new home, and based on favourable findings, influenced others in his family and neighbourhood in Pennsylvania to move to Upper Canada.[6]

John Raymer was at first content to be a farmer, but somehow he caught the fancy to learn the art of cheese making. In 1866 he travelled to Evans Mill, New York, to learn about the process. Upon returning to Markham, he established a cheese factory in connection with the family farm, assisted in this endeavour by his father-in-law, Samuel Reesor. Farmers would bring their milk to the factory, and when the cheese was cured by the fall they would pay the factory two cents a pound for the finished product. The rest of the cheese was retained by the factory owner. Cheese made at the Raymer Cheese Factory was sold at a store in Markham Village, and probably at the cheese factory as well.[7]

The Raymers' Box Grove Cheese Factory was such a success that the family decided to expand the operation and open another cheese factory in Unionville, on a half-acre property they purchased in 1869. About 1870 John Raymer, assisted by his brother Martin, built a cheese factory north of the Union Mills, on the east side of Main Street. It is said that an underground stream ran through the property. The former cheese factory building forms a part of the frame house that still stands on the site. The Raymer Cheese Factory was a large enough operation to be shown on a map of the village dating from 1878.

John Raymer had other interests besides farming and cheese making. He was a talented singing instructor in his community, and a strong supporter of his church. Although the numerous members of the Raymer family in Markham were Mennonites, this branch switched to the Methodist faith around the same time as the cheese-making enterprise began. Perhaps John Raymer was exposed to the Methodist view of Christianity while in New York and was impressed enough to make the change. His commitment to his new church was such that he was moved to provide an old granary on his farm to form the basic structure of a new Methodist church at Box Grove.

Tragedy struck in 1874 when John Raymer contracted smallpox and died while still a relatively young man in his late thirties. His brother Martin was also struck down by the disease. The family believed that an infected buffalo robe from Manitoba, purchased at Richmond Hill, was the source of the smallpox. John Raymer's widow, Christina, carried on the business, with the day-to-day work most likely being done by other family members or employees. The Unionville cheese factory continued to operate until at least 1877, as confirmed by the company ledger, and then was closed and sold.[8] The cheese factory building was afterward renovated and converted to a residence, expanded with a front-projecting wing.

Christina Raymer was eventually assisted in the management of the remaining Box Grove cheese factory by her son Franklin Raymer, as soon as he reached the age when he could make a meaningful contribution. According to local history, the business endured until 1900 or 1901. The building's foundation could still be seen in 1991, but today the former Raymer farm is part of a new residential community developed in the 2000s and all traces of the cheese factory have disappeared.[9]

Looking at the house at 233 Main Street today, it is difficult to imagine that it began as a utilitarian industrial structure. Its design and materials reflect the late Victorian vernacular houses being built in the neighbourhood during the 1870s and 1880s, most of which were of frame construction, clad in vertical tongue-and-groove wood siding, and designed with forms and details influenced by the Gothic Revival and Italianate architectural styles. The segmentally headed windows and steeply pitched cross-gabled roof are typical of the time period. The paired round-headed windows on the street-facing gable are similar to those seen on a couple of other 1870s houses in the village, suggesting that the cheese factory was transformed into a residence by the same builder. The wraparound verandah of the house is an attractive later addition, designed in the Edwardian Classical style that was much used in the early twentieth century.

Unionville Railway Station, 7 Station Lane, 1870

In nineteenth-century Ontario the railway was a powerful symbol of progress. Until the arrival of railways in the mid-nineteenth century, transportation of people, goods, and raw materials over any kind of distance was

difficult. Roads were not always dependable and not all areas were located within easy distance of canals and other water-related transportation routes. Limitations on transportation meant that communities large and small were mainly self-sufficient. Places like Unionville, located in the midst of an agricultural heartland, were local centres that supplied almost everything its inhabitants needed, from carriages to coffins.

Given the importance of railways in the development of communities across the province, there must have been considerable excitement in Unionville when it was announced that the Toronto and Nipissing Railway line was to be built through Markham Township. The directors of the Toronto and Nipissing Railway, incorporated in 1868, sought out local investors to help finance the railway venture, and were successful in securing a bonus of $30,000 from the Township of Markham to ensure a station stop or two would be built within the boundaries of the municipality. The narrow-gauge railway would extend northward from the Grand Trunk Railway line between Toronto and Scarborough to ultimately reach the town of Coboconk.[10]

After the initial excitement created by the news of the railway passing through Markham Township, imagine the dismay that must have overtaken the residents and business owners of Unionville when they learned that the new railway line would not be coming to their village, but would pass by to the south. Unionville's hope of becoming an important place would most certainly be over, as progress would favour other centres benefitting from being a station stop on the railway line.

Fortunately for Unionville, Hugh Powell Crosby, the MPP for the riding of York East, was an influential resident of the village and a former member of the railway's provisional board of directors. Crosby was successful in convincing William F. McMaster and the rest of the board of directors of the Toronto and Nipissing Railway to alter the route planned for the line so that it would pass through the south end of Unionville on its way from Scarborough to Uxbridge.[11] The line cut an arc through William Eckardt's subdivision of village lots to the west of Main Street, effectively cutting the emerging residential neighbourhood in two. Streets and lots on the east side of the tracks developed slowly over time as houses were built there one by one, but on the west side of the tracks the land seems to have been sterilized for development and the proposed network of backstreets and lots was not to be. On the east side of Main Street, the line passed through the properties of James Eckardt and William Eakin with minimal disruption to the village plan.

In the latter half of 1870, not long before the railway opened, a frame station scaled to suit the size of the village of Unionville was constructed on land purchased from William Eckardt.[12] Eckardt saw an opportunity to take advantage of the station location and registered a plan for Station Lane and a series of building lots along its path. The station ground brought other business activity to the area and had the effect of altering the focus of village development, both commercial and residential, from the area around and to the north of the Union Mills to the south end of the community.[13] Mail that was formerly brought to Unionville's post office by horse-drawn stage coach now arrived by train. Communication was further improved with the installation of a telegraph line along the tracks by the Montreal Telegraph Company. In terms of shipping and receiving goods, the speed, capacity, and reliability of rail transport easily outstripped that provided by teams of horses hauling heavy wagons.

In the railway's heyday there were two or three passenger trains running both ways six days of the week, as well as the constant traffic of freight trains serving the ever-growing needs of commerce. In 1882 the Toronto and Nipissing Railway amalgamated with the Midland Railway, and before long the narrow-gauge track was changed to the mainstream standard gauge to assure compatibility with the numerous rail lines that existed before their nationalization following the First World War.[14] In 1884 the line was leased to the Grand Trunk Railway, which acquired it outright in 1893. In 1923 the rail line serving Unionville became part of the Canadian National Railway.

Growth and prosperity promised by the coming of the railway lasted into the early twentieth century. However, in time, smaller communities like Unionville that had high hopes for their future based on the railway connecting them to an almost unlimited range of destinations saw industry drawn away to large urban centres like Toronto. The era of self-sufficient communities was over as the cities grew with business, industry, and population, while rural areas lost population and went into decline.

These changes were not all doom and gloom for Unionville. The village remained an important local centre serving the surrounding agricultural community, and even if businesses and industries did not expand to any great degree, village lots continued to be developed as farmers retired to town and people who wanted to live outside of the city could commute to and from their places of employment on the train. Unionville was fortunate not to lose its railway service as the province's rail network began to shrink in the face of improved roads and highways and the resulting car and truck traffic.

In 1982 GO Transit assumed the operation of the VIA Rail commuter line that connected Unionville with Toronto. Unionville Station was a busy place as the residents of the village that had grown into a bedroom community for Toronto made their daily journey to work, enjoying the comfort of train travel rather than enduring a long drive along congested roads and highways. The GO Train continues to run though Unionville and rumble past the old station, but no longer stops in the village. Instead, a new Unionville Station a little farther to the south, with a much larger parking lot, now serves commuters.

Unionville's historic train station, one of the oldest remaining railway stations in Canada, was very nearly lost on two occasions. In 1978 the station was damaged by fire. Following the suspicious fire, CN Rail was not interested in repairing the outdated structure and wanted to demolish it instead. Although the station's appearance was not the best, thanks to a dowdy cladding of red Insulbrick, the building held a great deal of affection with local residents, who lobbied effectively for its preservation.

The Town of Markham acquired the Unionville train station and its surrounding property, and in 1989 the station underwent restoration on its original site to serve as a community centre. The exterior has been returned to the grey-and-green colour scheme it had when it was part of the Grand Trunk Railway system. Inside, the general passenger waiting room can still be seen at the west end of the building, and the freight room is at the east end, now a gathering place for community events. Between them, where the station agent's office and a baggage room/ladies' waiting room were, is a kitchen and washroom serving the modern-day use of the building.[15]

The design of the Unionville Railway Station is close to that of the humble frame workers' cottages in the neighbourhood, with a simple rectangular plan, board-and-batten siding, medium-pitched gable roof, and six-over-six windows — all echoes of the Georgian architectural tradition, but without the strict symmetry. A deep overhang, supported on stout timber braces, shelters the station platform, which is still used from time to time when the York-Durham Heritage Railway runs a special train along this historic route. Unlike its slightly larger sister station in Markham Village, the Unionville Railway Station doesn't have the trackside box bay window that would have enabled the station agent to see up and down the line as trains approached or departed.

The Queen's Hotel, 174 Main Street, circa 1871

No building better captures the optimism that must have been felt in Unionville with the arrival of the railway better than the Queen's Hotel. In its position at the first bend in the route of Main Street, the Queen's Hotel is a landmark that perfectly terminates the view as one

City of Markham

travels up the road from the south. It figures prominently in archival views of the village, and today remains one of Unionville's most photographed historical buildings.

Before there was a hotel on this property there was a store, operated by George Hubertus, on a village lot purchased from Frederick Eckardt in 1852. History does not record what sort of merchandise was sold there, but it must have been one of the first stores in Unionville's village core because it was listed in the township assessment rolls in 1852. Before becoming a merchant, George Hubertus was a schoolteacher at the Colty Corners school at the crossroads of modern-day Kennedy Road and Major Mackenzie Drive. His father, Julius Hubertus, a German immigrant, was a schoolteacher as well. At this time, classes were held in a log building rather than the fine brick schoolhouse that replaced it in 1862.[16]

In 1859 the property was sold to John Stephenson, the blacksmith that had worked alongside Hewlett Eckardt in his wheelwright shop next door before taking over the business. The Hubertus family seems to have left Markham by then. John Stephenson probably rented out the store to another business for the next decade, until he

seized the opportunity presented by the coming of the railway to redevelop the property for a more lucrative use.

A modern hotel in a fashionable architectural style, with all of the amenities a traveller could expect in a hotel in an up-and-coming place important enough to be a station stop on a new railway line was an obvious choice. A hotel with a dining room and drawing room for the more genteel visitors, a barroom for the thirsty locals or travellers, stabling for horses and well-appointed lodgings would be an asset to the community, only a short distance from the railway station. Commercial travellers or salesmen could display their goods in a room reserved for this special purpose. Unionville's other hotels, all older frame buildings north of the mill, would have difficulty competing with a new brick hotel so conveniently located.[17]

The Queen's Hotel, almost certainly named in honour of Queen Victoria, the beloved reigning monarch of the British Empire during the era of Confederation, was built circa 1871, coinciding with the opening of the Toronto and Nipissing Railway through Markham. A spacious hotel ballroom known as Victoria Hall was later constructed over the driving shed behind the hotel, which became a popular venue for concerts, dances, and other community functions. The Magistrate's Court was held in the hotel, and Township Council also met here from 1874 to 1927. Previously, council meetings were held in Size's Hall at the Union House, later renamed Hunter's Hall. The Queen's Hotel became a popular place for city people travelling to the annual Markham Fair to stop for lunch as a highlight of their day trip to the country.[18] An open balcony wrapped around the south and east sides of the building, sheltering the ground-floor entrances while providing a space for visitors to enjoy a view of the village and take in some fresh air. The balcony had a railing composed of wood panels with decorative cut-outs, a rather unusual but nonetheless attractive feature of this building.

John and Jane Webber were the first proprietors of the Queen's Hotel. They were English immigrants with previous experience in the hotel business in Markham, having operated a hotel called the Beehive at nearby Hagerman's Corners. The Webbers secured a liquor licence for the Queen's Hotel in 1873, which was no doubt good for growing their business. In addition to having numerous well-furnished guest rooms, the hotel offered room and board for those in need of modest accommodation before finding more permanent quarters in the community.

Mrs. Webber is said to have been a talented cook who prepared excellent meals for the hotel's dining room, including the oyster suppers that were so popular in Ontario during the last quarter of the nineteenth century. She made regular train trips from Unionville into Toronto to shop for the things that were needed to maintain the Queen's Hotel's reputation as a first-class establishment. The beautiful furnishings of the drawing room, described by Grace Harrington in her recollections of the hotel as it was during her childhood in the opening years of the twentieth century — rich, red, wall-to-wall carpeting, marble-topped parlour tables, elegant sofas, and ornate lamps — were no doubt an indication of Mrs. Webber's discerning eye for quality and elegance.[19]

John Stephenson sold the Queen's Hotel to the Webbers in the summer of 1879 for $3,300. By this time, John Stephenson was busy in his new position as Markham township's clerk and treasurer, an appointment that he held until 1898. The hotel business seemed to run in the Webber family. Their daughter Matilda married Orson Hemingway, who was the hotel keeper at the

Beehive Hotel at Hagerman's Corners after John and Jane Webber relocated to Unionville. Orson and Matilda Hemingway's son, Moses Hemingway, took over the operation of the Queen's Hotel when his grandparents decided the time was right to step back from the family business and pass it on to a new generation.[20]

After the Webbers and the Hemingways, the Queen's Hotel was run by a series of proprietors who carried on in spite of the challenges that came about as Victorian Ontario faded away and the modern era was being ushered in at the turn of the twentieth century. The first of these changes was "local option," a government policy that allowed municipalities to decide if they wanted to be "dry" or not. Markham voted in favour of the prohibition of liquor sales in 1905, which was damaging to the hotel trade to say the least.[21] Many country hotels closed, but the Queen's Hotel somehow carried on, and continued to operate as a hotel, even after full prohibition came about during the First World War.

The second thing to impact the hotels of small-town Ontario as the new century progressed was the advent of the automobile, which soon began to overtake the horse and railway, means of travel that had traditionally provided a steady stream of patrons at a time when life moved at a slower pace. With travel becoming so much more convenient and fast in comparison with the modes of transportation of the past, people didn't require overnight stays for many of their journeys and hotel rooms no longer in demand for travellers became boarding-house accommodation or sat empty behind dusty windows. Such was the fate of the Queen's Hotel.[22]

A period of stability for Unionville's old hotel came about in 1924, when it was purchased by Talbert Findlay and his brothers Howard and Milton.[23] Talbert Findlay, who had been the village barber since about 1914, had his shop across the road from the Queen's Hotel. Perhaps he day-dreamed about one day owning the hotel while he trimmed the whiskers and hair of Unionville's gentlemen, glancing out the window at the object of his desire from time to time.

The Findlays kept the dining room at the north end of the building, and turned the former barroom at the south end into a pool hall. Between the pool hall and the dining room, Talbert Findlay installed a new barbershop behind a large picture window with a coloured-glass transom sash above. His relocated shop was a bright space with a fine view of the daily activity on Main Street. After a while, the old hotel dining room evolved into an ice cream parlour.

The Findlay family continued to own the Queen's Hotel into the 1970s when Unionville's renaissance was just beginning. By that time, the hotel's balcony had dis-appeared and the building, like some of the other old buildings on the street, began to look like it had seen bet-ter days. In spite of being a little rundown, the Queen's Hotel had been little altered from its original condition and for this reason was a good candidate for restoration.

The fortunes of this local landmark changed for the better when, in the 1980s, it was doubled in size with an addition to the rear in the same architectural style. At the same time, a portion of the unique balcony was recon-structed, and the hotel was reborn with retail space on the ground floor and offices above. Today, the three-storey Queen's Hotel remains as much of a local landmark as it was when it first opened its doors in 1871. Although it is not an ornate building or overly ambitious structure, it is an exceptionally well-preserved example of a com-mercial building designed in a vernacular interpretation of the Second Empire style that was in vogue during its period of construction. The wood-shingled mansard roof, punctuated with a series of peaked dormers, readily defines the architectural style as Second Empire. At the same time, the patterned brickwork with quoined corners and "eyebrows" over the segmentally headed windows is a little more generic to the 1870s in southern Ontario, a decorative and colourful treatment for brick buildings of all types that stayed in fashion until about the 1890s.

The Doctor's House, 198 Main Street, 1872

This brick house, with its distinctive double bay windows, is locally known as "The Doctor's House" for its early association with a series of medical doctors who lived in it. The first was Dr. Thomas Philip Eckardt, for whom this prestigious house was built in 1872. The present colour of the brick is the natural variegated buff to salmon produced by the local clay, but originally the brickwork was stained a dark red to give it a more even tone. A small patch of this colouring that escaped sandblasting can still be seen on the north gable-end wall, adjacent to an electrical box.

Thomas Philip Eckardt was a son of Philip Eckardt Jr. and Susannah Hegler. He grew up on a farm south of Unionville, at the southeast corner of what is now known as Main Street and Highway 7. The Eckardt farmhouse still stands on its original site, hidden from view amidst a development of townhouses on Meadowbrook Lane. In 1851 Thomas Philip Eckardt was nineteen years of age and living at home. Shortly thereafter, he pursued a career in the medical field.

In the latter half of the 1850s, Thomas Philip Eckardt attended the Massachusetts Medical College of Harvard University in Cambridge, Massachusetts. He earned his doctor of medicine in 1859.[24] The subject of his dissertation was "The Pulse — Its Condition and Variation in Health, and the Indications it Affords of Disease." It appears that following graduation, Dr. Eckardt remained in the United States, where he may have set up a medical practice for a short time. By 1862 he was back in Canada, pursuing additional medical training at the University of Toronto.[25] Perhaps his decision to leave the United States was motivated by the outbreak of the American Civil War in the spring of 1861, and the doctor chose to remove himself from potential service in the Union army.

After completing his further medical education at the University of Toronto, Dr. Eckardt returned to Unionville, living on the family farm south of the village once again before he married Abigail "Abby" Robinson on April 2, 1866. Fine photographic portraits of Thomas Philip Eckardt and Abigail, perhaps taken at the time of their wedding, are found in the Unionville Women's Institute's Tweedsmuir History scrapbook in the collection of the Markham Museum. In his photograph, the doctor has the longish, wavy hair, trim moustache, and artistically unkempt beard typical of the time period.

Abigail was a daughter of Andrew Robinson and Mary Whaley of Markham Village. One of her brothers, Wesley Robinson, was a medical doctor who had graduated from McGill University in Montreal in 1872.[26] Did Wesley Robinson's decision to become a doctor result from the influence of his brother-in-law? It certainly seems possible.

At the time of his marriage, Dr. Eckardt held a position of considerable prestige in his community. In Mitchell & Co.'s directory of 1866 his listing appears: "ECKARDT, THOMAS P., M.D., physician, surgeon and coroner for York and Peel." His work must have taken him far from home on numerous occasions. There is a local tradition that Dr. Eckardt lived in the adobe-brick house built by Frederick Eckardt, now addressed 206 Main Street.[27] This would have been in the early years of his marriage, before the brick house a few doors down the street was completed in 1872. The new house was of a scale and quality suited to a family of distinction in the community. Jennie Harrington, who grew up in Unionville, remembered that local children admired the peacock that Dr. Eckardt kept on the property.[28]

Dr. Eckardt wasn't the only doctor in the village. Dr. Charles Justice had a practice in Unionville from the late 1850s until at least the early 1870s. He followed Dr. N.R. Reed, who had died in 1857. Dr. Charles Justice, M.D., was known as a surgeon. He resided in the northern section of the village, according to census and assessment records, and dabbled in property investments to augment his income as a medical practitioner.

Tragically, Dr. Eckardt died at the age of forty-seven in 1880, leaving his wife with an infant daughter, Muriel, and their older daughter, Hattie, age thirteen.[29] The doctor had been attending a patient some distance from home when he went to sit down to rest in another room of the residence he was visiting. When someone went to check on him some time afterwards, Dr. Eckardt was found dead. The cause was determined to be Bright's disease, an affliction of the kidneys.[30]

Several years after her husband's death, Abigail Eckardt and her daughters moved to a smaller house at 151 Main Street, next door to the original Congregational church that became a Presbyterian church about 1880. The family's larger brick house was rented out to other doctors. The first was Dr. Alexander Robinson, from 1887 to 1892, followed by Dr. John Watson, from 1895 to 1899. After Dr. Watson came Dr. Roswell Henry Trumpour, who at first rented then later purchased the property from Abigail Eckardt in 1914. Hattie Eckardt became a missionary for a time, and was the organist in the Presbyterian Sunday school. She remained single for many years, then later in life married George Whaley. Her younger sister, Muriel, remained unmarried and died in 1910.

In 1936 Emma Trumpour's executors sold the property to Frank and Mabel Roberts. The Roberts family were followed by other residential owners until 1978, when the doctor's house became a restaurant. It remains so today. During removal of wallpaper in one of the main rooms, the owner discovered the date "1872" inscribed upon the bare plaster, confirming the date of the building's construction.

The Arch Tree House, 128 Main Street, circa 1873

The Arch Tree House is named for the old, arched cedar trees in the park-like north yard of the property that, for many years, served as a beautiful backdrop for

wedding photographs. Couples being married at Central United Church, directly across the street, would use the extensively landscaped garden of this large property as a picturesque setting for their photographs on their special day, thanks to the generosity of the owner. Unionville remains a popular place for wedding photography to this day, but now portraits are taken in the more public places in the village, such as the Millennium Bandstand, train station, and the gazebo near the site of the old planing mill.

The board-and-batten house on the south half of this property was built circa 1873, when Clarissa Ann Summerfeldt purchased a building lot from William Eckardt in his subdivision of village lots near the railway line, registered that same year. The property was enlarged with the purchase of the adjoining lot to the north a few months afterward. This northerly lot, never built upon, is the location of the "arch tree" and the garden that surrounds it.

Clarissa Ann Summerfeldt was the daughter of John Henry Summerfeldt and Euphemia Hagerman. She was likely named after her grandmother, Clarissa Ransom Summerfeldt. The family farm was on Lot 29, Concession 4, northwest of the crossroads community of Cashel. Her mother was widowed in 1870 when Clarissa Ann's father and sister Mary Ellen drowned in the Buttonville mill-pond, most likely during a family outing.[31] In a community like Markham Township, with no large lakes within its boundaries, millponds were popular places for swimming and boating. From time to time, these artificial ponds claimed the lives of poor swimmers unprepared for deep water or an accidental spill from a boat. After this tragedy, the eldest son, William Summerfeldt, took over the family farm, while his mother and surviving siblings Clarissa Ann and Murray moved into the village of Unionville.

It isn't clear why Clarissa Ann or "Clara" Summerfeldt was the one to purchase the building lots in Unionville, rather than her mother. She was unmarried and without a profession that would provide an income to finance buying a property and having a house built upon it. Although Clarissa Ann Summerfeldt entered into an agreement to rent the family home to her mother for life for the nominal sum of $1 a year, which gives the impression that she had moved away, she continued to live there. After residing with his mother and sister for a period of time, Murray Summerfeldt moved out of Unionville, first to Cherrywood, where he met and married Jeanette Wood. He later moved to Mount Albert, and finally Cannington, where he operated a furniture and under-taking business. Euphemia Summerfeldt died in 1912 and Clarissa Ann Summerfeldt in 1925. The property stayed in the Summerfeldt family until 1940, when Murray and Jeanette Summerfeldt sold to Lionel Middleton.

The Arch Tree House is a simple vernacular building, with some of the characteristics of the Gothic Revival style but none of the distinctly Gothic Revival ornamentation associated with it. The house has an L-shaped plan with a north and east facing ell that contains a deep Edwardian Classical–style verandah, no doubt an addition of the 1910s. A canted bay window on the street-facing gable end is the only enhancement of the basic form of the building. Even without the decorative details that dress up other late Victorian residences in the vicinity, the Arch Tree house has a quiet, crisp beauty about it that comes from its good proportions, board-and-batten siding with moulded battens, and medium-pitched cross-gabled roof, all set within a garden landscape that seems to embrace it.

Robert and Henrietta Harrington House, 141 Main Street, circa 1873

Architectural pattern books, many published in the United States in the second half of the nineteenth century and widely available across North America, guided the work of many local builders. For houses designed to be suited for country settings, there were three different classes of dwellings: cottages, farmhouses, and villas. Cottages were the smallest of these, generally one-and-a-half storeys in height and compact in plan. Farmhouses were larger versions of the cottage. When it came to the home of a gentleman, the villa was the largest and most sophisticated country dwelling.[32] For the Robert and Henrietta Harrington House, one of the most prestigious historic residences in Unionville, the term "villa" seems to fit.

Robert Harrington's family came to York County from Cleveland, Ohio, in 1804. Some members of the family settled in Markham Township, others in Scarborough Township.[33] Robert Harrington kept a store in Armadale, a crossroads community that straddled the border between Scarborough and Markham Townships, centred at the intersection of Markham Road and Steeles Avenue. He was Armadale's first postmaster when a post office was granted to the community in 1869.[34] Today little remains of this rural hamlet. A couple of old sugar maple trees stand on the southwest corner of the intersection in front of a modern bank, close to where the old store once stood.

Robert Harrington resigned from his position of postmaster after only one year, having decided to become a carpenter and builder. About 1874 he relocated to Unionville, and worked on jobs that ranged from repairs to existing buildings to the construction of entire houses in both Markham and Scarborough townships.

In 1873 Josiah Hall, a mason, was employed by Robert Harrington to build a fieldstone foundation for a new house on William Eakin's property. This was an important year for William Eakin. He was Markham Township's newly elected reeve and the owner of a new planing mill on the east side of Main Street, just north of the Toronto and Nipissing Railway line that had been built through the village in 1871. Historically, it was known as a sash and door factory. Previously, William Eakin had been a partner with his brother George in the Unionville Carriage Factory. The carriage factory later produced agricultural implements as well as an assortment of horse-drawn vehicles, operating until about 1871.[35]

Robert Harrington built a spacious and elegant Italianate villa on Josiah Hall's foundation. Hall likely did the brickwork as well, since Robert Harrington was a carpenter by trade. Seeing potential for business in the neighbourhood, one year later Josiah Hall moved to Unionville from the Scarborough Township community of Woburn. He built his own home on Station Lane and thereafter constructed numerous houses and churches in Unionville and other parts of Markham Township before moving to Toronto in the mid-1880s.

Assessment and census records tell us that in 1881 Robert Harrington was a carpenter living on a property he rented from John Gormley, on part of Lot 13, Concession 6, north of the bridge over the Bruce Creek.[36] At the same time, William Eakin was a sash and door maker living on Lot 12, Concession 6, in the heart of the village. Based on historical records, it appears that William Eakin, not Robert Harrington, was the first resident of the brick house at 141 Main Street, and William Eakin continued in the planing mill business until he sold the property to Robert Harrington in 1881.[37]

Robert Harrington's 1881 purchase included the beautiful house overlooking the mill property that he had worked on in 1873, as well as the planing mill. Not long after William Eakin sold his business and home, he moved away to embrace the opportunities then offered by the opening of the Canadian West. In 1883, while serving as Markham Township's reeve for the sixth time, he resigned his position, which was taken up by Thomas Williamson. William Eakin began his new life in Canada's western provinces as an agent for the Saskatchewan Land and Homestead Company. He later had a distinguished career in public service when he was elected to serve as the Liberal representative for the riding of Saltcoats in the Northwest Assembly, and in 1898 was appointed Speaker, a position he held for two terms. The Northwest Assembly governed Saskatchewan and Alberta.[38]

Robert Harrington was assisted in the planing mill by his sons, Delos and George. The mill machinery was not run by a water wheel but by steam power. The mill produced dimensional lumber, but also wood siding, mouldings, windows, doors, blinds (window shutters), bargeboards, spandrels, and brackets. In other words, all of the decorative elements in wood associated with the often exuberant buildings of the late nineteenth century were produced there. The output of Harrington's Planing Mill can still be seen throughout Unionville and for miles around.

Robert Harrington retired from the business in 1896, leaving his sons Delos and George to carry on. The planing mill continued under Delos Harrington, and after 1928 under George Harrington's son Arthur, until it was sold out of the family in 1960. Fire claimed this local landmark in the late 1970s, a terrible loss for old Unionville.[39]

The Harrington House remains as one of Unionville's finest old homes. For several years it has housed a real estate office rather than a family. It sits somewhat aloof from the traffic of Main Street, fronting on the original road allowance that runs through the broad floodplain of the Rouge River a little farther to the north of the property. The house, rendered in patterned brick and a full two storeys in height, has a blocky form, low-pitched hipped roof with bracketed eaves, and a commodious front verandah, all hallmarks of the Italianate mode of building that vied with the Gothic Revival as the style of choice in post-Confederation Ontario. The double doors of the main entrance, topped by a coloured-glass transom light, segmentally headed windows framed with functional louvered wood shutters, and the ornate woodwork of the front verandah are all original features that have been exceptionally well maintained on this historic treasure.

Job and Elizabeth McDowell House, 14 Eureka Street, circa 1874

When this house was new it was on the outer edge of the built-up part of Unionville. William Eckardt was not able to realize any significant returns from his subdivision of village lots laid out in 1856 until the arrival of the railway. Once the railway line and its associated station were established, some fine new houses were built on the lots fronting on the west side of Main Street, while more modest homes, mainly those of tradesmen and labourers, were constructed on the backstreets.[40]

Job McDowell was an Irish-born weaver. His wife, Elizabeth Bodkin, bought Village Lot 20 from William Eckardt in 1874, and the family built a modest board-and-batten-sided house on the property.[41] Like many of the other working man's dwellings in the area, the McDowell House was a one-and-a-half-storey frame building designed in a simplified rendition of the Georgian architectural tradition. Its six-over-six windows would have been old-fashioned for its time, when windows with two-over-two glazing were generally being used for new buildings, or in the updating of old ones.

Weavers were not as common in nineteenth-century Unionville as other trades, perhaps because the village didn't have a woollen mill in it or near enough to attract weavers to the area. Census returns from 1861 and 1871 tell us that there was at least one weaver, Alexander Cotter, in the neighbourhood before Job McDowell. We don't know what type of products were made by Alexander Cotter or by Job McDowell, but a clue may be found in the history of the hamlet of Buttonville, an early mill village west of Unionville where an airport was later established. In that community, in the mid-nineteenth century, the Sutton family wove carpets on a large loom they brought over from England when they emigrated to Canada West.[42]

In the late 1880s or early 1890s, Job and Elizabeth McDowell altered the conservative design of their home with two additions. A verandah was built across the front, with fretwork brackets and a fan-shaped decorative treatment on the gable ends, reflecting the Queen Anne Revival style of the time period. More significantly, a two-storey

canted bay window was added to the south end of the house, to take advantage of the light and warmth offered by that orientation. From the south, the character of the little house was so different from that of the east that it looked like two different buildings, depending on the observer's point of view. The bay window had the effect of making the McDowell House seem larger than it really was.

Elizabeth McDowell sold the family home in 1913 to Eleanor Stiver, the wife of local entrepreneur Reuben A. Stiver, who had an interest in many Unionville properties, particularly in this neighbourhood. Mrs. Stiver promptly sold the property to Thomas Tran, who owned it until 1920. The Ogden family, who owned the property until 1959, didn't alter the house very much, even though there was a strong trend to modernize in the post-war period. In fact, until 2014, when significant additions were made, the former weaver's house had remained one of the few older buildings in Unionville that had not been subject to gentrification.

Andrew and Martha Nicholson House, 136 Main Street, circa 1874

In nineteenth-century communities where a gristmill was in operation, there was sure to be a cooperage nearby to supply the barrels needed to store and ship the flour produced there. Unionville was no exception.[43] Andrew Nicholson and his brother George were coopers who had established their business in the village as early as 1866, based on their listing in Mitchell & Co.'s directory of that year. The Nicholsons were Irish immigrants.

Barrels and kegs were also useful for containing other foodstuffs and beverages such as cider or whiskey. They

steep centre gable, and one-and-a-half-storey height. This style of domestic vernacular architecture, emblematic of the Ontario countryside from the 1860s to 1900, blends the balanced form of the Georgian architectural tradition with the verticality and decoration of the Gothic Revival. Although houses of this style were very common in Markham Township, very few were built in Unionville. This example is noteworthy for the crispness of its design and its fine state of preservation. The house has vertical tongue-and-groove siding, well-suited to its style, and still has the original two-over-two windows. In a departure from the Gothic Revival, the builder chose to use a round-headed window in the front gable instead of one with a pointed-arched top.

had to be strong and watertight to protect the contents. Their construction required specialized tradesmen who employed tools expressly designed for that purpose, including curved wooden planes designed to follow the contours of the staves or wooden strips that formed the body of the barrel. Iron hoops, produced by a local blacksmith, were used to securely bind the staves together.

The Nicholson cooperage was located on a rented property north of the railway tracks, on the northwest corner of Main Street and Station Lane. It was constructed on the top of the bank adjacent to a tributary of the Rouge River that flowed through the planing mill property across the road. In 1874 Andrew Nicholson purchased the property from William Eckardt. The house at 136 Main Street may have already been built by this time, or perhaps a more modest dwelling was replaced once Andrew Nicholson became the owner. The cooperage was most likely operated in a workshop somewhere on the same property. The building no longer stands.

The Nicholson House follows the design of the Classic Ontario farmhouse, with its symmetrical facade,

The Village Hardware Store, 159 Main Street, circa 1874

Hardware stores have been a staple of small-town Ontario for generations — at least before the arrival

of the "big box" home improvement outlets that have replaced many locally owned and operated businesses. The old-time hardware stores had a certain smell to them — a pleasant smell, which seemed to be a mixture of oiled hardwood floors, rubber, and metal. Nails were sold by weight out of bins, and if your window was broken and you needed a piece of glass cut, the store proprietor would cut it for you on the back counter while you waited.

Unionville's old hardware store was just such a place. The building is believed to have been constructed about 1874 by John Eckardt, as a combined store and residence. John Eckardt was a son of George Eckardt and Isabella Robinson, who farmed the east hundred acres of Lot 11, Concession 6, east of the village. John Eckardt worked here as a merchant for a couple of years, then sold the property to follow his father's example and pursue the life of a farmer instead of a merchant. The store was rented by John Dunn to Reuben A. Stiver, who opened a hardware business there beginning about 1877. A few years later he decided to give up the hardware business as a speciality in favour of becoming a general merchant, and in 1885 moved into the commercial building now addressed as 182 Main Street, which he rented from Salem Eckardt.[44]

William Padget of Unionville, a member of Markham Township Council from 1868 to 1871, and Alexander Hay of Toronto bought the property from John Ramsay in 1888 and opened Padget and Hay Hardware and Horse. William Padget's son George went on to establish a hardware store in Agincourt, a village in Scarborough Township. William Padget's interest in local politics carried on into the twentieth century. He was appointed one of the first trustees of the Police Village of Unionville when it was formed in 1907.[45]

In 1917 George Padget sold the property to Archibald Brownlee, who operated a tinsmith shop to the south of Padget and Hay's store. The next year the hardware store was sold to John W. Graham, who ran a hardware store here for a brief period before selling to Joseph W. Perkin in 1919. Perkin Hardware operated from the premises from that time until the late 1970s.[46] Unionville's first telephone exchange was located in the building in 1900. When the automobile age was well underway, a gasoline pump was installed. The year was 1927. In 1964 Perkin Hardware became part of the Home Hardware group. The business expanded to include the sale and delivery of furnace oil.

Reginald R. Perkin was the last proprietor at the Unionville store. The hardware store relocated to larger quarters on Woodbine Avenue, south of Buttonville, after a fire in the late 1970s. Perkin Hardware still operates today under the ownership of Reginald Perkin's sons as one of Markham's longest-established businesses.

The design of the Village Hardware Store follows a plan from a time when the owner of a small-town business lived in the same place he or she worked. In some cases, the residential quarters were on the upper floors of a commercial building, which would be the norm in a business block typical of a town or city environment. In the village setting of a place like Unionville there was more frontage to work with, and the buildings were individual structures rather than joined together in a row. This allowed for an L-plan shape, where the store was placed close to the street, and the residence recessed, allowing for a private front-yard garden for the pleasure of those who lived there. The Unionville Hardware Store follows this plan, but because it is located on a piece of land constrained by the river valley at the rear, the recessed area is only large enough to accommodate a verandah in the ell.

The Unionville Hardware Store was originally sided in board and batten, which had been covered over with modern claddings for many years. A renovation undertaken in 2007 restored the exterior to board and batten, and reinstated a verandah in the place where the original must have existed in the past. The presence of a door in the gable above the former residential part of the building is an indication that the old verandah likely included a small balcony overlooking the street.

The simple pilasters and cornice framing the storefront are from the 1870s time period. The current storefront is largely a product of the early twentieth century, with its angled, recessed entryway and large showcase windows with leaded-glass transom sash above. The clear glass arranged in a geometric pattern is typical of the 1910s. Curvilinear bargeboards decorating the gables reflect a Gothic Revival influence in the building's design, as does the steeply pitched gable over the verandah.

In 1978 a major fire nearly destroyed the building. Much of the roof and rear portion of the structure were damaged, but fortunately the storefront and most of the facade of residential portion survived. The heavily damaged parts of the building were reconstructed in their original form, incorporating the front part that escaped the devastation.

Josiah and Phoebe Hall House, 4 Station Lane, circa 1874

Josiah Hall was Unionville's premiere builder in brick in the 1870s.[47] He was an Irish immigrant, born near Dublin in 1837. In 1860 Josiah Hall came to Canada, first living in Scarborough Township near the village of Woburn. According to the 1861 census, he was

employed as a shoemaker during his early years in his new country. By 1871 Josiah Hall was still residing in Scarborough, but his career had changed to brick mason. Perhaps he had learned his new trade in Canada, or maybe he could not find construction work right away and settled for shoemaking until his situation changed. His household consisted of his wife, Phoebe, born in Ontario, two young daughters, and his widowed mother, Eliza. A son, Josiah, had sadly died at only one day old. His weather-worn marble headstone at the Bethel Pioneer Memorial Cemetery on the east side of Kennedy Road, just south of Eglinton Avenue, is a melancholy reminder of the high rate of infant mortality in the days before modern medical care.

In 1874 Josiah Hall purchased two adjoining village lots from William Eckardt on Station Lane, with the intent of moving from Woburn to Unionville. His name was already known in the community from advertisements he placed in the *Markham Economist*. At 4 Station Lane, Josiah Hall built a one-and-a-half-storey brick house for his family, and a large stable and storage shed that probably served as his workshop as well. He is described in some sources as an architect and a builder, but there is no documented evidence that he had formal architectural training. His trademark style was the Gothic Revival, sometimes mixed with elements of the Italianate style, rendered in patterned brick, perhaps inspired by architectural pattern books or the work of other builders of his day. He built a number of houses in Unionville and elsewhere in Markham Township, but is perhaps best known as the builder of several churches in the late 1870s and early 1880s.[48] In the case of the churches, he executed the designs of professional architects. When the Primitive Methodist church in Unionville was built in 1879, Josiah Hall, a lay preacher in the congregation, was one of the contributors to the building fund as well as the contractor.[49]

Josiah Hall's residential work was lighthearted and decorative, constructed of red brick with buff-coloured brick accents, historically called white brick, combined with lacy bargeboards and picturesque plan outlines. Segmentally arched windows and canted bay windows were common design features of his attractive, comfortable houses. Although the overall form of Josiah Hall's houses followed the Gothic Revival model, for his residential work he used round-headed windows in his steep gables instead of the pointed-arched style, which was reserved for the churches he built. His house on Station Lane is typical of his signature style, with two exceptions. The first is that there is no bay window. The second is the wooden treillage of the verandah, an attractive feature of this home, but possibly a replacement for turned posts and fretwork more characteristic of the 1870s time period.

In addition to houses and churches, Josiah Hall was also the builder of the grammar school in Markham Village.[50] In 1881 he was one of several bidders for the construction of the town hall in Markham Village, but the lowest bidder got the job.[51] There are likely other buildings in Markham Township that were built by Josiah Hall waiting to be discovered through further research, some still standing and others demolished as farmland became subdivisions.

By the early 1880s Unionville's building boom was winding down after a flurry of construction activity in the 1870s. This decline in work likely led to Josiah Hall's decision to sell the family home in 1885 and leave the village in search of new building opportunities in Toronto, where neighbourhoods were rapidly expanding in places like Yorkville. In Toronto's streetcar suburbs of the late nineteenth century, street after street of two- and three-storey single, double. and row houses on narrow urban lots were being built to fill the demand for inexpensive housing. Since Toronto was then known as a city of brick, the potential work for a skilled brick mason must have seemed almost limitless.

After the Hall family left for the opportunities of Toronto, the house was owned by a series of others. A noteworthy later owner of the Hall House was Joseph Havelock Chant, one of the sons of local cabinetmaker Christopher Chant, who bought the property in 1926. Havelock Chant had worked for the Midland Railway beginning in 1883, and later the Grand Trunk Railway, until he retired in 1929. He lived here until 1951.[52]

Through all the years and owners, the house has been very well maintained, with its original character kept intact. It is an excellent example of Josiah Hall's residential work. Only the stable has disappeared from the property, which is regrettable because of its refined design, with doorways decorated with semi-elliptical arches.

George and Frances Pingle House, 15 Station Lane, circa 1874

Station Lane was formally established in 1873, when William Eckardt created Plan 335. In addition to providing access to the station ground from Main Street, building lots were created along the length of the street. Lot J was an awkward piece of land bounded by Station Lane, Eureka Street, and the railway tracks, probably better suited to an industrial use due to its proximity to the railway right of way than as a place to build a house.

George Pingle, a labourer, purchased this triangular lot in 1874 for the modest sum of $100. The location of the lot next to the noise and activity of the railway line made it an affordable choice for a family of limited means. Here, George Pingle and his wife, Frances, built a small house of balloon-frame construction, following the basic Georgian model of a symmetrical, one-and-a-half-storey worker's cottage. The house had an entrance door centred on the front wall, flanked by a pair of identical two-over-two windows. There was nothing fancy about the Pingle House, but for a labourer to own his own home, it must have provided a measure of contentment.

George and Frances Pingle lived in this small house with their five children, as we know from the 1881 census. Ten years later, George Pingle's occupation is given as farm labourer, and the eldest daughter, Maud, is a dressmaker. There were still seven people inhabiting the seven rooms under this roof in 1891. One wonders how a farm labourer could earn enough to support a family and own a home at this time. The income earned by their daughter probably helped.

The Pingles also supplemented the family income by having sold the west portion of their land, probably with a house built upon it, to Jemima Biles, a widow, in 1879. This frame house, addressed 33 Eureka Street but with its front facing Station Lane, was sold back to the Pingle family in 1891 by George Biles. Since Frances Pingle's maiden name was Biles, George Biles must have been related to her. In 1920 the administrators of Frances Pingle's estate sold the house at 15 Station Lane to James Denny.

In more recent times, renovations removed the front door from the former Pingle House, and the front windows were enlarged and glazed with modern windows with plastic grilles that didn't fit the style or period of the house. Then, in 2007, a new owner added an addition to the east end of the house, in effect creating two house volumes side by side, joined with a link that preserved the form of the older portion of the building. As part of the expansion and renovation of the house, the altered features of the facade were restored, including the front door that had been missing for so long. One feature that was discovered too late in the restoration to be reinstated was the original siding of wide, vertical tongue-and-groove boards. Instead, narrow clapboard was used, another historically appropriate treatment.[53]

John and Mary Stephenson House, 133 Main Street, circa 1875

One of Unionville's most architecturally interesting and attractive houses is connected with a remarkable success story. John Stephenson was a Canadian-born blacksmith of English descent. He got his start in the trade in Cashel, a crossroads community some distance to the north of the village but still within the boundaries of Markham Township.[54] By the early 1860s he was married and had moved to Unionville to work alongside Hewlett Eckardt in his carriage-making and wheelwright shop.[55]

Hewlett Eckardt decided to make a big move in 1863, relocating to California, while John Stephenson elected to stay where he was and continued to work as

a blacksmith in the brick wheelwright shop that had been built by Hewlett Eckardt's father, Gottlieb Eckardt, in the 1830s. The shop still stands at 166 Main Street.

John Stephenson had a good head for business. He saw opportunities to advance his situation and seized them.[56] The first good decision he made was to purchase a large piece of strategically located commercial land next door to the shop where he worked. When the Toronto and Nipissing Railway came to Unionville in 1871, the next big thing he did was to take the bold step of building a three-storey brick hotel on his property, much closer to the new station than any of the older hotels on the street.

The Queen's Hotel was a successful venture thanks to the railway, the location, and the famous hospitality of John and Jane Webber, experienced hotel keepers who ran the business on John Stephenson's behalf. While still working at his trade, he had the good fortune to be appointed as township clerk and treasurer in 1874, taking over for local merchant and former postmaster George Eakin. In 1879 John Stephenson sold the hotel to the Webbers, who had decided to put roots down in Unionville.

In 1875 John Stephenson bought a village lot in James Eckardt's new subdivision of village lots, just south of James Eckardt's house and farm lane. This farm lane was named Maple Lane for the large maple tree that stood at the rear of the lot purchased by John Stephenson. On this property a spacious frame house was built for the Stephensons, possibly by local builder George Robinson, who built a number of other picturesque frame houses in the south part of Unionville.[57]

In the 1890s John Stephenson opened the J. Stephenson & Co. Bank in the south wing of his residence.[58] This is the first indication of a bank in the village, remarkable for the fact that it was started by an individual and that it was operated from a private home. The bank operated for about ten years. During this time, John Stephenson continued in his position as township clerk and treasurer until 1899, when Charles H. Stiver took over. The family's success allowed the Stephensons the resources to provide their son George Henry Stephenson with a first-rate education that enabled him to become a barrister in Toronto.[59]

After the J. Stephenson & Co. Bank ceased to operate in 1901, a new bank opened in the village called the Sovereign Bank of Canada. It was located on the west side of Main Street on a property that was later occupied by a modern post office that opened in 1961, now addressed 186 Main Street.[60] The Sovereign Bank didn't last too long, closing in 1908. A branch of the Standard Bank of Canada became established in Unionville by 1910, managed by a Mr. Hutcheson. About 1920 the Standard Bank moved their branch into a new Edwardian Classical–style brick bank built for lease by local entrepreneur Art Brown in the front yard of his residence, now 158 Main Street. The Standard Bank merged with the Canadian Imperial Bank of Commerce in 1928. Eventually, the Unionville branch moved to a new building on Highway 7, and the old building was demolished in the 1980s.

John and Mary Stephenson's house is an outstanding example of vernacular architecture with a somewhat understated influence of the Gothic Revival, all the more valuable for its exceptional state of preservation. The main block is gable-fronted, with its broad, street-facing gable ornamented with a wooden quatrefoil. This decorative element is repeated in the steep gable of the sidewing that housed the J. Stephenson & Co. Bank. The house still has its original, segmentally headed windows and an impressive entrance framed

with a transom light and sidelights. A pair of French doors provides an elegant means of accessing the covered front porch. An unusual aspect of the design of the Stephenson House is the tall, steeply pitched gable of the sidewing, which contains a pointed-arched window. The angle is so pronounced it almost gives the impression that the builder had run out of room and needed to compress the gable to fit it in the available space.

James and Sarah Jane Eckardt House, 137 Main Street, circa 1875

Some of Unionville's best examples of late Victorian domestic architecture are to be found on the east side of Main Street, between Highway 7 and the railway crossing to the north. This Main Street frontage was originally the farm of Gottlieb Eckardt, one of the sons of Philip Eckardt and Ann Elizabeth Koepke. Lot 11, Concession 6, Markham Township was one of several properties granted by the Crown to William Berczy. In 1804 Berczy sold the 200-acre property to a speculator, John Gray. Gray held onto the land for a number of years before selling to Philip Eckardt in 1827. He didn't live there, but made the west half of the property available for the use of his son Gottlieb Eckardt, and the east half to another son, George Eckardt.

Gottlieb Eckardt is often associated with the brick wheelwright shop that he built and operated a little farther to the north on Main Street, but he is best remembered for his role in the Upper Canada Rebellion of 1837 as a supporter of William Lyon Mackenzie. Gottlieb Eckardt was one of a group of residents in the Unionville area that were briefly incarcerated for their activity and rebel sympathies during the time of the rebellion.[61]

On this property, taking advantage of the Rouge River that ran through it, Gottlieb Eckardt operated a sawmill. The approximate location of the sawmill and the millpond that served it is shown on maps of Markham Township dating from 1853 and 1860. According to the reminiscences of Gottlieb Eckardt's grandson A.J.H. Eckardt, the sawmill was established by Philip Eckardt in the early nineteenth century.[62] It was mentioned in Gottlieb Eckardt's will, and ceased to operate not long after his death in 1852. According to the 1851 census, a pump-making workshop operated by William Eckardt, one of the sons of Gottlieb Eckardt and Catharine Helmke, was located on the same property.

James Eckardt, another of Gottlieb Eckardt's sons, inherited the family farm in 1852. The original house on the property was frame and one-and-a-half storeys in height. The location of the old house may have been in the vicinity of the present residence at 137 Main Street, if the small rectangle shown on Tremaine's map of 1860 is at all accurate.

James Eckardt married Sarah Jane Size, a daughter of local hotel owner Anthony Size, in 1859. The family first lived in the old frame house on the property that had been built by Gottlieb Eckardt many years before, but by 1875 a new house of brick was constructed. At the same time the new house was built, the Main Street frontage of the farm was subdivided by Plan 401 into forty-nine village lots.[63] This plan created Maple Lane and Eckardt Avenue. The lots on Main Street were the first to be sold and built upon, but the lots on the side streets were not developed until the 1910s through the 1920s. After the death of Sarah Jane, James Eckardt remarried in 1893. His second wife was named Agnes Cowan.[64]

The circa 1875 house, located just south of the railway line, is one-and-a-half storeys high and built of the variegated brick locally produced at the Snowball brickworks. The architectural style reflects the influence of the Gothic Revival in its irregular plan shape, its picturesque, many-gabled roofline, and the pointed-arched window in the steep gable over the front porch. The asymmetrical arrangement of windows on the street-facing facade is unusual, particularly with respect to the window to the right of the two-storey canted bay window. This ground-floor window, with a wooden canopy over it, was once a door leading into the entrance hall before the door was moved around the corner to open onto the porch. A second door within the porch was changed to a window when the other front door was relocated. Another unusual feature is the treatment of the overhanging eaves of the portion of the house containing the bay window. It seems to suggest that perhaps the builder had intended to apply some decorative woodwork to accent the gables and thereby mask the differences in the gable and wall planes.

Certainly this spacious brick house was a reflection of James Eckardt's stature in the community as the owner of a large farm, justice of the peace, licence inspector, and president of the East York Agricultural Society. The original segmentally headed windows, framed by operational louvered shutters, are characteristic of the 1870s and lend a great deal of authenticity to this fine old house. Few historic buildings remain unchanged through the generations, and 137 Main Street is no exception. About 1908 an Italianate-style box bay window, with a series of round-arched windows with Art Nouveau–style leaded glass in the transom lights, was installed on the south side of the house. In the 1910s the original front porch, with its ornate turned posts and decorative brackets, was replaced with a heavier Edwardian Classical porch typical of the time period. This later porch is interesting for its gently curving contour. At the back of the house, the posts from the first porch can still be seen, relocated to support a newer porch.

Thomas and Catherine McDowell House and Shoemaker's Shop, 161 Main Street, circa 1875

Before the days when boots and shoes were mass produced, it seems that even the smallest of old Ontario villages had a resident boot and shoemaker or a cobbler. Footwear was custom made in small shops to fit the owner, and repaired again and again until it could be worn no more. Every farmer in the Unionville area would have required a sturdy pair of leather boots to deal with the heavy, sticky clay that was found below Markham Township's rich, fertile soil. In the nineteenth century there was a curious custom, still unexplained, of placing an old shoe or boot in a wall cavity or under the floorboards of a house before construction was completed. These oddities turn up from time to time in the longest-settled parts of Ontario, when old houses are renovated or demolished.[65]

Thomas McDowell established a shoemaker's shop on the east side of Main Street in the mid-1870s. He bought a lot from George Eakin in 1874, and shortly thereafter constructed a small frame house in the Ontario Gothic Revival style. Thomas McDowell was not the first or the only boot and shoemaker in the village. His competitors were John Size and David Johnston, whose establishments were located in the north end of Unionville, past the gristmill and bridge. John Size was in business as early as 1861.

At first, Thomas McDowell worked at his trade from a room in his house. As his business grew, he constructed a shop at the north end of his house, and from that time on the south part of the building was reserved for use as a residence. As it turned out, perhaps three shoemakers in the small village of Unionville was one too many. The McDowell family decided to relocate to the crossroads community of Cashel in the early 1880s, buying a three-acre property from Alfred Spofford in 1882. Thomas and Catherine McDowell then sold Spofford their Unionville house and shop.

After re-establishing themselves in their new community, the McDowells were content to stay for a few years, then in 1889 they left Markham altogether and moved to Amaranth Township in Dufferin County, northwest of Orangeville.

For much of its history, the former McDowell shop served as the village barbershop, another mainstay of small-town Ontario, particularly important when men found it fashionable to grow whiskers great and small. The village barbershop was the domain of men, where the regular customers would have their own personal shaving mugs and brushes kept on a shelf right in the shop. The barbershop was a social place where one can imagine that all kinds of topics were discussed and debated between the barber and his patrons. The barbershop was no doubt a less boisterous environment than the local barroom, and therefore those whose opinions differed were less likely to come to blows.

Unionville's barbershop was not without its trademark red-and-white-striped pole out front, as confirmed in the recollections of Grace Harrington, born in the village in 1897. Ben Dixon was the first barber to operate in this location, which he purchased in 1893. The next barber, William "Billie" Brodie, set up shop here in 1901, and apparently he was also a taxidermist.[66] It was William Brodie whom Miss Harrington recalled as the village barber when she was a child. In her reminiscences, she wrote about a travelling showman visiting Unionville with a trained bear that for a few pennies would dance for the spectators. The bear was kept tied to a pole at the back of the Brodie's yard, down in the valley.[67]

Talbert Findlay came from Thornhill to Unionville in 1914 and set up a barbershop with one of his brothers where William Brodie had been until 1910.[68] In 1924

Talbert Findlay and his brothers Howard and Milton purchased the Queen's Hotel, directly across the street from the barbershop, and moved the business to a space between the hotel's barroom and dining room. The large plate-glass window with coloured panes of glass at the top marks the location of the Findlay's old barbershop.[69] Another barber, Gord Kerswell, plied his trade in Findlay's old shop from the late 1940s into the 1950s, after the Unionville Library vacated the space.

Today both the board-and-batten shop and the adjoining residence are in commercial use. As with most of the other older buildings in the commercial core of Unionville, an addition has been made to the rear to provide more space for the businesses operating there. The oldest part of the building has the characteristic L-shaped plan, where the store is the most prominent portion, close to the street and sheltered with a wooden awning, and the residential portion is recessed to allow space for a covered porch. The ogee-topped Gothic Revival window in the steep centre gable of the former house is a noteworthy feature of 161 Main Street. This style of pointed-arched window was used far less frequently in vernacular interpretations of the Gothic Revival style in this part of Ontario. This is one of only two examples remaining in Markham. It is nicely framed within the street-facing gable, decorated with lacy bargeboards and a turned finial.

Christopher and Elizabeth Chant House, 147 Main Street, circa 1876

Christopher Chant was an English immigrant from the county of Somerset. The family first settled in St. Catharines in the early 1840s, where Christopher Chant

apprenticed and learned the trade of cabinetmaker.[70] During this time period, cabinet furniture was made individually by order by master craftsmen, not mass produced as became the norm later in the century. Cabinet shops were found in communities large and small, often combined with the service of undertaking, coffin making, and supplying the furnishings of a proper Christian burial.

By the 1850s Christopher Chant had relocated to Markham Township, first setting up shop at Hagerman's Corners, a crossroads community to the south of Unionville.[71] By the time of Mitchell & Co.'s directory of 1866, he was based in Unionville. In 1873 Christopher Chant purchased Village Lot 14 on the east side of Main Street from George Eakin, which contained a frame workshop with a loft above. This structure had served as the Unionville Carriage Factory, operated by George Eakin and his brother William, in the 1860s. It still stands at 147A Main Street, altered after a fire that occurred in the 1950s, and clad in corrugated metal panels.[72]

The family lived in the loft above the shop until 1876, when a fine new house was constructed for them by

local builder Josiah Hall. This house, designed in a vernacular version of the Gothic Revival style, is similar to several other L-plan, one-and-a-half-storey residences in the area built by Josiah Hall in the 1870s. His use of patterned brick, segmentally arched windows, canted bay windows, and sculptural, curvilinear bargeboards were part of his trademark style. Remarkably, the original bellcast-roofed verandah, complete with its turned posts and fretwork, has survived unaltered. Instead of a pointed-arched window, the steep gable over the verandah contains a round-arched window as its focal point.

According to the 1881 census, Christopher Chant was assisted in the business by three of his sons, Herman, Joseph Havelock, and Clarence. The Chants produced custom furniture and also kept a stock of ready-made pieces on hand in their warehouse. The business specialized in undertaking and funeral services, and even had a horse-drawn hearse available for hire. Later, the undertaking business was purchased by the Wright family of Richmond Hill, along with the hearse and the undertaking and funeral-related furnishings.[73] These rare and unusual artifacts were preserved by the Marshall family who eventually took over the business from the Wrights.

Clarence A. Chant did not continue in the family business, but pursued higher education and an academic career. Dr. Clarence A. Chant founded the Department of Astronomy and Astrophysics at the University of Toronto in 1905.[74] He played a major role in the establishment of the world-class David Dunlap Observatory near Richmond Hill in 1935, and resided in Elms Lea, the former farmhouse of William Marsh, located on the same property as the observatory dome and administrative building. Many significant discoveries were made at this distinguished research and teaching facility before it was closed and sold by the University of Toronto in the first decade of the 2000s.[75] Light pollution from the development that had grown up around the formerly rural site had gradually diminished the effectiveness of the telescope in viewing the celestial realm.

Christopher Chant lived in his Unionville home until he died in 1915. His widow, Elizabeth Croft Chant, remained there until 1930. The Chant House has changed very little since the time of its construction, even though it has served as an office and commercial space since it was last inhabited as a residence.

The noted Canadian artist A.J. Casson painted a view of the Chant House while visiting Unionville to see his colleague Fred Varley, when he was living with the McKay family in his later years. The painting is done in the distinctive style in which Casson depicted small-town Ontario. In 1942 the house was purchased by the Township of Markham to become the municipal office, where it remained until a larger, modern building was constructed south of Buttonville in 1953.[76] Given the extent of development and the population of Markham today, it is difficult to imagine how different a place Markham was when all the business of the municipality could have been done within this small village residence.

George and Dorothea Robinson House, 306 Main Street, 1876

The identity of the builder of a vernacular house is usually unknown. Land records can tell us who originally owned a property and building so we can say it was built for a certain individual or family, but the name of the actual constructor is usually more difficult to pin down. The board-and-batten house at 306 Main Street is a happy exception to that rule.

George Robinson was an English-born carpenter who married into the Eckardt family.[77] We don't know exactly when he came to Upper Canada, but we do know that in 1847 he bought a small piece of land on the west half of Township Lot 19 in the 6th Concession of Markham, in a rural area north of Unionville. There he lived with his wife, Dorothea, and their two young children, Elizabeth and Joseph, in a one-and-a-half-storey frame house he likely built with his own hands. John Lee, a carpenter apprentice, lived in the same household as the Robinsons.

When the census-taker for the 1851 census asked George and Dorothea about their religious affiliation, they both declared that they were members of no church — an uncommon position to take in nineteenth-century Ontario, when most people were devoted churchgoers. Later, the Robinsons would embrace the Lutheran faith of Dorothea's family, so much so that George Robinson would become the builder of the Lutheran parsonage.

Although there must have been no shortage of work for a carpenter and builder in mid-nineteenth-century

Markham, a time when the agricultural community was well-established and thriving thanks to the township's fertile soil, in the early 1860s George Robinson decided to try a different trade. He moved the family to a rented one-and-a-half-storey frame house in Unionville and was employed as a machinist, probably in association with a carriage maker or blacksmith rather than working on his own.[78] This change in career didn't last too long, because in Mitchell & Co.'s directory of 1866 he was listed as a builder and carpenter. He may have built the house the family lived in at 205 Main Street. All the while, the Robinsons retained the ownership of their property north of Unionville.

By the early 1870s, the Robinson family had moved back to the rural home they owned, and George Robinson once again identified himself as a carpenter. His oldest son, Joseph, had joined his father in the trade. With the purchase of some additional land in 1872, the property was increased in size to just under nine acres; however, it was not long after returning to his original home that George Robinson decided to sell the land and purchase a village lot on the east side of Main Street, south of the railway line. In 1876 he bought a building lot in James Eckardt's subdivision of 1875. The property was next door to the south of what would become the site of a new Methodist church in 1879.

Construction of a new house for the Robinson family began shortly after the purchase of the lot. Fortunately for modern-day historians, two of the Robinson children, George and Eugene, signed their names on the inside surface of the wall sheathing of their new home while it was under construction, and included the date of October 1876. This valuable piece of documentation, covered over with lath and plaster as the house was completed, remained as a hidden time capsule until the house was renovated in the mid-1980s and the names and dates were discovered by the owners.

In addition to designing and constructing his own residence, George Robinson is credited with building a number of the attractive frame houses that still line Unionville's Main Street, including the Lutheran Parsonage and the Esther Summerfeldt House.[79] He favoured picturesque but modestly ornamented styles, clad in board-and-batten or vertical tongue-and-groove siding. Bay windows and the segmentally arched windows that were in vogue in the 1870s were often used in his houses. Even without the bargeboards that decorated other mid- to late-nineteenth-century houses in Unionville, George Robinson's houses have a delightful feeling of lightness and playfulness in their character. His designs may have been inspired by architectural pattern books, mainly of American origin, that were widely available at the time. These pattern books tended to feature plans and designs for frame houses in the Gothic Revival, Italianate, and Second Empire styles, each of which appear to have been referenced in George Robinson's buildings.[80]

For his own house, George Robinson used an L-plan layout, one-and-a-half-storey height, board-and-batten siding, and a steeply pitched gable roof — all features that reflect the Gothic Revival style that was particularly favoured in the 1870s, but without the lacy bargeboards or lancet windows usually associated with this style. A two-storey canted bay window on the street-facing gable end wall, capped with a low-pitched hipped roof, and a bellcast roofed verandah in the ell added interest to the front of the house. Today, the chamfered posts with a star-shaped fretwork applique on a flattened mid-section remain to hint at what must have originally been a highly decorated verandah, now missing the brackets and spandrels that almost certainly were once there.

The Robinson family sold their Unionville home in 1894. After that, two of the granddaughters of the Reverend John Dieter Petersen, a Lutheran pastor that served the Berczy settler community from 1819 to 1829, resided here along with a boarder who lived in part of a rear addition that also contained the kitchen.[81] After serving as a private home for many years, in 1965 the former Robinson House was purchased by Donald Deacon, MPP, and his wife, Florence. They donated the property to the church next door, which had become Central United Church after church union in 1925. For a time, the church used the old house as a youth drop-in centre named the Village Inn, and then for a Sunday school and other church-related functions.

In 1985, after the congregation of Central United Church decided to expand their facility to serve their growing ministry, the Robinson House had to be removed to make way for a large new addition. Instead of demolishing this fine old building, the church allowed a local real estate agent to move it. A location was found at the north end of Unionville, on the west side of Main Street, which kept the building within the same historic community in which it was constructed. The house was moved to its new site, placed on a new foundation, and converted back to residential use with minimal changes to its exterior appearance. Fortunately, over the years the house had been very well cared for and only minimally altered, preserving most of its original details right down to the functional louvered shutters on the windows. In addition to the discovery of the date of construction during renovations, the original exterior colours were also found. When first built, the house had pale grey siding accented with brownish-red trim.[82]

Dr. Albert Pingle House, 121 Main Street, circa 1877

Albert R. Pingle was a medical doctor who served Unionville from 1878 to 1883.[83] Depending on the source consulted, the spelling of his surname varies between Pingle, Pingel, and Pringle. He was a son of George Pingle and Eleanor Robinson, and grew up on a farm north of Unionville, between the crossroads communities of Colty Corners and Cashel.[84] In 1877 Albert Pingle bought a lot from James Eckardt, and shortly thereafter a house was constructed on the property. This fine frame house has a pair of tall, narrow round-headed windows in the street-facing gable, a distinctive feature also seen on two other Unionville residences dating from the same time period, one of which is the Weatherall double house across the street.

Dr. Pingle had ambition beyond his medical profession. Seeing the flurry of building activity that had occurred in his neighbourhood since the arrival of the Toronto and Nipissing Railway, the doctor decided to try his hand at land speculation. In 1879, not long after the construction of his new home, Dr. Pingle purchased William Weatherall's sizable piece of Main Street real estate. The Weatherall property consisted of three of the village lots laid out in William Eckardt's subdivision of 1856. The lots had frontage on Main Street, Union Street, and Euclid Street, which created an opportunity for further subdivision.

Plan 570, consisting of eight village lots that by today's standards would still be quite large, was registered in 1881. The subdivision is an historic example of what would now be called residential intensification. Unfortunately for Dr. Pingle, he had missed the building boom, which had begun to subside in the late 1870s. Many of the newly created lots were not built upon until the twentieth century, when Unionville transitioned from a rural village to a suburban community.

In 1881 Albert Pingle was unmarried and sharing his home with his widowed mother, Eleanor Pingle. Two years later he decided to sell to another medical doctor, Dr. William J. Mitchell, who is said to have been a boarder in Esther Summerfeldt's house at 123 Main Street before buying this property in 1883. Dr. Pingle relocated to London, Ontario.[85] Dr. Mitchell remained here until 1888. From 1904 to 1925 the former Pingle House served as the residence or manse for the Presbyterian church minister and his family.[86] The house was conveniently located a short distance to the south of the Presbyterian church, which is now known locally as the Veteran's Hall but was built as the Congregational church in 1879.

The Pingle House is a truly vernacular building that combines elements from different architectural styles but in a way that harmonizes to create a beautiful, picturesque whole. The house has the basic L-shaped plan, one-and-a-half-storey height, and steeply pitched cross-gabled roof that were used again and again in the last quarter of the nineteenth century, derived from the Gothic Revival style. However, instead of pointed-arched windows and bargeboards, the Pingle House has as its focal point a pair of round-headed windows incorporated within a decorative round-headed surround. Within the arch of the surround is a fretwork applique that adds an extra touch of refinement and says much about the design sensibilities of the builder. This feature shows the influence of the Italianate style, which was popular in Markham Township in the 1870s through the 1880s, but more so in Markham Village than in Unionville.

In the early 1900s, the house was altered with the addition of an Edwardian oval window next to the front door, and a new, larger verandah that was heavier in proportion than the light, bellcast-roofed verandah from the 1870s, shown in an old photograph. At the same time, a portion of the front wall was covered in narrow clapboard, while the rest of the original vertical tongue-and-groove siding remained untouched. Further additions have been made to the house over the years, but they have been kind to the historical integrity of this remarkable heritage building. In 1990 the Edwardian verandah was removed and the original verandah design reconstructed, complete with a bellcast roof, turned posts, and fretwork brackets, all based on the old photograph of this house and its neighbours taken around the turn of the twentieth century.

Stiver-Summerfeldt Store, 182 Main Street, circa 1877

This building is sometimes said to be the oldest store remaining in Unionville, but research and the store's

architectural details point to a date of construction in the mid to late 1870s. The two-storey board-and-batten sided store, for many years one of Unionville's many antique stores, was likely built by James Hunter, who purchased the property for $400 in 1877 then sold it to George McDowell in the same year for $1,000. Salem Eckardt, the local auctioneer, bought the store in 1882 and rented it out in the 1880s and 1890s. In 1881 it was rented by Benjamin Fenwick, who had previously operated a general store farther south on Main Street, along with his brother James W. Fenwick, before he relocated to Vaughan Township, and later Toronto. Benjamin Fenwick was married to Aurella, the daughter of Salem and Catherine Eckardt.

Reuben A. Stiver, the son of Robert H. Stiver and Ann Bell, ran a general store from this location, beginning in 1885 and continuing until the mid-1890s, when a relative, Charles H. Stiver, took over the business.[87] In addition to being a merchant, Reuben Stiver invested in local real estate and bought and sold many properties in Unionville. Some of the vacant properties he bought were developed with modest houses that were sold not long after they were built, mainly on lots within William Eckardt's subdivision of 1856. In 1910 his business letterhead identified his occupation as "Lumber Dealer."

Reuben A. Stiver grew up on a farm to the northwest of Unionville. His father, Robert Stiver, was a staunch Reformer in his politics, so much so that he claimed to have taken part in the Upper Canada Rebellion of 1837.[88] His son chose the career of merchant rather than farmer, and about 1877 opened a hardware store in a building constructed by John Eckardt, then owned by John Dunn, now addressed 159 Main Street. After several years in the hardware business, Reuben A. Stiver decided to switch to being a general merchant and relocated to the store at 182 Main Street. He retired in 1895. By this time, the Stivers lived in an ornate frame house two doors down from the Methodist church. This house, now known only from archival photographs, was probably built by William Eakin during his ownership of the property between 1878 and 1882.[89] Its most arresting feature was a mansard-roofed tower with triangular dormers, unique in Unionville. Unfortunately, this architectural treasure was destroyed by fire in the 1920s. Another house was built on the site by Dr. McKay about 1930.

According to family history, Reuben A. Stiver and his wife, Eleanor "Ella" Mustard, enjoyed travelling and often vacationed in the United States.[90] Their favourite destinations were the southern states and California. Their travels were chronicled in correspondence published in the *Markham Economist* newspaper at the turn of the century. The fact that a newspaper would carry the details of a local family's vacation is a reflection of the intimate nature of communities like Unionville at the time.

Charles H. Stiver ran the store from 1896 to about 1901. In 1899 he had been appointed township clerk, a position he held until 1917. His business interests expanded in the early 1900s when he partnered with his brother Francis and started Stiver Brothers Coal and Seed.[91] Stiver Brothers had their business office in a store at 186 Main Street, in a building that had housed the Sovereign Bank in the early 1900s and which later became the site of Unionville's new post office in 1961, after the old building was demolished.

Above the store was a spacious meeting room locally known as "Stiver Hall." A variety of public gatherings happened in the hall, which was accessed by an outside stairway. The village band used the space for their practices. Eventually the area was partitioned to provide an apartment, and Stiver Hall was no more.

After the Stivers, Abner Summerfeldt, who served as township reeve in 1903 and 1904, ran the store from the early 1900s to the 1930s.[92] Next, the business was operated by the Connells, who later relocated to another building across that street that had once housed John Devlin's harness shop, and sometime after that G.A.M. Davison's Ford dealership showroom.

The interior arrangements of a turn-of-the-century, small-town Ontario general store were wonderfully described in Grace Harrington's reminiscences of old Unionville:

> Next door [to the Sovereign Bank] was Summerfeldt's General Store. On the right hand side as we went in was the candy counter. What candies we could get for 1 cent! — a bag of mixed candies, a licorice whip, a marshmallow broom on a stick — all day suckers, etc. The groceries also were on this side. On the other side were yard goods, patterns, thread, etc. At the back — shoes, rubbers, men's overalls, etc. There were living quarters above the store.[93]

The Stiver-Summerfeldt Store has an interesting plan outline. Its gable end faces the street, which is typical for a commercial establishment on a main street, but the structure extends deep into the property, with a distinctive bend following the contour of the side property line. The storefront is noteworthy, first because it has survived the changing tastes of the retail market, and secondly for its Eastlake style, characteristic of both the furniture and some of the architecture of the circa 1877 date of construction. This style was used for the embellishment of both commercial and residential buildings in architectural pattern books of the time. The regular, machine-made, geometric decoration of the storefront's cornice and pilasters is reminiscent of the treatment used on furniture of the 1870s and 1880s, often referred to in the antique trade as "Jacques and Hay" after the prominent Toronto furniture manufacturer.

Warren Bishop Jr. House, 7 Victoria Avenue, circa 1877

William Eakin, owner of the Unionville Planing Mill, created a small subdivision of village lots on the south side of Victoria Avenue in 1873. Of the eight lots created by Plan 348, Lot 1 at Main Street contained the planing mill. Lot 2, where 7 Victoria Avenue stands today, was next door to the east. In 1881 three more lots were added, leading to the creation of Victoria Lane. Today, Victoria Avenue, a narrow, winding road overlooking the Rouge

After Warren Bishop Jr. moved on, the house was owned by a succession of others. The Meyer family lived there beginning in 1889. Grace Harrington, the granddaughter of Robert Harrington, owner of the planing mill after purchasing it from William Eakin, recalled her memory of this little house:

> There was a little stream running through the mill property. In the spring it would flood and carry some of the planks away. They would usually be caught in a culvert under the railway track…. There was a house below the hill on Victoria Avenue which would be almost surrounded by water in the flood. We called it "The Ark." The Meyer family lived there at one time.[95]

River valley, is the most authentic village-like setting to be found in all of Unionville. To walk along this street is to savour the atmosphere of a different time.

In 1877 a labourer, Warren Bishop Jr., purchased the east part of Lot 2, next door to the planing mill, for $40. This low value is an indication that it was a vacant lot at the time. Warren Bishop Jr. was related to First World War flying ace Billy Bishop, and was a member of a local family of house and barn builders based in Box Grove.[94] A modest frame house was soon built on the lot by Warren Bishop Jr., perhaps with the assistance of some of his family members. Like many other workers' homes of its time, this house retained the familiar symmetry of the Georgian cottages of the early days, but incorporated more up-to-date features, such as balloon-framed walls, two-over-two windows, and a steeper roof pitch in tune with the popularity of the Gothic Revival. Warren Bishop Jr., whose occupation is variously given as teamster or labourer in the Markham Township Assessment Rolls, was employed by the planing mill from time to time.

During the "discovery" of Unionville by old house enthusiasts in the 1960s, not all of the old houses in the village remained preserved in their original form, or were restored to their earlier appearance. Some houses, like this one, were updated for modern-day living without a thought to keeping their small-paned windows, panelled doors, or wood siding. When the house at 7 Victoria Avenue was remodelled in the 1960s, the owners placed the building on a new foundation, rearranged windows to suit a new interior plan, and covered over the old vertical wood siding with neat white aluminium siding. A convenient carport was added to the east side of the house. Only the basic shape and underlying structure of the 1870s house were kept in the renovations, making the true age of the building recognizable to savvy observers of century homes, but to others making it look like just another renovated older home.

Margaret Robinson House, 117 Main Street, circa 1878

This nice example of a village house in the Second Empire style has a history that links back to the turbulent times of the Upper Canadian Rebellion of 1837. In 1878 Margaret Robinson bought a building lot on the east side of Main Street from James Eckardt. She was the widow of John Robinson, a farmer of English birth who in his youth had been a supporter of William Lyon Mackenzie and his mission to reform the colonial government of his day through armed rebellion. John Robinson was involved in the rebellion to such a degree that he was arrested in February of 1838 and sentenced to three years of incarceration in Kingston, to be followed by banishment.[96] In late 1830s Upper Canada banishment meant a one-way trip to Van Diemen's Land, now Tasmania, an island off the coast of Australia.

John Robinson's outlook seems to have improved, because it seems that he was not banished after all, and it wasn't long until he was back to farming at Colty Corners,

a crossroads community north of Unionville centred at an intersection known today as Kennedy Road and Major Mackenzie Drive East. Around 1850 his prospects must have been good, because by then he was able to afford to replace his old dwelling with a new brick farmhouse in the Ontario Regency Cottage style. This house, originally located on land that is now part of the Angus Glen community, was relocated to Markham Heritage Estates in 2002 and restored after being "rediscovered," hidden behind an extensive remodelling of the 1940s.

John Robinson's first wife was Julia Ann Stiver. After her death during the 1860s, at a comparatively young age, John Robinson remarried. In the nineteenth century widowers didn't stay unmarried for long, especially when there were children to care for and a household to manage. His second wife, Margaret Telford, was twenty-six years his junior. The age difference between him and his first wife had been about the same.

Margaret Robinson found herself widowed in 1876. She decided to move from the family farm into the village of Unionville, and in 1878 had a modest but well-designed house constructed for herself and her three unmarried daughters who were still living at home. According to the 1881 census, the oldest daughter, Abigail, was a dressmaker. Ten years later, Margaret was sharing her home with her youngest daughter, Eleanor Devlin, and Eleanor's infant son, Harvey. Eleanor was married, but her husband didn't seem to be living with her at the time.

In 1907 the house was sold to Alexander Pingle. He resided there with his unmarried sister, Lucy. Like the Robinsons, the Pingles had previously farmed in the vicinity of Colty Corners. The families likely knew each other before they connected through the purchase and sale of the Robinson House in Unionville. Historical accounts of this house say that it was built in 1907 for Alexander Pingle, but the style and details of the house, so similar to the circa 1879 Esther Summerfeldt House only a few doors up the street, suggest a date of construction in the 1870s.[97] By 1907 the Second Empire style was long out of favour and it is doubtful that a new house would follow a style so decidedly out of fashion at the time. The similarities between the two houses strongly suggest that George Robinson, a local builder who is known to have constructed Mrs. Summerfeldt's house, was also the builder of Margaret Robinson's house, except perhaps for the red-brick veneer, since he was a carpenter and not a mason.

The Margaret Robinson House was built with an L-shaped plan that provided a perfect place for a porch in the street-facing ell. At a later date this porch was enclosed with modern windows that were at odds with the style of the house, but during an expansion of the house in the 1980s that also included restoration work the porch was opened up again to show off its elaborate turned posts and fretwork decoration.

The tall mansard roof of the Margaret Robinson House has a bellcast shape that flares out at the eaves. It was clad in patterned wood shingles when first built. The fascia boards have a decorative lower edge in a small repeating "sawtooth" pattern that is also seen on the canted bay windows that grace the front and south sides of the house. The roof is accented with gabled wall dormers with finely detailed bargeboards and small turned finials, an indication of the builder's attention to detail. The use of a plain red brick in the late 1870s, when most other brick buildings were being finished in brick laid in a pattern of red and buff, is an unusual feature of this house.

On the other hand, the segmentally headed windows with louvered shutters are typical of the period of construction. The shutters were installed during the 1980s restoration.

Weatherall Double House, 118 Main Street, circa 1878

Census records tell us that by 1851 a blacksmith by the name of John Grundy had established a home and shop on Lot 11, Concession 5, a property owned by King's College, later the University of Toronto. This property, which fronts on the west side of Main Street, was purchased by William Eckardt, the son of Gottlieb Eckardt, in 1856. William Eckardt created a subdivision of village lots on part of his farm lot in 1856, which later formed the southwestern residential neighbourhood of Unionville when it began to develop after the arrival of the Toronto and Nipissing Railway in 1871.[98]

In 1861 William Weatherall, an English-born blacksmith, purchased a village lot from William Eckardt at the southwest corner of Main Street and Euclid Street. The property extended all the way back to Union Street. It seems likely that this lot contained the house, and possibly also the blacksmith shop formerly occupied by John Grundy. A one-and-a-half-storey frame house at 5 Euclid Street, altered but still recognizable as a mid-nineteenth-century dwelling, is believed to be the Grundy-Weatherall House, perhaps relocated onto a new foundation at a later date. Assessment records show that William Weatherall had been William Eckardt's tenant from 1856 until he was able to purchase the land where he lived and worked.

There are two common spellings of this family name, Weatherall being the earliest of the two and Weatherill being the later one. Variations in the spelling of family names as found in different official records, and even among family members themselves, was something that happened from time to time in the nineteenth century and more so before that.

William Weatherall enlarged his property holdings in 1874 with the purchase of the two adjoining village lots south of his property from Jane Lewis. Circa 1878 he built a double house on the newly acquired lot south of his original residence, on an existing fieldstone foundation. This may have been a remnant of a building constructed by the Lewis family, who had owned the properties from 1861 to 1874. This building may have been demolished or relocated by William Weatherall after he became the owner.

The double house at 118 Main Street is one of only two of its type to have been built in Unionville.[99] According to local history the house was built for one of the sons of William Weatherall and Mary Ann Northway so he could have his own home. Instead, so the story goes, he moved to Toronto, leaving the new house without a tenant. However, this seems unlikely since the only son

who was the right age to strike out on his own when the house was built was George, who was twenty-one at the time, and he stayed local after marrying Hannah Harrington, the daughter of the operator of the Planing Mill.[100] The next oldest son, Henry, was sixteen in 1878.

In 1879 the Weatheralls decided to sell all of their property to Albert R. Pingle, a local physician who lived at 121 Main Street. From the original three village lots, Dr. Pingle created a small subdivision of eight lots, Plan 570, in 1881, leaving the double house and main Weatherall residence on their own, smaller lots.[101] Henry Weatherall may have stayed behind after all and become a tenant of Dr. Pingle. William and Mary Ann Weatherall moved to a farm south of Unionville, where William tried his hand at farming. By the early 1890s the family had relocated again, this time to a village lot on the east side of Main Street, south of today's Highway 7, that they had purchased in 1880. The small frame house to which the Weatheralls retired was located at 65 Main Street, and was demolished several years ago.

In the 1970s the Weatherall Double House was made into a single dwelling with interior changes, but on the exterior the appearance of two residences with separate front doors was maintained. The house has a T-shaped plan with a rear kitchen wing that has been altered with the addition of a second floor and other extensions. The house looks large from the street view, but in reality the front section is only one-room deep. It is a vernacular building with its basic form based on the Gothic Revival style, with a steep centre gable and a vertical emphasis thanks to the narrow, vertical tongue-and-groove siding and medium roof pitch.

The paired, round-headed windows in the centre gable and on both gable ends are a distinctive feature of 118

Main Street. These windows, indicating an Italianate stylistic influence, were also used on two other frame houses in Unionville that were constructed at about the same time. This suggests the houses may have been the work of the same builder. Other windows on the house have segmentally arched tops typical of the 1870s. Functional louvered shutters enhance the effect of the windows in the Weatherall Double House. The front verandah is a bit of an odd mix of styles. The low-pitched hip roof, slender chamfered posts, and fretwork brackets reflect the original period of construction, while the railing, with its curved balusters, is a style of the early 1900s often used for Edwardian Classical porches that commonly replaced Victorian verandahs in the new century.

Gingerbread Cottage, 27 Victoria Avenue, circa 1878

This village house perfectly expresses the spirit of what vernacular architecture is in its small size, use of local materials, informal, individualistic design created by the carpenter who built it, and a measure of whimsy in its "gingerbread" decoration. The setting on the well-treed, winding Victoria Avenue, away from the constant traffic of modern-day Main Street, enhances the effect of what home meant to the ordinary working people of Unionville a century or more ago.

Today, Victoria Avenue is arguably the one residential street in Unionville that has retained the most of its nineteenth-century village character.[102] With the narrow street bordered by the Rouge Valley on much of its north side, development has been slow to overtake the little frame cottages that were constructed on William

Eakin's subdivision of 1873. Considering the selling prices of properties in the 2010s, it is remarkable to think that the lot where 27 Victoria Avenue stands sold to a Mr. George Ellis for a mere $30 in 1876.

George Ellis is not likely to have built on this lot, because in 1878, when he sold the property, it was only worth $50. The buyer was John Webber, the proprietor of the Queen's Hotel. The Webbers rented this small house, built circa 1878, as an income property. According to the township assessment rolls, an early tenant was William Ferguson, a carriage maker. Later, John Prentice and his family lived here. John Prentice was an auctioneer who is said to have learned his trade from Salem Eckardt. He was also a dealer in Massey-Harris agricultural implements in the community of Milliken, which straddled the boundary between Markham and Scarborough townships.[103]

Moses Hemingway, the son of Orson and Matilda Hemingway and the grandson of John and Jane Webber, was the executor of John Webber's estate. He acquired the property for a nominal $1 in 1910. Moses Hemingway ran the Queen's Hotel after the Webbers retired.[104] He didn't reside in the cottage on Victoria Avenue or in the hotel, but lived in another house in the village, at the northeast corner of Main Street and Highway 7. Moses Hemingway died in 1911. In 1914 his widow, Catherine, sold the property out of the family and continued to live in the larger house on Main Street.

While some of the modest frame houses on the street have been significantly enlarged, 27 Victoria Avenue has fortunately been treated with a gentler hand, with additions of a scale in keeping with the original character of the building. The cottage has an L-shaped plan, positioned sideways on the lot so that the ell faces west. This space probably had a verandah at one time, with a balcony in line with the steep centre gable and its so-called "suicide door." From the front, the house is only two bays wide, with a single door and window, an indication of a humble beginning. The delightful gingerbread trim in the gables is more properly called bargeboard in architectural terms. However, in this case gingerbread better suits its lighthearted, flowing design. It may be the work of a craftsman of more recent times, looking to add a bit of Gothic Revival whimsy to a simple cottage.

Old Lutheran Parsonage, 109 Main Street, circa 1879

History is not always neat and tidy. Sometimes the story of a historical building gets a little muddled when differing accounts get written down and repeated, with each story thereby gaining the status of legitimacy. Unionville's Old Lutheran Parsonage is one of those

places where the history doesn't quite agree and some of the answers are difficult to find.

The Lutheran Church played an important role in Unionville's early history. Most of the Berczy settlers and their descendants followed the Lutheran faith, given their German cultural background. By 1819 two Lutheran congregations were established in Markham Township under the leadership of Reverend John Dieter Petersen: St. Philip's in Unionville and St. John's in Buttonville. Another Lutheran church, named Zion, was located in the community of Sherwood in Vaughan Township.[105]

A turbulent period for the church community resulted from strongly opposing political opinions and conflicts that arose around the time leading up to the Upper Canada Rebellion of 1837. The Lutheran Church north of Unionville entered a period of decline after a split occurred in the congregation, where supporters of the government formed an Anglican Church and supporters of the Reformers stayed with the Lutheran faith. By 1850 the Lutherans of Unionville and their sister congregations started to regain their strength with the arrival of a new pastor from the United States. The name of the church was changed from St. Philip's to Bethesda, since the name St. Philip's had been taken by the Anglicans.

A welcome time of stability began when the Reverend Jeremiah Fishburn began his ministry and encouraged the construction of a new church building next to the Lutheran cemetery on the hill overlooking Unionville. He served the three local Lutheran congregations from 1852 to 1879. In the 1850s the parsonage where he resided was located in Buttonville. It was a very modest frame building that had originally been built as a tradesman's cottage.[106] In the 1860s and 1870s, the Reverend Fishburn lived in Vaughan, in the vicinity of Zion Lutheran Church.

Some historical accounts of the Lutheran Parsonage in Unionville say that it was built in 1867 and its first resident was the Reverend J.F. Bruch.[107] The location of a parsonage on the present site is supported by a notation on James Eckardt's plan of subdivision of 1875, where a block of land is labelled "Lutheran Homestead." However, census records do not show the Reverend Fishburn, or any other clergy for that matter, at this location in Unionville during this time. It seems curious that the Lutherans would go to such a great expense to erect a parsonage of this size and quality when their pastor lived elsewhere. Another fact that doesn't fit this account of the building's history is that the Reverend Bruch began his ministry in 1894, nowhere near the year 1867.[108]

An alternative history of the Old Lutheran Parsonage, better supported by primary source research, points to a construction date of circa 1879. In that year, James and Sarah Jane Eckardt entered into an agreement of purchase and sale with the trustees of the Lutheran Church to sell a plot of land for a parsonage. The trustees were Joram Eckardt, William Stiver, William Fierheller, and Alfred Quantz. A mortgage agreement associated with the sale is very specific about the purpose that the property is to be used for: "… the site of the Residence of an Evangelical Lutheran Clergyman and to permit such congregation or any person or persons disposed to erect such Residence for an Evangelical Lutheran Clergyman free access to the land for the purpose of erecting the same…."[109]

The site of the parsonage, as described in the agreement, was Lot 21 in James Eckardt's Plan of Subdivision No. 401, registered in 1875. The price was $400 for the land and premises. The mention of the word "premises" in the agreement suggests that the property contained a building at the time of sale to the church trustees, which seems somewhat at odds with the language elsewhere in the same document that describes a building yet to be constructed. Was there a small house or another type of structure on the lot deemed unsuitable for a parsonage, and therefore in need of replacement?

Local carpenter and builder George Robinson is believed to have designed and constructed the Lutheran Parsonage in 1879–80. The construction of the parsonage at Unionville at the end of the Reverend Fishburn's lengthy ministry seems to suggest that the congregation of Bethesda Lutheran Church hoped that if a fine residence was provided it might be an enticement for a new pastor to locate in the community. Nonetheless, church records show that in the 1880s the Lutheran congregation continued to have difficulty securing the services of a pastor willing to stay.[110] If the first clergyman to live in the parsonage was indeed the Reverend

J.F. Bruch, who came in 1894 after the departure of Reverend Edward Ritter, who lived there from the time of building until then? Did the previous succession of Lutheran clergymen live near the Buttonville or Sherwood congregations? One thing that is known for certain from a reading of the township assessment rolls is that Hugh Powell Crosby, the area's former MPP, rented the Lutheran Parsonage from the trustees during the 1890s, until a new house was built next door for him and his wife, Harriet, in 1900. Did the Reverend Bruch share accommodation with them?

After the Crosbys moved out, the Old Lutheran Parsonage was occupied by a series of pastors. In 1910, during the ministry of the Reverend Jacob Maurer, the church relocated from its original site north of the village to Union Street, in the heart of Unionville, bringing the church and parsonage closer together. The last clergyman to live in the Old Lutheran Parsonage was the Reverend N. Willison, whose ministry spanned the war years, 1914 to 1918. He was the first graduate of the Waterloo Lutheran Seminary, now Wilfrid Laurier University, in the city of Waterloo.

After the departure of the Reverend Willison, the church rented the house out to others, until the late 1940s when the property was sold. York County's Lutheran congregations took turns hosting their pastors. A new parsonage was built adjoining the church in 1950, so that the Reverend Fischer could live in Unionville.[111] Previously, the Lutheran pastor lived in the Vaughan Township community of Sherwood.

The new parsonage at Unionville was a more up-to-date residence than the building of 1879, and certainly more conveniently located. No longer needed by the church, in 1966 the Old Parsonage property was sold to Clair and Ruth Ingram, who furnished the house with Canadian antiques appropriate to the period of the building. Ruth Ingram was one of Unionville's most enduring antique dealers. It was the Ingrams who installed the ornate double doors, sheltered beneath the bracketed hood over the entrance, that contribute so much to the architectural interest of 109 Main Street. These doors were salvaged from the Toronto Conservatory of Music, demolished in 1962. The set of double doors that were original to the house, designed in a much simpler style than the doors that replaced them, were moved to a side entrance.

In form, the Old Lutheran Parsonage is similar to other residences attributed to George Robinson. Its picturesque, irregular plan, cross-gabled roof, and two-storey bay windows are some telltale features associated with the work of George Robinson. The use of flat-headed windows and roughcast stucco, the original exterior finish, was not typical of the houses he presumably designed and built. One noteworthy feature is the wooden quatrefoil ornament in the street-facing gable. When Markham's heritage advisory committee, Heritage Markham, was established in the mid-1970s, this architectural detail was adopted as the committee's logo, which remains in place to this day.

The Old Lutheran Parsonage has been altered in recent years with a large addition to the rear and north side. Regrettably the stucco finish that was such an important element of the building's character was replaced by modern board-and-batten siding at the time of the addition, likely in an effort to unify the old and the new. Modern windows with multi-paned grilles have replaced the original, simpler windows that were a combination of one-over-one and two-over-two glazing. Even still, the Old Lutheran Parsonage remains one of Unionville's most distinctive late Victorian residences.

Esther Summerfeldt House, 123 Main Street, circa 1879

The former home of Esther Summerfeldt is a remarkable heritage building for both the beauty of its design and its exceptional state of preservation. It is one of Unionville's most outstanding late-Victorian houses, and is particularly interesting because its historic character has been carefully maintained and is not the result of extensive restoration. Somehow the home's owners over the years resisted the temptation to modernize and remodel the old house in ways that would have compromised its originality.

Esther Summerfeldt was the widow of George Henry Summerfeldt. The Summerfeldts were among the Berczy settlers that arrived in Markham in 1794.

When they first arrived in Upper Canada, the family name was spelled "Sommerfeldt." George H. Summerfeldt lived on Lot 23, Concession 6, a farm property near the Markham Township crossroads community of Cashel.[112] Cashel was centred around an intersection that today is known as Kennedy Road and Elgin Mills Road East. An old hotel in the Georgian style, a substantial two-storey brick building, remains a landmark at the four corners. In the mid-nineteenth century Elgin Mills Road was a plank toll road that ran east-west across Markham Township, beginning at Yonge Street.

George H. Summerfeldt's first wife was Clarissa Ransom. By the time of the 1861 census he was a widower. Not long after the death of his wife he married Esther Davis, an American immigrant. Sadly, this second marriage was short lived, because by 1871 Esther Summerfeldt was a widow in her middle age.

Esther Summerfeldt stayed on the family farm for a while after her husband's death. After several years went by she decided to move from the farm into Unionville, and in 1877 bought a lot on the east side of Main Street from James Eckardt. According to local tradition, she employed George Robinson to build a new home on the vacant lot.[113] Another part of local tradition is that Mrs. Summerfeldt took on boarders to provide her with income. According to the 1881 census she shared her home with Peter Hagerman, a harness maker. Other boarders in the 1880s were medical doctors who served the local community, Dr. Robinson and Dr. W.J. Mitchell.

The estate of Esther Summerfeldt sold the house to Thomas Ogden in 1912, and in 1918 his estate sold to Ada Hood, the widow of John Hood, a Markham farmer. Ada Hood was a midwife, and many of the older residents of Unionville and the surrounding area were born in this house.[114] Before the establishment of hospitals in communities outside of Toronto, many villages in rural areas like Unionville, Markham Village, and Richmond Hill had birthing houses or nursing homes where women delivered their babies with the help of midwives rather than medical doctors. Doctors avoided a lot of travelling on country roads by relying on local midwives to deliver babies. It's not clear how long Ada Hood's role as the local midwife lasted, but she owned the property until 1968. Because of her half century of ownership, the house is locally referred to as the Hood House.

This house is an outstanding example of a village residence in the Second Empire style, unusual for its two front doors. Its frame construction seems to have encouraged the builder to embellish the modestly scaled house with decorative woodwork. The house is sided with vertical tongue-and-groove wood, which provides a simple, flat backdrop to the peaked window surrounds, the bracketed hood over the front door on the projecting portion of the L-shaped house, the bellcast-roofed porch with its turned posts and arched fretwork brackets, and the segmentally headed windows and their louvered shutters. The effect is enhanced with a period colour scheme in straw yellow, dark green, and white.

Similar to Margaret Robinson's house on the same street and thought to have been constructed about the same time, the bellcast-shaped mansard roof has gabled wall dormers accented with bargeboards and finials as well as decorative fascia boards with a sawtooth pattern. The same fascia boards can be seen on the canted bay window on the south wall, the porch, and the small hood over the door. Small "sandwich" brackets under the eaves add a further touch of Victorian flourish.

Central United Church, 131 Main Street, 1879

For a small country village, Unionville has a history of being well served by churches of many denominations. The number of choices churchgoers of the nineteenth century had within a short distance reflects the diversity of the population that lived in and around the village. Religion is often a good indication of a person's culture, and although Unionville is generally associated with a Germanic Lutheran heritage, people of other cultural backgrounds and religious affiliations lived here too.

At the time when Central United Church was built in 1879 as a Primitive Methodist place of worship, it was one of six churches in Unionville. The others included the Lutheran church and Anglican church on the hill overlooking the village, and the churches of the Wesleyan Methodists, Congregationalists, and Presbyterians in the village proper. Any families of the Roman Catholic faith had to travel to Markham Village or Thornhill to attend services.

The Wesleyan Methodists were the first Methodists to establish a congregation in Unionville.[115] In the mid-1840s they built a chapel on the west side of Main Street at the upper end of the village, just north of the Unionville Public School. In the 1870s the congregation included some of Unionville's most prominent citizens, including Hugh Powell Crosby, Frederick Eckardt, and Christopher Chant. Today no trace remains of Unionville's Wesleyan Methodist Church, which prospered between about 1844 and 1884. For a time the old church was used as a residence, before it was finally demolished.[116]

Unionville's Primitive Methodist congregation got its start a few years after the Wesleyan Methodists. The roots of the church go back to the late 1850s. The congregation was served by circuit preachers whose responsibilities also took them to Markham Village and Bethel. In 1879 the Primitive Methodist church at Unionville became the head of a larger circuit that included Markham Village, Ebenezer and Zion in Markham Township, and Malvern in Scarborough Township. In that same year Josiah Hall, a local builder, lay preacher, and church member, oversaw the construction of a fine brick church, designed by the distinguished Toronto architectural firm of Langley, Langley and Burke.[117] Josiah Hall is also credited with constructing Ebenezer Church in Milliken, a community that straddled the boundary between Markham and Scarborough townships, and the church at Wesley Corners in Whitchurch Township, today part of the Town of Aurora.

The Langley, Langley and Burke design, rendered in the early Gothic Revival style, is a richly detailed and colourful church building in red and buff brick, set on a raised stone foundation that provided space for a Sunday school before new classrooms were added in the 1980s expansion. The church is tall, slender, and elegant in its form, with a sense of dramatic verticality that is enhanced by buttresses and a central tower topped with a soaring broach spire. The dichromatic brickwork and lancet windows are characteristic of church architecture of the period. The overall effect of the design and materials is highly decorative and light.

In 1884 Unionville's Primitive Methodists and Wesleyan Methodists amalgamated as the result of the Methodist Church union, with church members from both groups electing to worship in the church of the Primitive Methodists. A similar coming together of church congregations occurred in 1925, when the Methodist and Presbyterian churches joined to form the United Church of Canada.

Central United Church continues to serve the community. In 1986, as the congregation continued to grow, a major addition was made to the rear and south of the church.[118] The addition is a postmodern interpretation of the Gothic Revival style in red and buff brick to relate to the design and materials of the 1879 structure.

The Old Veterans' Hall, 150 Main Street, 1879

A church, even when it is no longer a place of worship, is always a church thanks to the distinctive architectural forms used for these sacred spaces. This former church is seldom if ever referred to by local people as anything else but the Vet's Hall, even though its design boldly proclaims its original purpose.

The Congregationalists got their start in Unionville in the 1840s, providing an alternative to the Lutheran and Anglican approaches to Protestant Christianity that had established an early foothold in the community. Their first church was a frame building constructed

circa 1847 that still stands at 149 Main Street, right across the road. That building, converted to a residence in the 1890s and subsequently added to and remodelled, is no longer recognizable as a former church.[119]

By the 1870s the Congregationalists began to outgrow their original meeting place, and a new building was needed to serve the expanding membership. One claim to fame boasted by Unionville is to have a church designed by E.J. Lennox, who went on to design such Toronto landmarks as the Old City Hall and the King Edward Hotel. More precisely, the church was designed by the Toronto architectural firm of McCaw and Lennox before Lennox went on to establish his own practice in 1881.[120] Edward James Lennox apprenticed with William Irving from 1874 to 1879, then briefly partnered with William Frederick McCaw. Unionville's Congregational Church, built in 1879, was an early work of Lennox's, before he embraced the Richardson Romanesque style that he became so well-known for. It has been said the look of the church was inspired by a church seen by the minister while travelling in the United States.

Unionville's Congregational Church is an unusual building. Its character is somewhat heavy and angular when compared to the more lightly proportioned churches designed in the early Gothic Revival style that are its contemporaries, such as the nearby Methodist church built in the same year. The architectural style of the Congregational church has been classified by at least one architectural historian as Queen Anne Revival and others as Gothic Revival. It certainly is a hybrid, difficult to slot into one particular category. The timber steeple, with a steep pyramidal spire sitting atop an open timber framework, the bracketed eaves, and the decorative projecting upper front gable are distinctive features associated with the American Queen Anne Revival and Stick styles popular during the period of construction. Other details of the design are more conventional aspects of the Gothic Revival, such as the buttresses at the corners and sidewalls, the large pointed-arched window on the front, facing east, and the entrance porch with its plank double doors and wrought-iron hinges. Decidedly unconventional are the tall, narrow windows on the north and south sides of the building, flat-headed except for their wooden heads in a trefoil arched pattern, and capped with shed-roofed wall dormers. This treatment is most unlike what one would expect to see on a church.

While other faith groups in Unionville and elsewhere in Markham Township were building symmetrical churches with towers centred on their front wall, the Congregationalists chose an asymmetrical design with a corner tower. Later, this form would become the most common for new churches, as seen in Bethesda Lutheran Church and St. Philip's Anglican Church, so this group was on the cutting edge of church architecture when they agreed to this design.

The new church was built on a piece of land donated by one of its most faithful members, Mark Braithwaite, a general merchant and the village postmaster at the time.[121] In addition to his store, Mark Braithwaite owned a farm that bordered on Unionville's western edge. The church was constructed on a part of that farm, a little to the south of the Braithwaite store and residence. An archival photograph exists that shows cows pastured in the foreground of the Congregational church.

The *Canadian Independent*, the journal of the Canadian branch of the Congregationalist Church, reported on the laying of the cornerstone of the new building during the summer of 1879.[122] At this memorable event the church pastor, E.D. Silcox, was present, along with a gathering of church dignitaries and church members. The ceremonial laying of the cornerstone, including the placement of papers, coins, and other objects deemed to be of interest to some future persons who might chance to reopen it, was done by James Fraser, Esquire, of Toronto. After a lengthy address on the importance and prospects of the Congregationalists, an enticing spread of tea and peaches was laid out in the old frame church across the road for the enjoyment of those assembled for this auspicious occasion. Afterward, people were free to stroll about what the chronicler of the day's events described as "the pretty little village." Then, quite suddenly, the day turned dark and stormy with furious wind, rain, thunder, and lightning, prior to the closing lecture of the day given by the Reverend T.W. Handford.

The opening service was held on February 19, 1880. The Reverend Handford returned to preach the dedicatory sermon.[123] That May the Reverend Silcox announced that he would be stepping down

from his position as provisional pastor so that a regular pastor could take charge of his church.[124] The Congregationalists secured the Reverend E. Ebbs to occupy the pulpit of their fine new building, and for a while all seemed well. One noteworthy event to take place in the Congregational church was a performance by the esteemed Canadian poet Pauline Johnson, recalled by Jennie Harrington in her reminiscences of old Unionville.[125]

In January of 1881 the church proudly celebrated the anniversary of the Sunday school, however, in spite of this ambitious building project and the leap of faith that inspired it, the fortunes of Unionville's Congregationalists would soon change.[126] Perhaps the storm that occurred following the cornerstone ceremony was a bad omen. About a month after the Sunday school anniversary, a fire, started when a twelve-lamp chandelier fell to the floor, badly damaged the interior.[127] The church was repaired, but two years later was closed for what was hoped at the time to be a temporary situation.[128]

By 1894 the number of members had declined to the point that the church was disbanded and the building and property was sold to the Presbyterians, who had been meeting in the original frame Congregational church since 1880. The Presbyterians worshipped in the brick church until 1925, when the United Church was formed and many Presbyterians decided to join with the Methodists. The church was given to a local group of Presbyterians that decided not to become part of the newly formed United Church.[129]

After the church was no longer being used for services, in 1927 the Presbyterians sold the building and property to the municipality, who used it as a community meeting hall and council chambers until 1949, when it was sold to the Unionville District Veterans' Association. The church bell was taken down from the tower and given to Central United Church, the congregation that absorbed the Presbyterian members who had decided to join with the Methodists. Other than removing the bell, the Unionville Veterans changed very little of the appearance of the former church, unlike the Markham Veterans' Association, which altered their meeting place, another former church, in their effort to create a less church-like meeting place. In the mid-1950s, Murray Evans, a local roofing contractor who had repaired the roof after a fire, organized the creation of the unique copper weather vane that sits atop the steeple. For a small financial contribution, the families of veterans of the Second World War could have their names engraved upon it. The weathervane proudly bears the words "Unionville Veterans," but the names can no longer be read.

The Unionville District Veterans' Association met here from the 1950s until the late 1990s. Since 2002 the former church has been in private ownership and has served as retail space.

James Eckardt Tenant Farmer's House, 24 Maple Lane, circa 1880

Maple Lane began as the lane from Main Street leading into James Eckardt's farm. It was later formalized as a public road when a plan of village lots was registered for the Main Street frontage of the Eckardt farm in 1875. It is remarkable that in the 2000s Maple Lane still leads to a farmstead at the end of the street. It has been many years, however, since the fields have been cultivated and livestock and crops have been sheltered within the barn.

James Eckardt was an individual of some importance in his community. He was a successful farmer, a justice of the peace, a licence inspector, and, for a time, president of the East York Agricultural Society. In 1875 he built a spacious brick farmhouse, which stands today at 137 Main Street, a little to the north of where Maple Lane and Main Street intersect.[130]

About 1880 James Eckardt built a modest frame farmhouse, well set back from Main Street, just outside of the village lots that were laid out along Maple Lane. The farmhouse provides a focal point at the end of the street, with the Rouge River valley forming a picturesque backdrop behind it. To the south of the farmhouse stands a full-size barn, larger than the town barns and stables that served many village residences when Unionville was still a rural village. The first phase of this barn may have predated the construction of the farmhouse and the subdivision next to it.

The one-and-a-half-storey farmhouse appears to have been designed to serve as a dwelling for a tenant farmer, who would run the day-to-day operation of the farm on behalf of its distinguished owner. David Eakin was possibly the first resident farmer there as he was noted on the property in the 1881 census.

From the street the farmhouse has the appearance of a Georgian-tradition cottage, with a centre door flanked by a window on either side. The hip-roofed front verandah, now enclosed as a sunroom, previously had chamfered wood posts and was decorated with fretsawn brackets. The vertical V-groove tongue-and-groove siding and two-over-two windows are original features, typical of the period of construction.

From the south side view, the farmhouse follows the L-shaped plan that was so often used in the last few decades of the nineteenth century. In the ell that once had an open verandah off the kitchen wing, there is now an enclosed space. Centred above the closed-in side verandah is a steep Gothic Revival gable. Instead of a pointed-arched window, the gable contains a flat-headed window, an indication that after all this was a tenant farmer's house of modest design and construction.

The barn is a remarkable survivor from the agricultural past of the village, unexpected in the context of present-day Markham. Based on the layout of the foundation and the structure of the post-and-beam frame, it appears that the

barn was built in two phases. The first phase was a long rectangular shape, probably with a simple gable roof. In the early 1900s the barn was expanded to the north, squaring up the plan shape and altering the roof from a gable to a gambrel roof. The gambrel roof, sometimes called a hipped roof by old-time farmers, can span a greater depth of building due to its broken slope. This roof style was commonly used for new barns, or renovated barns, from the 1890s into the early twentieth century.[131]

The Old Bakery, 31 Victoria Lane, circa 1885

The old bakery on Victoria Lane looks more like a stable than a bakery, and that is because it probably started out that way. It was constructed in the mid-1880s as an accessory building for a house at 31 Victoria Avenue, first owned by Maria Wilson, the widow of Thomas Wilson. This village lot was part of a small extension of William Eakin's subdivision of village lots that also created Victoria Avenue in 1873. Plan 489, registered in 1881, added three new building lots to the original eight. Maria Wilson's house, the last one on the street, overlooked the Rouge Valley to the north and east.

In 1910 George P. Court, a baker, purchased the property. He and his wife, Eleanor, were English immigrants. George Court worked at the bakery at the rear of Brown's store at 156 Main Street. The bakery was started at this location by Arthur Brown, who bought out the business and delivery route of another local baker in 1891. After Arthur Brown's death, Mrs. Brown continued the business with the assistance of a number of family members, and built a new bakery equipped with a brick oven. After renting out the bakery to a series of operators, it was eventually sold to Brown's Bakery of Toronto. It was during that time that George Court was employed there.[132]

Older people can remember door-to-door milk delivery, but in the late nineteenth and early twentieth century other staples were delivered by horse-drawn wagon as well, especially in the city. Bread and other baked goods, fresh vegetables, and tea were among the items sold by entrepreneurs with regular routes. Bread baked at the Brown family's bakery, and later Brown's Bakery of Toronto, was delivered this way on a daily basis, except of course on Sundays.

George Court converted the stable adjoining his residence into a bakery at some point, possibly as an auxiliary place of production for the main bakery behind the Brown's store. Either that or perhaps he used his training to start his own bakery business after leaving the employ of Brown's Bakery. This was not a retail bakery where customers would enter and find an array of tasty-looking baked goods in a glass-fronted showcase. Rather, it was small-scale industrial operation that must have produced a wonderful aroma in the vicinity whenever bread was baking in the oven. Baked goods were delivered throughout the community.

After the death of George Court, his wife and children continued to live in this beautiful, secluded spot, and the bakery operated for a time under the supervision of Mrs. Court. The Court bakery was known for its bread and Chelsea buns.[133] Walter and Douglas Court sold the family home in 1984. The bread oven and numerous baking pans were left behind in the old bakery for later owners to find and puzzle over. They were still there in 1996, when a new owner wondered about the history of the property and why there was a bread oven in the weather-beaten, unpainted shed on the lane next to the house. The date "1910" was cast on the metal door of the oven. By this time the old bakery was beginning to lapse into picturesque decline, with a notable sag in the roof and a patchwork of mismatched doors and windows. From the outside, only a stove pipe hole on the west gable end hinted that what looked like a stable had actually been a bakery in the early 1900s.

Fortunately, the old bakery building was rescued from its dilapidated state, restored, and converted to a single-car garage, revitalized with a colour scheme of barn red trimmed with white. The board-and-batten siding, with moulded battens rather than plain ones, is an indication of a better class of construction, even for a utilitarian structure.

Charles E. Stiver Carpenters' Shop, 17 Euclid Street, circa 1886

There was a time when every residence in old Unionville had some type of outbuilding in its yard. Some were stables and driving sheds. Some were general storage buildings. Others might have been chicken coops or workshops. Many contained an outhouse as an accessory

— most often a two-seater. As the nineteenth century transitioned into the twentieth century, some of these utilitarian buildings were converted to garages to house automobiles, if they were the right shape and size. Over time, most of these urban barns disappeared as village life turned into suburban life. The Charles E. Stiver Carpenters' Shop is a noteworthy exception to this trend.

Charles Edward Stiver was the second son of William Stiver and Susan Hesk, a member of a farming family that lived to the west of Unionville. Their old farmhouse, altered but still recognizable as a heritage building, is now a small community centre known as Warden House, located a short distance to the north of Markham's Civic Centre. At the time of the 1881 census Charles Stiver was twenty years of age and living at home with his parents and siblings. He was unmarried, and his occupation was given as "millwright." Historically, a millwright was a mechanic that constructed the machinery of mills.

Charles E. Stiver married Annie Johnson and left the family farm to settle in Unionville. He changed careers, abandoning his training as a millwright and instead learning the trade of carpentry, which was probably much more in demand as the village grew in the last quarter of the nineteenth century.[134] He worked with his younger brother, Frank Stiver, and several of his sons. The Stivers moved into a new house at the southeast corner of Euclid Street and Eureka Street that had been built about 1886. The house was constructed by Reuben A. Stiver, a relative who was an ambitious local entrepreneur with an interest in a number of Unionville properties, probably as a speculative venture. Charles E. Stiver is said to have worked on the very house he would come to own when it was completed. A few years after the house was built a wing was added to the front, and the frame exterior was updated with brick veneer in a pattern of red and buff brick.

On the same lot, a spacious urban barn was constructed by Charles E. Stiver to contain his carpentry shop and function as a drive shed and stable. The building likely housed tools, ladders, and other equipment as well as lumber and building components. No doubt there was a sturdy workbench and a selection of sawhorses.

Charles E. Stiver and his brother had become carpenters and builders at a time of major change in their trade. With the addition of planing mills to sawmills, where lumber was shaped by machines and many components of buildings were produced with the aid of specialized machinery such as bandsaws, the level of skill required by carpenters significantly changed. The era of the hand-crafted house was over. No more would it be necessary for carpenters to plane roughsawn planks into dimensional lumber, or to spend hours producing casings and baseboards using moulding planes.

By 1911 Charles E. Stiver described himself as a builder and contractor. He was a serious churchman, serving the Unionville Primitive Methodist Church as a lay preacher for many years.[135] He would have still been active in the church when the Methodist and

Presbyterian churches merged to form the United Church of Canada in 1925.

The former carpenters' shop has been well cared for and has become integrated with the house with a well-designed link that preserves the character of both buildings. The barn-like building has an L-shaped plan, a loft, and diamond-shaped windows in the gables. Its red-painted, tongue-and-groove siding enhances the traditional barn look of the building, so much a part of the nineteenth century but in reality serving the purpose of a modern-day garage.

George and Hannah Weatherill House, 77 Main Street, circa 1890

Unionville's residential Main Street did not begin to extend south of Highway 7 until the late nineteenth century. Development began in 1878, when Edward Eckardt, the son of Philip Eckardt Jr., decided to sub-divide the front of his farm into village lots.[136] Plan 445, surveyed by Peter S. Gibson, created a row of building lots on Main Street, beginning from Highway 7, locally known as Dufferin Street at the time, and ending at the bridge over the Rouge River. In the midst of the new village lots was a road called Rouge Avenue, which was intended to extend eastward from Main Street. The river valley just beyond Main Street was an effective barrier that prevented Rouge Avenue from being opened as a travelled public road.

In the late nineteenth century a number of Edward Eckardt's village lots were bought up and built upon, mostly with modestly scaled houses. Lot Number 6, at the north corner of Main Street and the unopened stub of Rouge Avenue, was purchased by George Weatherill in 1888. He was a farmer that cultivated a rented property on the west side of Main Street, south of Highway 7.[137] About 1890 builders associated with the Unionville Planing Mill constructed this simple L-plan frame house clad in vertical tongue-and-groove siding. George Weatherill's wife was Hannah Harrington, daughter of Robert Harrington, the owner of the planing mill. Like a number of the houses erected by the planing mill's builders in the latter part of the nineteenth century, the Weatherill House has the picturesque form and sense of verticality characteristic of the Gothic Revival style. However, the decorative elements so often associated with this style are not part of this design; rather, the house has a simplified architectural treatment without bargeboards or brackets. The large, plate-glass windows with patterned glass in the transom sash above were coming into fashion in the 1890s, so the Weatherill House would have been seen as being quite up-to-date for its time. In the early 1900s a porch was constructed in the ell facing Main Street, with Edwardian Classical detailing that blended well with the overall clean lines of the circa 1890 residence.

The Weatherills sold to John Taylor in 1913, moving

to a more up-to-date brick house on Eckardt Avenue.[138] In 1948 William and Eva Fry became the owners. Eva Fry was the assistant postmaster in Unionville, and later in her career she was in charge of a post office in Scarborough Township to the south of Markham.

For some reason the gentrification of Unionville that took effect north of Highway 7 never really caught on south of the highway. A number of the older houses, particularly the smaller frame ones, were demolished in relatively recent times and replaced by new residential development, in spite of the heritage protection afforded by the heritage district. The Weatherill House, however, has survived the transition on the street. In 2002 the house was placed on a new foundation and underwent an extensive restoration that returned the wood siding and other elements of the building to their original appearance.

Moses and Catherine Hemingway House, 105 Main Street, circa 1896

Standing at the gateway to old Unionville at Main Street and Highway 7, this simple frame building is the first indication that people see of the historic streetscape of the village beyond. Although it is not an elaborate structure by any means, it is nonetheless a landmark at this busy street corner. For many years 105 Main Street has served as an office and other commercial uses, and has been greatly extended, but its residential character still remains easily recognizable.

Although this building was a house for much of its history, it had an industrial beginning that is not obvious from its appearance. In 1896 the Unionville Butter and Cheese Manufacturing Company Limited purchased two

adjoining village lots from James and Agnes Eckardt. Not much is known about this short-lived business. It was Unionville's second cheese factory, and it came along almost two decades after the Raymer Cheese Factory farther north on Main Street had ceased to operate.[139]

The butter and cheese factory building was damaged by fire only three years after it opened, and that seems to have been the end of the business.[140] Perhaps the owners did not carry a sufficient amount of insurance to rebuild, or any at all. How much of the building survived the fire is not clear. After the fire the company sold the property, and either a new structure was built on the original foundation or the damaged building was repaired. In either case, the former factory was converted to a residence, in much the same way the old Raymer Cheese Factory was remodelled to serve as a house in the late 1870s.

In 1903 Moses "Mose" Hemingway, proprietor of the Queen's Hotel, purchased the property. He was the grandson of John and Jane Webber, the longtime owners of the hotel.[141] Moses Hemingway's parents, Orson "Ton"

Hemingway and Matilda Webber Hemingway, ran the Beehive Hotel at Hagerman's Corners. In 1891 Moses Hemingway was single and living at the Queen's Hotel with his grandparents. At the time, he was a mail courier.

By the turn of the century Moses Hemingway was married to Catherine Good and had taken over as the hotel keeper at the Queen's. At the time he purchased the property at 105 Main Street the conversion of the butter and cheese factory into a residence had probably been completed by a previous owner. Moses Hemingway was a community-minded individual. When Unionville achieved a level of self-government within Markham Township by becoming a "police village" in 1907, he was one of three local businessmen elected as village trustees.[142] The others were George Dukes, a butcher, and William Padget, the owner of the village hardware store. The first meeting of the newly elected trustees took place in Hemingway's temperance hotel, the Queen's Hotel, at 174 Main Street.[143]

Ownership of the house was transferred to Catherine Hemingway, Moses Hemingway's wife, in 1908. By the time of the 1911 census she was widowed but stayed on in the family home until 1920, when the property was sold. Over the years the house was used as a nursing home by the Dukes family, a real estate office, business offices, and a spa. In the mid-1980s the former house was enlarged with an addition to the rear that adds to the building's prominence on Highway 7.

It is difficult to place the Moses and Catherine Hemingway House within an identifiable architectural style category. In this respect it is a true vernacular building, attractive for its clean lines and good proportions, but without any decorative elements. Like many of the other frame houses built in Unionville at around the same time period, it is sided in vertical tongue-and-groove wood in a style associated with the work of the Unionville Planing Mill. For the most part, few changes have been made to the building, even through all of the uses it has had. An old photograph shows that the window design was originally simpler and without pane divisions, and the large front window had a leaded-glass transom light. Early on there was a spacious porch in an Edwardian Classical design. Most unusual about the former home of the Hemingways is a canted bay window on the second floor on the north side of the building, while a somewhat larger bay window is found on the ground floor on the south side.

Unionville's transition from a Victorian Ontario village into a community of the modern era is perfectly captured in this archival photograph that shows Ira White's mill-owner's house converted to an automotive repair shop in the 1920s.

Markham Museum Archival Collection

Unionville's Second Century

In the early part of the twentieth century Unionville was still very much a Victorian village, with a grist-mill, planing mill, general stores, and blacksmith shops. As the new century progressed, Unionville was transformed. Horses, carriages, and wagons were replaced by cars and trucks, blacksmiths were replaced by mechanics, and the mills that bookended the commercial centre of the village were destroyed by fire. Unionville continued to grow in the 1900s, with comfortable red-brick houses in the early years, followed by an explosion of suburban growth in the 1960s and onward.

Hugh Powell and Harriet Crosby House, 111 Main Street, circa 1900

It's not necessarily the showiest of Unionville's old houses that are the ones with the most compelling stories. Some houses stand out simply by virtue of their architectural style, excellence of preservation, or their ornamentation, and in these ways they are primarily of architectural interest. Others, like 111 Main Street, are of the plainer sort but have remarkable historical associations.

The former residence of Hugh Powell Crosby, one of Unionville's most interesting and influential early residents, is a house that has not undergone the gentrification that many of its neighbours have experienced. Its buff-coloured brick is painted a dusky maroon, accented with black shutters that tend to make the house recede into the landscape rather than stand out from it. It's not the architecture but the history of the house and its former inhabitants that make 111 Main Street worth a second look.

Hugh Powell Crosby was a member of an Irish-American family from the State of New York. His grandfather, William Crosby, came to Upper Canada in 1807 and purchased land in Markham Township in 1812. His father, Chauncey Crosby, lived at the south end of Markham Village on the west side of Main Street, at about the point where the on-ramp for Highway 407 is now located. Chauncey Crosby was a distinguished member of his community, serving as a justice of the peace in addition to being a farmer and a merchant.[1]

Hugh Powell Crosby initially followed in his father's footsteps, working as a merchant in Markham Village in the early 1850s. He married Harriet White, the daughter of Ira White, owner of the Union Mills, and through this family association came to be the proprietor of the gristmill and sawmill at Unionville while his father-in-law pursued other ventures elsewhere in the province.[2] Census records from 1861 through 1881 indicate Crosby's occupation as merchant miller, and Mitchell & Co.'s directory of 1866 lists Hugh Powell Crosby as the proprietor of the Union Flour and Grist Mill and also a sawmill proprietor.

While the management of the milling operations at Unionville must have kept Hugh Powell Crosby very busy, this ambitious gentleman was eager to expand his horizons and take on additional responsibilities. Crosby was the municipality's first clerk and treasurer after the incorporation of Markham Township in 1850, a post he held for a decade. He was a founding trustee of the new grammar school at Markham Village when it got its start in 1858.[3] From 1866 to 1872 he was captain of No. 9 Company of the local militia at Unionville, at a time after the American Civil War when the Irish-American Fenians posed a threat to the security of British North America.[4]

More than anything else, Hugh Powell Crosby had political ambitions. He was a supporter of Reform political ideals in the time leading up to Confederation. Although he was not successful in winning the nomination for the federal House of Commons, he did win the provincial nomination and ran as a candidate for the Reform or Liberal Party in the election of 1867. Crosby was elected as the member of the Provincial Parliament for the riding of York East, serving in the Ontario Legislature for two terms spanning the years 1867 to 1874.[5] During that time he served on a number of standing committees, including the standing committee on railways.

Hugh Powell Crosby's interest in railways was an important benefit to Unionville, when the Toronto and Nipissing Railway, incorporated in 1868, was considering its route through Markham Township.[6] The original plan was for the new railway line to pass through Markham to the south of the village of Unionville. At the time, Unionville was not a major centre, but a modest-sized village that the railway didn't consider significant enough to warrant a station stop. Through Crosby's political influence with the railway company's board of directors, a change to the route of the railway was achieved to the benefit of Unionville and its business owners, which ushered in a period of growth and prosperity for the village.

By the mid-1880s, Hugh Powell Crosby had retired from the milling business. In the 1890s the Crosbys lived in the Lutheran parsonage at 109 Main Street, to the south of the business district of the village, which they rented from the parsonage trustees.[7] A new house was built for them on a group of three adjoining village lots purchased from Reuben A. Stiver in 1900. This property was located next door to the north of the Lutheran parsonage, so they must have been able to keep a close watch on the progress on their new residence as it was being constructed. The Crosbys soon moved into what would have been a modern residence in its day, the first in Unionville to have a concrete basement rather than a fieldstone foundation that was the usual type in Markham in the nineteenth century. Builders associated with Robert Harrington's planing mill were employed to construct this fine new home for its distinguished occupants.[8]

The concrete foundation is not the only modern feature of the Crosby House. It was built with buff-coloured brick that began to be used in the area in the 1880s in place of the orange-salmon coloured variegated brick produced by the local Snowball brickworks. The house has a large cottage window in the front gable-end wall, featuring a single plate-glass window topped with a rectangular transom light. Other windows in the house have one-over-one glazing, without the pane divisions usually seen in the previous century.

Overall, the house reflects a vernacular interpretation of the Queen Anne Revival style, with its irregular plan outline and gables. The box bay window on the south gable end, with a balcony over, overlooks an expansive lawn and landscaped area. It must have been a pleasant place to sit before the days of the automobile and the ever-increasing traffic on Main Street. When first constructed, the Crosby House had a light but richly decorated hip-roofed porch in the street-facing ell, which was replaced in the early 1900s by a somewhat heavier porch with Edwardian Classical lines. In recent years, this later porch has been modified with turned posts and fretwork brackets that approximate the earlier treatment.

An unusual and understated feature of the Crosby House is the square entrance tower in the ell, containing the front door on its south-facing wall within the porch. It is not clear if a portion of the tower above the roofline was intended by the builder but not completed, or if the upper portion was removed when this type of feature was no longer in style. Typically, a tower of this time period would have been capped with a pyramidal or mansard roof. Whichever is the case, the nearly flat roof of the entrance tower has a feeling of unfinished business about it.[9]

Hugh Powell Crosby died in 1905. The house was given to the nearby Methodist Church to serve as a manse to house the minister and his family, replacing an older and smaller manse on Victoria Avenue. The ministers of the Methodist, and later the United, church resided here until 1965, when a more modern dwelling was purchased, closer to the church itself.[10] Since that time the Crosby House, with its fascinating historical associations hidden behind a rather unassuming facade, has been used as a private residence.

Hugh Powell and Harriet Crosby are commemorated in Unionville in the name of Crosby Memorial Arena at the top of the commercial centre of the village, thanks to their son William H. Crosby. William H. Crosby achieved considerable success after moving to Buffalo, New York, following a brief career as a schoolteacher in the Whitevale community of Pickering Township to the east. He made his fortune in the establishment of a metal-stamping industry that began by supplying parts for the assembly of bicycles. When the age of the automobile arrived, William H. Crosby used his business savvy to grab hold of this new opportunity and his plant switched to the fabrication of parts for automobiles.[11]

William H. Crosby provided the funds for the Crosby Memorial Community Centre, which opened in 1928, and an adjoining athletic ground on the site of the original Crosby residence near the Union Mills, named in memory of his parents.[12] The arena itself may have been changed over the years, but the Crosby family is still commemorated in the name of this popular facility.

Stiver Brothers Grain Elevator and Feed Mill, 9 Station Lane, Early Twentieth Century

When Canadians think of grain elevators, the image that most often comes to mind is a series of brightly painted, angular structures strung out along a railway line, set against the backdrop of the Canadian prairies.[13] To see a structure of this type in southern Ontario is a little unusual. The Stiver Brothers Grain Elevator and Feed Mill on Station Lane is a reminder of a time when wheat was a staple crop in this part of Canada, a crop that enabled the early settlers to not only get themselves established in a new land, but to prosper.

In the early 1900s grain elevators and other storage buildings were constructed next to Unionville's Grand Trunk railway station. Hiram Powers, a newcomer to Unionville at the turn of the century, may have been the builder of at least one of the grain elevators, since he is known to have built one in Gormley Station in 1907. In the 1901 census his profession was given as "grain buyer," and in 1911 "grain dealer." The land these buildings occupied was leased from the railway.[14]

About 1910, or perhaps a little earlier, brothers Charles and Francis "Frank" Stiver started a business they called Stiver Brothers Coal and Seed. Then, in 1916, they purchased and repaired the fire-damaged structures of the Matthew Grain Company to the west of the station to develop their business. Stiver Brothers was beginning to prosper when a major setback shocked the Stiver family and the whole community. Charles Howard Stiver, who was the township clerk as well as a co-owner of Stiver Brothers, died suddenly and tragically in 1917. His wife, Marein, likely with the help of Frank Stiver, stepped into his place in the operation of the business, which would have been quite something in those days. When her son, Ewart, returned from the

First World War, he took over running Stiver Brothers' Unionville operation along with his brother Howard.[15]

Stiver Brothers owned grain elevators and had business offices in both Unionville and Stouffville, a larger village farther north on the railway line. Frank Stiver ran the Stouffville branch. They also had a warehouse in Aurora. In 1950 the business expanded once again, adding a warehouse in Uxbridge. The Stivers sold grain, seed, feed for livestock, coal, and cement. Locating this type of business next to a railway line was typical of grain elevators across the country, a convenient way of shipping and receiving bulky goods. Carloads of grain shipped from the Canadian west would arrive at the Stiver Mill and their contents unloaded for storage in the elevator's several grain bins. The chopping work required for the production of livestock feed was at first done at the Union Mills, the venerable old gristmill at the head of Main Street's commercial core.

After the gristmill was destroyed by fire in 1934, Stiver Brothers added a feed mill to their operation. A storage building to the east was moved up against the grain elevator to house a diesel engine that ran the chopping and mixing machinery. About 1950 storage sheds were constructed on the west side of the grain elevator. Four years later, Charles H. Stiver's sons Ewart and Howard moved the business office and store from the building that once housed the Sovereign Bank on Main Street to a new, rather utilitarian building on Station Lane, opposite the mill. They continued on until 1968, when Dominion Coal and Building Supplies became the railway's tenant in the mill. After that business closed, the municipality became the owner in 1993, with the purchase of the land and building from Canadian National Railway.[16]

For years the battered, silver-painted building, locally known as the Stiver Mill, sat empty and deteriorating. It was a heritage landmark without a purpose, preserved but not really saved. Committees were formed then faded away. Ideas were put forward, but never implemented. Then, in the 2010s, a group of dedicated heritage volunteers was formed to work with the municipality to give the abandoned structure a new life. The Unionville Conservancy helped guide the way to the development of a restoration plan, and the Stiver Mill Farmer's Market drew people to the site to promote the need to really do something this time around. The turning point came in 2012 with federal infrastructure money awarded to the project to add to municipal funding, and not long afterward the restoration was underway.

Work on the Stiver Grain Elevator and Feed Mill, now called the Stiver Mill Cultural Centre, was completed in the spring of 2014.[17] The ground floor has been repurposed for use as community meeting space containing displays relating to Markham's milling history, while the elevator acts as an artifact that helps tell the story of this last remnant of Unionville's role as a service centre for the surrounding agricultural community that existed prior to large-scale suburban development. A key component of the project was to change the silver-painted metal siding to barn red. This was the only significant alteration to be made to the exterior, a bold visual cue that the structure has been renewed and is entering a new phase of its history.[18]

The grain elevator is of plank-on-plank, or cribbed, construction, above the timber frame main-floor level. Plank-on-plank is an old method of building that consists of roughsawn lumber stacked horizontally and nailed together for stability to form a solid wood wall.[19] The elevator's design is similar to the iconic slope-shouldered grain elevators of the Canadian West, once a common part of Canada's prairie identity but one that is rapidly disappearing from the landscape. Unionville's grain elevator is one of the last in the region.

The exterior of the Stiver Brothers Grain Elevator was clad in corrugated metal panels at an early date, to protect the underlying wood structure from the weather. The addition was clad in pressed-metal panels in a narrow clapboard pattern, a precursor to the aluminium siding that became popular in the 1960s. In the restoration, the siding has been replaced with new material, as the old siding was simply too damaged to be restored. Inside the building much of the machinery, grain bins, and chutes remain as artifacts accenting this new community facility.[20]

Delos and Jennie Harrington House, 130 Main Street, 1905

When Delos Harrington and Jennie Hemingway first married, they lived in a rented house owned by Robert Harrington, a few doors away from the planing mill. Their original home, a frame house now addressed 25 Victoria Avenue, was built in 1896.[21] It was a humble beginning for the man who would take over the ownership and operation of the family business in that same year.

Delos Harrington was the eldest son of Robert Harrington and Henrietta Green. He and his brother George worked alongside their father in the operation of the planing mill, which the family had owned since 1881, when it was purchased from William Eakin. When Robert Harrington decided to retire in 1896, his sons bought the mill and continued to produce dimensional lumber and all manner of wooden building components, both structural and decorative. It wasn't long before George sold his share in the planing mill and Delos Harrington became the sole proprietor of one of Unionville's most successful and long-lasting businesses.[22]

In 1905 the Harrington family decided it was time to build a new house in the village and move from the working man's neighbourhood of Victoria Avenue to a location on the more prestigious Unionville Main Street. Jennie Harrington had been willed a property on the west side of Main Street, south of the railway line, by her grandmother, Jane Webber, co-owner of the Queen's Hotel. Jennie Harrington also acquired an adjoining lot owned by the Webber family at the same time, providing a spacious double lot which is said to have contained an old orchard with some apple varieties no longer cultivated, including strawberry apples and "sheep's nose" apples.[23]

According to Delos and Jennie Harrington's daughter Grace's account of her childhood in Unionville, the house site had a small building used by the railway to store equipment for the section men looking after the tracks. There was also an old blacksmith shop on the property, a two-storey structure of brick that in some sources is described as a wheelwright shop. This old building is thought to have been owned by Walter Walker, but earlier may have been the blacksmith shop of John Grundy and William Weatherall. Delos Harrington had the shop carefully dismantled and the bricks cleaned for reuse in the construction of his new house.

Perhaps it was no accident that Delos Harrington's new house was made of brick rather than wood, to proclaim to his neighbours his success in the family enterprise. Wood houses were for his customers and employees, not for the planing mill's owner. Not only was the new Harrington residence a substantial two-and-a-half-storey red-brick building on a large lot, rendered in the latest modern style, it was the first in the village to have an indoor bathroom.[24] The added conveniences of electricity and a telephone came several years later. A particularly attractive feature of the property was a front-yard fence composed of intricate sawn balusters produced by the planing mill. Its late Victorian character contrasted with the Edwardian simplicity of the house. A portion of this unique fence remains today, a rare survivor from the early 1900s.[25]

The Harringtons lived here until 1944, when they sold to Edwin Newton. After that the house was purchased by Clark and Jean Young when they retired from their farm east of Hagerman's Corners. Clark Young was a champion ploughman.[26] In 2000 a new house in a traditional style, designed to complement the former Harrington residence, was built in the large yard north of the house. The intricate wood fence once graced the front of the old house as well as the new one until it was removed by a subsequent owner who did not appreciate its special significance.

The Harrington House was designed in an early twentieth-century interpretation of the Queen Anne Revival style, but is similar in form to an American Foursquare, except for the deep, wraparound verandah and shallow, projecting bay on the north side. The north-facing gable has patterned wood shingles and contains a beautifully detailed attic window with a Classical surround that resembles a shallow portico. On the south wall is an oriel box bay window. The large, plate-glass window of the parlour, with it ornamental transom window above, is an indication of the modernizing influence of the new century. Decorative details such as the paired Doric columns on the verandah show the influence of the Edwardian Classicism that was popular at the time of construction, while the paired brackets of the cornice recall something of the Italianate style of the previous century.

Charles H. and Marein Stiver House, 202 Main Street, 1907

Two old houses stand somewhat aloof from the busyness of Main Street, the former home of Hewlett Eckardt at 158 Main Street and this one, the Charles H. Stiver House. Many local people in the Unionville area remember this house as the local funeral home, which it was from 1969 to the 1980s. More recently the atmosphere

is livelier as a popular restaurant and bar that forms the backdrop to a spacious outdoor patio. According to a Stiver family history, published for a family reunion, the house is rumoured to have a resident ghost.[27]

Charles Howard Stiver was an entrepreneurial type of person. From 1896 to around 1901 he ran a general store that had previously been operated by Reuben A. Stiver, a relative, at 182 Main Street. He had less time for the store once he was appointed township clerk in 1899, taking over for John Stephenson, the former blacksmith and original owner of the Queen's Hotel.[28] In 1916 he and his brother Francis bought the former buildings of the Matthew Grain Company next to the railway station, and Stiver Brothers expanded to become a long-standing landmark business on Station Lane.

The history of the property where 202 Main Street stands is not well known. Prior to the construction of the Charles H. Stiver House, in 1907, there were large stables and sheds but no house on the lot between the adobe-brick cottage at 206 Main Street to the north

and the former home of Dr. T.P. Eckardt to the south. These buildings may have originally been associated with 206 Main Street but were later severed off. According to information preserved in the pages of Unionville's Tweedsmuir History, compiled by the local Women's Institute, the barns were used by prominent local auctioneer Salem Eckardt, who lived in the house at 197 Main Street. A perusal of the deeds for the property confirms that the lot was owned by Salem and Catherine Eckardt, and by 1904 was owned by Catherine Eckardt's heirs. Charles H. Stiver and Abner Summerfeldt purchased the lot in 1906, and in 1907 Abner Summerfeldt, who had taken over the general store by this time, sold his share in the property to his business partner.

Charles H. Stiver's life came to a tragic end in 1917, when he drowned in Lake Wilcox, near Yonge Street in Oak Ridges.[29] This was in the midst of the First World War, a troubled time for many families who had sons fighting overseas. After Charles's death, his widow, Marein Burkholder Stiver, courageously assumed the day-to-day operation of the Stiver Brothers branch in Unionville until her son Ewart returned from the war.

The late Charles H. Stiver's wife and unmarried daughters, Dorothy and Helen, continued to live in the family home for many years, before the property was sold out of the family.[30] Marein Stiver lived a long life as an active member of her community, passing away in 1965.

The architecture of the Stiver House and its building materials strongly suggests it may have been constructed by the same builder who worked on the home of Delos and Jennie Harrington at 130 Main Street. John Miller is one possibility as the builder, since he was active in the community at the time of construction of both houses.[31] Like the Harrington House down the street, the Stiver House had running water provided by a tank in the attic, positioned to create water pressure by the force of gravity. Notwithstanding their many similarities, the former home of Charles and Marein Stiver is somewhat grander in scale than the Harrington House, with a larger floorplate and more of a distinctly irregular plan.

The Stiver House is a superb example of the early twentieth-century phase of the Queen Anne Revival style, with the influence of Edwardian Classicism. The house displays many of the architectural features that define this blend of styles, including a two-and-a-half-storey height, red-brick walls, steep hipped roof with dormers, deep verandah supported on Classical columns resting on brick pedestals, and stylized decorative motifs inspired by the buildings of ancient Greece and Rome. Bracketed eaves, a small second-storey balcony, and accent windows add an extra touch of refinement. The same portico-like attic window surround and patterned wood shingles that are found on the Harrington House appear in the north gable of the Stiver House, while the front dormer is larger and of a different design than the one on the Harrington House, and has a small, decorative oval window within a closed pediment.

Inside is a brick fireplace with a bold, round-arched shape framed by radiating brick voussoirs that reflects the Richardson Romanesque style that was current a few years earlier, mainly in urban settings such as Toronto.[32] The fireplace is a noteworthy high-style feature of this impressive house, unexpected as its design contrasts with the otherwise classic Edwardian character of the exterior and interior.

Edwin and Verdilla Dixon House, 108 Main Street, circa 1910

Unionville's most ambitious and elaborate early twentieth-century residence stands at the corner of Main and Pavilion Streets. Pavilion Street was named long before the Dixon House was built. History doesn't record why William Eckardt chose this particular name, but it is unlikely that in the mid-1850s he would have guessed that one day a fine house with a large corner pavilion would be built on this corner lot.

Edwin Dixon grew up on a farm to the northeast of Unionville, located on the east ninety acres of Lot 14, Concession 6. His parents were George and Elizabeth Dixon. Their farmhouse was located in the centre of the property, and along the frontage there was a series of five other houses on smaller lots, south of a Bible Christian church. At one time this community was locally known as Quantztown, named after one of the Berczy settler families that had settled in the area. Today no trace remains of the Dixon farmhouse, but the cemetery associated with the Bible Christian church can still be seen next to the woodlot on the west side of McCowan Road, a little south of 16th Avenue.[33] The last remaining house from Quantztown was relocated to Markham Heritage Estates in 1991, where it has been restored back to its mid-nineteenth-century appearance.[34]

Edwin Dixon was the youngest of George and Elizabeth Dixon's seven children. His older brother, Benjamin, followed in his father's footsteps and became a farmer, but was also a taxidermist. Edwin likely learned to be a taxidermist from his older brother. He prepared and stuffed birds and other animals shot by hunters, to serve as trophies of their exploits. One of his biggest customers was Robert Armstrong, who sold stuffed, mounted moose heads to Loyal Order of Moose chapters all over the country for decorating their lodge rooms. Grace Harrington's reminiscences of Unionville as it was in the early 1900s tell us that Ed Dixon displayed his work in the windows of his shop, which was located in the front section of Christopher Chant's cabinetmaking shop and undertaking establishment at 147A Main Street.[35] This was a rather interesting combination of activities under one roof, but after all, the work of a taxidermist and undertaker are similar in that the goal is to make the deceased seem as lifelike as possible, under the circumstances.

In 1911 Edwin Dixon purchased the shop from Christopher Chant, and 147A Main Street was then entirely devoted to his studio. His business letterhead proclaimed him to be "Ontario's Leading Taxidermist" and listed a number of the large Canadian mammals that he specialized in mounting. A sign on the front of the building, painted on wooden slats much like those of a window shutter, read "Edwin Dixon" on one side, and "Taxidermist" on the other, a kind of optical illusion depending on from which direction the sign was viewed.[36] In an archival photograph dated 1910 in the collection of the Markham Museum, Ed Dixon is shown touching up one of his pieces on the wood-lined wall of his studio, surrounded by mounted deer heads. Given today's sensitivity around animal rights, this photograph seems odd, but at that time many households proudly displayed such trophies on their walls.

Another oddity about the work of Edwin Dixon is the fact that he lived in such a large and impressive house that rivalled those of the local doctor and the owners of some of major businesses in the village. Was the trade or art of a taxidermist so lucrative that it would enable him to afford such a fine home as this? Chances are that Edwin Dixon must have had some other source of wealth, perhaps family money.

The property at 108 Main Street was purchased by Edwin Dixon in 1910, and it is supposed that the house was built that same year. In the 1911 census, Edwin (with his name recorded as Edward) Dixon was thirty-four years of age and unmarried. This was a large home for a single man. It was not until 1936 that he married Verdilla Doner. She was thirty-five; he was sixty. They owned the property until 1944, having sold it not long after Edwin Dixon retired.

The year 1910 seems to have marked a building boom in Unionville. Most of the new houses being constructed in the village around that time were two to two-and-a-half storeys and built in red brick. They followed the popular styles of the day, which included the Queen Anne Revival and Edwardian Classical. Unlike their late Victorian neighbours, the houses of

Unionville's second century were simplified in their details, lacking the applied elaborations that belonged to the previous era. The Dixon House combines the form and some of the detailing of the Queen Anne Revival with a number of the characteristics of Edwardian Classicism, such as the Tuscan columns of its spacious verandah, supported on brick piers.

What sets the Dixon House apart from its contemporaries is the round corner pavilion at the north end of the verandah, with its conical roof creating the effect of a bandstand. A projecting balcony on the second floor, centred over the main entrance of the house, has a rounded front and conical roof that echoes the design of the corner pavilion. When it was built, the Dixon House must have been a show-stopper in Unionville. The village taxidermist was doing well. Today, the former home of Edwin and Verdilla Dixon remains as impressive as ever.

William and Hannah Caldwell House, 201 Main Street, 1910

George C. Caldwell was a veterinary surgeon from Scotland who first established his practice in Markham Village. His wife, Susannah, was a milliner and dressmaker and together they worked and raised their family on Main Street, Markham Village, from the mid-1860s until the mid-1870s. By the time of the 1881 census, the Caldwell family had relocated to the village of Unionville. George C. Caldwell's profession was then given as "blacksmith," while his wife carried on with her career as a dressmaker.[37] It was not unheard of in the 1800s that a blacksmith could be skilled in both the art of metalwork and in the treatment of animals, most particularly horses. Perhaps by the time of the move to Unionville, George C. Caldwell, aged fifty-six, was less robust in his constitution and could no longer work with the heavy, large animals.

The Caldwell family lived on the east side of Main Street, a few doors down from the Union Mills. The property had previously been owned by Thomas Allison, a wheelwright, who had been a tenant of Philip D. Eckardt but had purchased the quarter-acre village lot in 1874. It was only one year later that the property, containing a small house and a workshop, was sold to George C. Caldwell for $550.

In his early years in Unionville, George C. Caldwell was assisted in the blacksmith shop by his younger brother, William, who lived in the same household along with his wife, Charlotte. George and Susannah Caldwell's oldest sons, David and George H., worked with their father in the blacksmith shop as well. They also had a younger son, named William, who was a student and, though not actively involved in the family business, was no doubt learning the art of metalwork by observing his father, uncle, and brothers.

The Caldwell blacksmith shop was set close to the road, and the house the family lived in was located in the backyard, well away from the activity of Main Street. In 1881 the household was quite crowded, with four adults and six children, two of whom would have also been considered adults by their age. Ten years later, George C. Caldwell and his wife, Susannah, had moved in with Miss Jane Neville, a dressmaker who lived on the same side of Main Street, just south of a building that housed John Devlin's harness-maker's shop. Miss Neville's residence was attached to a one-storey building that contained the village library, where she served as the librarian in addition to operating her dressmaking shop. The living quarters were separated from the library by a heavy red curtain.[38] George C. Caldwell continued to work as a blacksmith, but Susannah left the dressmaking to Jane Neville and was in the millinery business after the move. George C.'s brother William and his wife had left the village.

George H. Caldwell, his wife, Mary, and his brother William stayed on in the family home. By the time of the 1891 census William Caldwell, now twenty-one years of age, had learned the trade of "general blacksmith" and was working alongside his father and brother. As the twentieth century began, William Caldwell was in charge of the shop. His father was retired and his brother George H. Caldwell had moved to Headford, another Markham Township mill village, where he operated a blacksmith shop and from 1905 to 1907, served as the village postmaster. About 1900 William Caldwell married Hannah Ellis, a relative of the Harrington family, owners of the Planing Mill. In the early years of the marriage, he continued on as a blacksmith, but soon changed his occupation to carpenter,

working with wood rather than metal. William Caldwell got a job at the Planing Mill, likely as a benefit of his new family relationship to the Harringtons. He and his bride moved to a rented house near his new workplace.[39] The blacksmith shop was rented to another blacksmith by the name of Samuel Allen.

Thanks to the incredible detail provided by the series of fire insurance maps of Unionville's commercial centre produced by the underwriter's association, we know that in 1910 a new house was under construction on the site of the blacksmith shop, which had been removed from the property by that time.[40] This was a new home for William and Hannah Caldwell. There is a local story that during the building of the house he would sometimes walk up the street carrying lumber and other building components from the planing mill to the construction site. Not long after the couple moved into their new home on Main Street, William Caldwell had another career change, this time working for local entrepreneur G.A.M. Davison at his new Ford dealership and garage.[41]

Elements of the Queen Anne Revival style and Edwardian Classicism, popular in the early 1900s, can be seen on the Caldwell House. Architecturally, the house is similar to a number of other frame residences built by carpenters employed by Harrington's Planing Mill in the 1890s and early twentieth century. These houses have clean lines and a sense of verticality expressed in the use of vertical V-joint tongue-and-groove siding and a full two-storey height. Cottage windows in the front with a large, single pane of plate glass topped with a flat-headed transom sash, wood-shingled gables, and horizontally oriented attic windows in those gables are common features of houses built by the Planing Mill in the 1910s.

The Caldwell House was one of the last in the commercial core of Unionville to be fully converted from residential to commercial use.[42] For years a small frame garage belonging to the house sat close to the sidewalk, an oddity among the stores and restaurants that were all around it. Finally, in 1996, the old house was renovated and added onto, transformed into a popular coffee shop. The renovations kept most of the original character of the Caldwell House intact, while adding space in a way that altered the formerly open front porch by creating a sunroom effect, and stretching out the bay window on the south side. The garage was replaced by a patio overlooking Main Street. No trace remains of the first house on the property. That was removed not long after the new house was built in 1910.

Powers-Maynard House, 268 Main Street, circa 1910

This house was built next door to the site of one of Unionville's earliest hotels, the Union House, operated by Anthony Size.[43] The hall associated with the hotel, first called Size's Hall but later known as Hunter's Hall, was where Markham Township Council met from 1850 to 1873. Anthony Size was in the hotel business as early as 1851, according to the census of that year. The Union House was a spacious two-storey frame building that also housed the family, including their son William, who built a hotel on the opposite side of the street, a little to the south of this location, circa 1860. Anthony Size later combined his hotel-keeper occupation with farming. By 1881 he had retired from both careers. The old Union House burned down in 1919 after serving as a private house and farm implements dealership for a number of years.[44]

About 1910, Hiram Powers built a new brick house south of the former hotel. When he first came to Unionville, around the turn of the century, he was a grain dealer, with an interest in a grain elevator next to the Unionville train station.[45] Not long after his arrival in the village he switched careers to become an active local builder. A few years before constructing the house at 268 Main Street, Hiram Powers lived in the former William Size hotel, the Crown Inn, at 249 Main Street, which he had renovated and made into a comfortable home for his family.

In 1919 Mark and Hannah "Annie" Maynard purchased the house at 268 Main Street, along with fifteen acres bordering the millpond, from the Powers family. The Maynards were English immigrants who had previously lived in Toronto before moving to Unionville. Mark Maynard was trained as a mason in his youth in Sussex, England. He emigrated to Canada and settled in Toronto where there was much work for bricklayers as the prospering city grew at a fast pace in the latter part of the nineteenth century and early years of the twentieth century.[46] Brick was the building material of choice, preferred over wood for reasons of fire safety in the neighbourhoods of closely packed houses in Toronto's ever-expanding suburbs.

The Maynard sons learned the trade from their father and were part of the family business, constructing many houses in Toronto's east end. The Maynards worked on the construction of the brick kilns and tall red-brick chimneys of the Don Valley Brickworks.[47] One of the chimneys remains today, an enduring landmark in the valley seen daily by untold numbers of commuters as they make their way to and from work along the Don Valley Parkway.

As an expert brick mason, it made sense that Mark Maynard would purchase a brick house rather than a frame one when he moved to Unionville. With a critical eye from years of experience in the trade he must have been pleased with the work of Hiram Powers and his choice of red pressed brick. The house was designed in the simplified style of domestic architecture favoured in the early twentieth century, with a hipped roof and projecting, gabled bays, elements typical of the Queen Anne Revival style but without the more decorative treatments seen on earlier examples. The house has large cottage windows capped with robust concrete lintels. A prominent feature is the exceptionally spacious wraparound verandah, originally supported on stout, full-height columns. In the 1920s the columns were replaced by shorter ones that rest on brick pedestals.

Although the move to Unionville was based on the premise of retirement, Mark Maynard did not stay idle. He served as a village trustee, and in 1923 established a business next to the Stiver Brothers Feed Mill and Grain Elevator, farther west along the railway line near Eureka Street. His sons Albert, Jim, and Charles were partners in this new business venture. The Maynards sold livestock feed, coal, fuel oil, and wood.[48] Mark Maynard also operated a planing mill at the north end of Markham Village, opposite the train station that served the same railway line as the station in Unionville.[49] After Mark Maynard's death in 1928, his sons carried on with the business at the Unionville depot, which endured until 1976.

In addition to his active business life and role as a community leader, Mark Maynard indulged in his hobby of keeping exotic birds. In good weather, the deep verandah of the family home was a perfect setting for Maynard's parrot cages. The birds were a delight to the other villagers, and one can only imagine the things they might have been trained to say to the curious passersby.[50]

Annie Maynard stayed on in the family home after her husband's passing, until she died in 1933. The Maynard's former home was significantly expanded with a complementary frame addition in the early 2000s. This addition allowed for the preservation of the old house while increasing its size and amenities to meet the standards of the large custom homes that have defined the character of this part of Main Street since the 1990s.

Bethesda Lutheran Church, 20 Union Street, 1910

One of Unionville's most historic places is tucked away on a backstreet in the southwest part of the village, in the midst of a long-established residential neighbourhood.

If you didn't know it was there, you might never see Bethesda Lutheran Church. Unlike most historic villages and towns, where the churches are typically situated on main streets, this church sits removed from the traffic and activity of a well-travelled road.

Similar to how the church is removed from Main Street, Bethesda Lutheran Church is also a fair distance away from the place where it was originally built. In 1819 the Reverend Johann Dieter Petersen was invited to come from his home in Pennsylvania to minister to a group of sixty-seven German-speaking families that had settled in Markham Township, under the leadership of William Berczy, in 1794. Previously, the spiritual needs of the Berczy settlers were taken care of by the Reverend George Sigmund Liebich (spelled "Liebrich" in some sources), who accompanied them from their original home in Europe to serve as pastor, teacher, and doctor, until a family tragedy ended his ministry only a few years after his arrival in Markham Township.[51]

Lutheran churches under the Reverend Petersen's charge were built in Unionville and Buttonville in Markham Township, and in Sherwood in Vaughan Township. Philip Eckardt donated a plot of land for a church and cemetery on his hilltop farm on Lot 17, Concession 6, north of the present village, and a church was built there in 1820. Before then, services were held in Philip Eckardt's hewn-log house on the same lot.

Reverend Petersen retired in 1829 and the next clergyman to assume the pulpit proved to be an interesting and ultimately disruptive character who split the congregation apart a few years later. The Reverend Vincentius, or Vincent, P. Mayerhoffer was a native of Hungary, originally a Franciscan monk who had served as a chaplain in Napoleon's army before moving to America and becoming a Protestant convert. He later came to Upper Canada where he took his holy orders in the Church of England, now known as the Anglican Church. Although St. Philip's was nominally a Lutheran congregation, the form of service under the Reverend Mayerhoffer was essentially Anglican.[52]

All went well at St. Philip's until the political climate in Upper Canada, and in particularly York County, became quite heated and polarized in the 1830s. This was the beginning of a turbulent time of conflict between the ruling elite of Upper Canada, based in York, renamed Toronto in 1834, and the Reform-minded farmers of the agricultural hinterland that surrounded the young city. Many of the residents of Unionville and its surrounding area were supporters of William Lyon Mackenzie, the charismatic leader of the Reform movement. They were also among the members of St. Philip's Lutheran Church.[53]

Unlike a large number of the members of his congregation, the Reverend Mayerhoffer was a strong supporter of the political elite that had welcomed him and allowed him to become ordained in the Church of England. As the mood darkened and the anticipated rebellion loomed closer, his views became too much for the Reformers in his church, and he was barred entry on Ascension Day in 1837. Although the Reverend Mayerhoffer attempted to regain control of the church with the aid of political allies, the Lutherans were successful in expelling him from the church by legal means. If they had not taken this action, in only three months, by terms of legislation that provided that a church that went ten years without ordained clergy of its own denomination would automatically transfer to the Church of England, the property would have officially become Anglican.[54]

The Reverend Mayerhoffer and those members of the congregation that supported him established St. Philip's Anglican Church across the road. The Lutheran Church was renamed Bethesda. After a few tentative years, Bethesda Lutheran Church secured a new pastor, and by 1862 the congregation was in a position to build a new church in brick in the early Gothic Revival style. This church, with pointed arched windows, a centre tower capped with a metal spire, and trimmed in patterned brick, was similar to churches being built by many other Protestant congregations in the mid- to late-nineteenth century.

As Unionville developed with the arrival of the railway in the early 1870s, the concentration of population that supported the church had moved south. By the early 1900s the area around the church remained rural, and in 1910 the congregation decided to relocate into the more populated part of the community. The cemetery remained to mark the original place of worship, but the church building was dismantled so that the brick and other materials could be reused to erect a new building.

The new site, in the midst of William Eckardt's 1856 subdivision of village lots, was at the southwest corner of Union and Euclid Streets. The new church, like the old one, has Gothic Revival influence in its style, but is different in character to the church building of 1862.[55] The new Bethesda Lutheran Church was designed in an Edwardian interpretation of the Gothic Revival, with its entrance in a corner tower. The top of the squarish tower has a crenellated parapet rather than a tall spire, which was typical at the time of reconstruction. The new church was constructed of plain red brick rather than the patterned red and buff brick of the earlier building. Local contractors John Miller, mason and bricklayer, and Frank Stiver, carpenter, worked on the rebuilding project. Their names were recorded on documents preserved in the cornerstone for future generations to discover.

Over time a number of additions and renovations have been made to Bethesda Lutheran Church. One significant change occurred in 2012, when the congregation decided to add a metal-clad spire to the top of the tower as a tribute to the 1862 church on the hill.

Davison Ford Dealership, 189 Main Street, circa 1913

While the coming of the railway was a catalyst that changed Unionville in the late nineteenth century, the arrival of the automobile ushered in a period of even greater change in the early twentieth century. A handful of Unionville's leading citizens owned automobiles at a time when the horse and buggy still remained the dominant form of personal transportation embraced by the majority of Markham Township's largely rural population.

Frank L. Stiver, who ran the Stiver Brothers feed mill in Stouffville, was one of these forward-thinkers. He owned a 1908 Tudhope automobile, a Canadian-made vehicle manufactured in Orillia by Tudhope Anderson.[56] It must have been quite a novelty in the area as the first of its kind, turning heads and impressing some people, while at the same time annoying others with its noise and fumes. Not long afterward, Hiram Powers, a local builder, purchased a Model T Ford, the iconic early automobile that has come to characterize the popularization and mass production of the motor vehicle.[57]

George A.M. "Art" Davison recognized the tremendous opportunity of being on the ground floor of an emerging industry. Already a successful entrepreneur as the owner of a general store and a member of a family with a knack for business, Art Davison secured a dealership from the progressive Ford Motor Company in 1912.[58] In 1913 he purchased property on the east side of Main Street, opposite his store and post office. This large frontage on Main Street became the site of the new automobile dealership.

At what is now addressed 189 Main Street, Art Davison built a garage for the repair of cars and trucks, and may have also served as a showroom before another building was acquired two doors down the street. Brothers Wilbur and Harvey Latimer were his mechanics. Davison's new building was utilitarian in character, with its light stud-framed walls clad in corrugated metal panels on the outside, and finished on the inside with horizontal tongue-and-groove wood. On the side walls, windows with a six-over-six glazing pattern may have been salvaged from some older structure and reused for the sake of economy. The street front exaggerated the scale and importance of the building with a boomtown front that concealed the low-pitched gable roof and simple structure behind it.[59]

The Davison Ford Dealership sold the company's trademark Model T automobiles and other vehicles, including Fordson farm tractors. Being in the heart of a thriving agricultural community, it is not surprising that gasoline-powered tractors would be big sellers. For two years running, the Davison dealership had record sales of Fordson tractors for all of Canada, an accomplishment so noteworthy that it caught the attention of Henry Ford himself. As a result of this success, Ford personally presented Art Davison with an award at a ceremony held at Toronto's distinguished Granite Club.[60]

Unionville's Ford dealership was an important local employer, and was a centre for the sale and repair of motor vehicles of all kinds. Later on, a gas pump was installed to serve the growing demand for accessible fuel for the emerging class of car drivers in the village and the surrounding area. As the business grew, it expanded with a showroom in the building that once housed John Devlin's harness shop at its south end and Mr. Morrison's tailor shop in its north end, today addressed 179 Main Street.

The Davison family's interest in raising Standardbred and Hackney ponies is a remarkable contrast with the motor vehicle business they brought to Unionville.[61] Their ponies won prizes at the Canadian National Exhibition and the Royal Winter Fair. The recognition received for this pastime led to Mrs. Davison becoming known as Canada's "pony queen."

In the early 1940s Fred Minton, said to have been Unionville's last blacksmith, had a shop at the rear of the building within its concrete foundation walls. He lived in the small frame house next door, which many years later became known as the Unionville House Restaurant. On the main floor of the old Davison building there was a carpentry shop, where John Epps repaired and repainted farm wagons.[62]

As Unionville began its transformation into a unique tourist destination in the 1970s, the old building, with its large open floorspace, served as a playhouse for a time. It next became a restaurant, with a new front with recessed double doors flanked by a series of arched showcase windows. The new look was designed to evoke the spirit of a late-nineteenth-century storefront, and this aspect of the old Davison Ford Dealership building has endured for so many years that it has become a heritage feature in itself.

In December 2007 a fire severely damaged the building. The rear portion of the structure was affected and much of the roof was destroyed. During the repair and reconstruction of the restaurant, original details of the building were revealed after long being hidden behind more recent finishes, confirming the early twentieth-century period of construction.[63]

Old St. Philip's Anglican Church, 218 Main Street, 1913

The early history of St. Philip's Anglican Church and that of Bethesda Lutheran Church are intertwined and rich in drama, not the usual church histories one typically reads about.[64] Unionville's Anglican congregation traces its roots back to 1829, when the Reverend Vincent P. Mayerhoffer arrived in the community to minister to the Lutheran population of William Berczy's German-speaking settlers. The Reverend Mayerhoffer had taken his holy orders in the Church of England at the residence of Upper Canada's lieutenant-governor, Sir John Colborne, in the Town of York. He was a strong supporter of the colony's established government and the Church of England that the ruling elite favoured. This alignment with the Tory political viewpoint became a significant factor leading to the formation of St. Philip's as an Anglican parish.

The original St. Philip's Lutheran Church, built in 1820 at the top of the rise of land north of Unionville, was located on donated land on Philip Eckardt's farm. For several years the members of the St. Philip's Lutheran congregation were content to worship under an Anglican clergyman and in the Anglican form, but as political tensions built up in the years leading up to the Upper Canada Rebellion of 1837, many church members found they could no longer support the Reverend Mayerhoffer and his Tory views. A rift occurred in the St. Philip's congregation, and those that supported the Reverend Mayerhoffer helped establish St. Philip's Anglican Church on his land across the road, and those who wanted to remain Lutheran remained in their church, which was renamed Bethesda Lutheran.

In 1839 the Anglicans built a modest-sized frame church, more on the scale of a chapel, in the early Gothic Revival style. A cemetery was located on the same property, a seventy-acre part of the east half of Lot 17, Concession 5. The Reverend Mayerhoffer had purchased this land from James Hopkins in 1832. In 1835 he deeded the land to King William IV, essentially donating it back to the Crown for the use of the Church of England. In fact, the property was not deeded from the Crown to the church until 1905, when the Incorporated Synod of the Diocese of Toronto became the owner.

Early maps show the large St. Philip's property as "Glebe." In 1846 the church was consecrated by Bishop John Strachan, who had been one of the leading figures in Upper Canada's Family Compact. This must have been quite an honour for the Reverend Mayerhoffer but very irksome for the Reform-minded Lutherans across the road, many of whom had participated in the 1837 Rebellion, or at the very least had supported that cause.

In a family history written about 1910, preserved in the cornerstone of Bethesda Lutheran Church in the village of Unionville, A.J.H. Eckardt recounted stories passed down to him by his great-uncles about pranks that were played on the Anglicans by some of younger members of the Lutheran church, in reprisal for some of the troubles of 1837. One story described how an effigy of the Anglican minister was placed atop the church roof one Saturday night, representing him driving a horse and wagon. This ridiculous sight greeted the minister and his congregation the following Sunday morning. Another story involved livestock being placed in the Anglican church on Saturday evenings, so that the next day the beginning of Sunday service would be delayed until the calves and heifers, and likely their droppings, could be removed.

The Reverend Mayerhoffer continued to serve the congregation of St. Philip's until 1848, and also founded Grace Anglican Church in Markham Village before he left Markham Township. V.P. Mayerhoffer moved on to another parish in Whitby, and died in 1859 at the age of seventy-five. His resting place is the cemetery of St. John's Anglican Church in Whitby, where his wife, Caroline, is also interred. The Reverend George Hill became the next rector at St. Philip's and a new rectory was built next to the church to replace the residence that the Reverend Mayerhoffer had been living in. The church carried on here for many decades and under the leadership of a succession of rectors, until the congregation decided to follow their former Lutheran neighbours and relocate into the heart of Unionville proper.[65]

In 1913 the frame church of 1839 was dismantled, and some of the building materials were reused in a new church just north of the Union Mills and south of the bridge over the Rouge River. The new church was markedly different in style from the old one, larger in size and clad in dark-red brick.[66] Designed with the influence of the Tudor Revival and Arts and Crafts styles that were more commonly used in residential architecture at the time, the new St. Philip's Anglican Church has a distinctly English flavour. Picturesquely sited near the former millpond, the church is nestled in mature trees and seems well-rooted in the landscape. Its side tower, decorated with a wood-shingled upper section and a broach spire, is perfectly scaled for a village setting. The church is unusual for its small, segmentally headed, grouped windows, a reflection of the Arts and Crafts design inspiration, while its steeply pitched roof reflects the Tudor Revival.

By the mid-1980s the congregation had grown to the point where a larger and more up-to-date facility was needed. The 1913 church was sold and in 1986 a new St. Philip's Church was built next to the historic cemetery at the original location on the hill. Today, Old St. Philip's is the home of the Village Church of the Nazarene.

John and Ellen Snowball House, 9 Eckardt Avenue, circa 1923

Brick making involves the baking of clay at high temperatures to create hard, durable, and uniform masonry units. The fact that Markham's most well-known and successful brick-making family was named Snowball is amusingly ironic. John Snowball Sr.'s first brickworks in Markham Township, established circa 1845, was located in the hamlet of Buttonville. His presence

there is noted in the 1851 census. It may be that the source of clay was the excavation of the millpond in the midst of the tiny hamlet where he lived.

John Snowball Sr. was a native of Yorkshire, England, where he learned the trade of brick making prior to emigrating to Canada in the early 1840s. He worked at a brickworks in Yorkville and married Ann Glue, the daughter of his employer, before deciding to start his own brick-manufacturing enterprise.[67]

Brick buildings were not common in the vicinity of Buttonville in the mid-nineteenth century. Most families in the hamlet and on surrounding farms lived in frame houses. The limited local market for brick probably influenced John Snowball Sr.'s decision in the 1850s to move nearer to the larger villages of Unionville and Markham, where there was much more building going on at that time.[68] The Snowball family lived on rented property on the east side of McCowan Road, south of Highway 7, where the western portion of Milne Park and part of Highway 407 are now located. There was a large deposit of clay available on this property to provide the raw material for the manufacture of brick, which was probably excavated from the banks of the Milne's millpond and the banks of the Rouge River.

Early brick from the Snowball brickworks is variegated due to the composition of the local clay deposits. Snowball brick is known for its distinctive blend of colours, ranging from salmon pink to orange to buff. Due to the variations in colour, which were not as well appreciated in the nineteenth century as they are today, the brick was often dyed a rich, dark red to create an even-toned brick. Over time the dyed brick surface deteriorated due to weathering, and for this reason most examples of the dyed-brick walls were cleaned by sandblasting before the damaging results of sandblasting soft local brick were realized. Later in the history of the Snowball brickworks, the brick was a more consistent orange-red colour.

John Jr. and William, two of the sons of John and Ann Snowball, were involved in the family business. By the 1870s the Snowball brickworks specialized in producing clay tile for draining wet farm fields, but still manufactured brick for construction.[69] They were not the only local suppliers of brick. In the *Markham Economist*, during the summer of 1875, Isaac O'Neill advertised that he had on hand 60,000 first-class red bricks at his brickworks near the Toronto and Nipissing Railway Station.

John Snowball Jr. worked with his father and brother at the brickworks for a number of years, then turned to farming around the turn of the century. In 1890 the family purchased the land they had previously leased, then two years later added to their land holdings through the purchase of an additional fifty acres on an adjoining lot. John Snowball Sr. died in 1897, leaving the operation of the business to William Snowball, who was still working as a brick manufacturer at the time of the 1901 census. In the 1910s John Snowball Jr. took over Snowball brick and tile from his brother William. The Snowball brickworks closed in 1923, after decades of manufacturing brick and tile in Markham Township, perhaps due to competition from larger manufactures such as the Don Valley Brickworks in Toronto.

The house at 9 Eckardt Avenue was built for John Snowball Jr.'s retirement to Unionville, and remained in the ownership of the family until 1959.[70] The building lot was purchased from William Risebrough in 1923, and the house is believed to have been built in that same year. The houses constructed on the less costly properties on the side streets of the village were smaller in size, and more simply adorned that those on Main Street.

The Snowball House is a typical example of an American Foursquare, a house form that became popular in the early 1900s for its compact shape, practical layout, and modern style.[71] The Foursquare vied with the bungalow as the comfortable home of middle-class families in North America in the first decades of the twentieth century. Large numbers of houses much like this were built in cities, towns, and rural areas, and many were constructed in Unionville and elsewhere in Markham. While frame was the usual mode of construction in the United States, in Toronto and its surrounding communities brick was the finish of choice, and in particular red brick. These houses are typically cubic in shape, two to two-and-a-half storeys with a hipped roof, and usually have a deep front verandah. In the case of the Snowball House, the front verandah is enclosed to form a sunroom, which may be an alteration of a verandah that was originally open.

Hiram and Sara Powers House, 4802 Highway 7, circa 1930

Hiram H. Powers was a grain dealer, carpenter, and builder who came to Unionville in the early 1900s.[72] He married Sara E. Rainey and first lived in the north end of the village. Their home was once a hotel known as the Crown Inn, which they rebuilt to suit the needs of their family about 1904. Powers built a number of houses in the Unionville area, and also worked on public works projects such as the Crosby Memorial Arena, which opened in 1928, and a concrete dam at the millpond.[73] He was assisted by his son Hartwell, who served as one of the village street lamplighters during the 1910s.[74]

In 1926 Sara Powers purchased a building lot on the north side of Highway 7 overlooking the Rouge River valley on a portion of what had once been the farm of James Eckardt, and before him Gottlieb Eckardt. The irregularly shaped property is east of Main Street, set apart from the built-up residential area of Unionville.

On this lot, about 1930, the Powers family built a one-and-a-half-storey, stucco-clad house in the Arts and Crafts style, along with a separate coach house at the back. At the northeast corner of the lot the land steeply drops off toward the Rouge River, which meanders through the valley below.[75] A partially unopened street called Second Street, established by a plan of subdivision in 1926, formed the original western boundary of the Powers property.

Hiram Powers turned his attention to land development after his move to Highway 7. In 1938 he bought a property at the southwest corner of Highway 7 and Main Street, and created East Drive and a series of building lots through Plan No. 2926. Many of these lots remained undeveloped until relatively recent times, probably due to a period of economic stagnation resulting from the Great Depression.

Hiram and Sara Powers lived in their home east of Unionville, known to the locals as "the pink house" because of the colour of its building materials, until 1943. After that the house had many residential owners, but by the 1980s had been converted to a brass-bed shop, when the brass-bed revival was at the height of its popularity. For many years after the brass-bed shop was closed, the Powers House was a vacant building in the midst of an area that had largely become a commercial strip along the highway. After a fire the coach house, with its residential quarters above, was demolished. In 2012 the old house underwent extensive repair and restoration for potential use as commercial office space.

The Powers House is one of the few residences built in Unionville and Markham Township to have been constructed in the Arts and Crafts style. The complex form of the building plan, steep cross-gabled roof with multiple gables, banked windows, stucco walls accented with wood-shingled gable ends, and a front porch with a clipped gable roof and heavy wood posts and brackets are features associated with English Arts and Crafts movement architecture, somewhat different in character from the look of houses influenced by the American Arts and Crafts movement but sharing many of the same elements. A sense of informality and asymmetry, simplicity of detail, use of natural, minimally processed building materials and finishes, and functional, open floor plans are the underlying principles of design associated with the Arts and Crafts movement, that was more of an approach to design than a clearly defined architectural style. The Powers House is a late expression of this mode of residential design, which had begun to fade in popularity after the First World War.

The Old Fire Hall, 170 Main Street, circa 1930

Unionville is fortunate that its commercial core never suffered a catastrophic fire like the ones that were the fate of many other older communities in Ontario. The biggest losses by fire were the Union Mills at the top end of the street, and the planing mill at the bottom. Not a bad record for a compact street of buildings mainly of frame construction. Firefighting techniques were quite basic before the advent of professionally trained firefighters and their specialized equipment in the twentieth century. Before then, communities outside of the city had to rely on volunteer fire brigades with minimal equipment that did their best when fire struck, but were hardly adequate to battle a fully engulfed burning building. Later, in small places like Unionville, the firefighters were still volunteers, but were better equipped. In the 1920s the village fire engine was stored in an automotive garage at the top end of Main Street's commercial district, owned by Harold Parkinson, a member of the local fire brigade.[76]

The building at 170 Main Street was Unionville's fire hall during a later period. It didn't start out as a fire hall, but was a commercial building constructed on the former site of a wooden storage building that stood between the old wheelwright and blacksmith shop and the Queen's Hotel. About 1930 the old storage shed was replaced with a slightly larger but simple structure of moulded concrete block, constructed by the Findlay family, owners of the Queen's Hotel. In 1933 this was Wilbur Latimer's Cockshutt Tractor Dealership and farm implement repair shop, rented from the Findlays. His brother Harvey worked here until 1942, when he became employed by Massey-Harris, the pre-eminent agricultural implements manufacturer of the day.[77]

An archival photograph in the collection of the Markham Museum shows the front of the Latimers' shop with advertisements for tires and farm machinery. It was an important business in an area with an agriculturally based economy, housed in a decidedly utilitarian structure. The texture of the sturdy concrete blocks that made up its walls represented, in the most conventionalized way, rock-faced, squared stone. It was a style of block used from the early 1900s to the 1930s, after which concrete blocks were typically smooth-faced.

Wilbur Latimer eventually closed his repair shop to work for Champion Farm Equipment in Brougham, Pickering Township. In 1957 the trustees of the Police Village of Unionville purchased the vacant building to be converted into a proper modern fire hall in the heart of the village. There was a dispatcher on site, but the firefighters were volunteers, called to duty when needed.[78] The front of the old building was altered with the removal of the shopfront and its replacement with two large garage doors. The central location of the site made it an ideal choice for a fire hall. As time went on and Unionville and the surrounding area grew in population due to residential development, the fire hall became too small for its purpose and was closed in 1977 when it was replaced by a larger, up-to-date facility in the community.

At around the same time as the retirement of the old fire hall, Unionville's quaint Main Street had transformed into a popular shopping district for antiques and specialty stores, and the building was reborn as Old Firehall Sports. An addition of reclaimed brick and a distinctive tower were added to the front of the original building, making it a local attraction which referenced its former role in the community. In 2009 another transformation took place when the Old Firehall Confectionary opened in the building, providing a nostalgic, old-fashioned candy-store experience.

Unionville's old fire hall has been much altered from its humble beginnings to become the building that it is today. A still-visible remnant of the early twentieth-century structure is a section of moulded concrete block that can be seen on the south side wall, a little in from the street line. The alterations made to the old fire hall in the 1980s changed a simple, utilitarian building into a local landmark that embraced the historical character of Main Street. However, the old fire hall is not in any sense a restoration, since it never had a hose-drying tower as suggested by its current appearance. The contribution that this fanciful interpretation of a late-Victorian fire station makes to the street is how it captures the spirit of optimism of the 1970s and 1980s, when the citizens of Unionville realized that the prosperity of their community could be secured by protecting and embracing its unique architectural heritage.

Maynard Houses, 36 and 38 Eureka Street, circa 1946

The Maynard family were among a later group of enterprising business leaders to come to Unionville in the early twentieth century. Mark Maynard, a brick mason of English birth who did most of his work in Toronto's east end, relocated his family to Unionville after buying a property in the northern part of the village in 1919. Rather than retiring from work altogether, Mark Maynard gave up bricklaying and construction for a new career as a dealer in livestock feed, wood, coal, and fuel oil. He and his sons Albert, James, and Charles established a sales depot adjacent to the railway tracks, a little west of the Stiver Brothers feed mill and grain

elevator.[79] The land where the business was located was leased from the railway and the paperwork for the leases was kept secure in the safe inside the station agent's office in the Unionville railway station.

The Maynard's depot was accessed from Eureka Street. As time went on, Mark and Annie Maynard's sons Albert and James ran the coal and feed side of the business. Charles Maynard and his two sons Charles Jr. and Harry sold the fuel oil and gasoline to the farming community.[80] Most of the products sold by the Maynards were brought in from the United States. Gulf Oil supplied the petroleum products. Being next to the railway station and the tracks was ideal for receiving bulk goods being shipped by rail from the U.S.

Charles Maynard Sr. and his wife, Blanche, bought a block of land on the west side of Eureka Street, a little north of the railway tracks, in 1938. After the Second World War was over in 1946 the north part was deeded to their son Charles Jr. and his wife, Katherine, and the south part was deeded to their other son, Harry, and his wife, Helen. On these equally sized lots two identical houses were constructed by Stan and Carman Stiver that were quite unlike anything else ever seen in the village before.[81] The new houses, rendered in an interpretation of the Tudor Revival style, look like they may have been purchased as prefabricated "kit" homes.[82] The long line of the roof structure required special beams to be brought in by the builders.[83] Side by side in these picturesque, small houses, Charles and Harry Maynard lived conveniently close to their workplace, though perhaps not so close that they could actually see the depot from their homes.

The Maynard Houses were designed as modest suburban homes, modern in plan but with a traditional appearance on the outside. They almost have a storybook charm about them, which at the time of construction would have been a pleasant contrast to the memory of the harsh reality of the war that had ended one year before. The steep gable roof and gabled, projecting front bay containing the entrance are signature features of this particular version of the Tudor Revival, which lacks the more common half-timbered stucco and wood treatment. The door, with its Classical detailing, is an indication of the eclectic nature of this style, and works well with the overall design. Although the two houses started out as identical, one now has replacement windows that create a subtle difference between them.

Unionville Public School, 300 Main Street, 1955

An account of the history of Unionville would not be complete without including Unionville Public School, even though it isn't one of those buildings that stands out as a particularly noteworthy structure. Markham is fortunate in having most of its nineteenth-century schools still standing and in active use as community facilities or other purposes. Franklin Street Public School in Markham Village, built in 1886, is York Region's oldest school building still being used for its original purpose.[84] One-room schoolhouses throughout

the municipality have been preserved and restored long after the last students and teachers were dismissed for summer vacation. Regrettably, Unionville's historic public school was not so fortunate.

The early history of schools in Unionville is a little vague. An early school is believed to have been located north of the Lutheran cemetery on the hill overlooking the village.[85] Perhaps it was affiliated with the church, but this is only speculation because no primary-source documents are known to exist to tell us anything for certain. Classes were very likely held in German rather than English at that time, since the majority of families living in the area were from the Berczy group of German-speaking immigrants. The Reverend George Sigmund Liebich, the Lutheran clergyman who accompanied the settlers when they came to Upper Canada and probably the most educated person in the group, could have been the first schoolteacher in Markham Township.

Another school was located in the area that later became the commercial centre of Unionville. Not much is known about this school either, other than that it was included in a List of Common Schools in Markham Township, dated December 1834, recorded in the Journals of the Upper Canada Legislative Assembly. It is rumoured to have been located near the site of the Unionville Planing Mill.[86]

By 1855 Unionville and the area around it had been split into two school sections, with a schoolhouse serving School Section No. 9 on part of Philip Eckardt Jr.'s farm at the southeast corner of present-day Highway 7 and Main Street, and another schoolhouse serving School Section No. 10 on the west side of Main Street, south of 16th Avenue.[87] The school site chosen for School Section No. 10 is the one that has endured to the present day.

The land was formally purchased from Anthony Size, innkeeper and farmer, in 1858.

A frame, one-room schoolhouse was built on this site some time before the map of Markham Township's school sections was drawn in 1855. It has been said that the schoolhouse was built in the 1830s, a simple clapboarded building with twelve-over-twelve paned windows and separate entrances for boys and girls on the gable end.[88] In style it was similar to the small rural chapels and meeting halls built throughout the township in the mid-nineteenth century, following a vernacular interpretation of the Classical Revival with its low-pitched gable roof, eave returns, and symmetrical "temple front" form.

In 1892 the frame school was replaced with a new, two-storey school in red brick. This new school contained two classrooms, and in 1928 it was one of first in Markham Township to have electric light.[89] It was designed with the influences of the Queen Anne Revival and the Romanesque styles that were in vogue at the time. Its large belfry was similar to the one on the local Congregational church. Unionville's new public school was a building with a distinctly urban character in a village setting. The residents of Unionville must have been very proud of their modern and fashionable public school.

After the Second World War, a growing population required the 1892 school to be enlarged, first with two new classrooms at the west end in 1949, then with a larger new wing added to the south of the original building in 1955. This new wing became the main part of Unionville Public School when the oldest part of the building was demolished in 1977.[90] Further additions followed as the community continued to grow. It is regrettable that the late-Victorian school that was once the pride of the community was lost at a time when the unique historical qualities of old Unionville were well on their way to being valued, preserved, and enhanced.

The present Unionville Public School, with additions, is a modernist building typical of its period of construction: spare in its design, flat-roofed, and equipped with large windows. As time goes on this style of single-storey school, once considered up-to-date, has itself become old-fashioned in the minds of today's educators. Thinking on school design has moved away from this rambling form, and for several years there has been a return to compact, two-storey schools that echo the form of urban schools of the 1920s.

The Unionville Planing Mill, 139 Main Street, 1986

The Unionville Planing Mill is a landmark building that defines the south end of the commercial core of Main Street, but only its name and site are of historical significance. The Planing Mill is actually a fairly recent structure that contains a restaurant and two levels of retail shops, built in the mid-1980s on the site of the original structure of the same name.

On this site in 1873 William Eakin, the township reeve, a farmer, and a former carriage maker, built a planing mill next to a tributary of the Rouge River.[91] The machinery of the mill was run by a stationary steam engine rather than by water power; however, water was still a necessity to provide the basis for producing steam. The main mill building was a two-and-a-half-storey, gable-roofed structure of frame construction, clad in board-and-batten siding. The engine house was a smaller masonry lean-to on the north side of the mill. The planing mill had multi-paned double-hung window of varying shapes and sizes and sat in the hollow by the stream at the southeast corner of Main Street and Victoria Avenue. The tracks of the Toronto and Nipissing Railway, running atop an earthen embankment, defined its southern boundary.

William Eakin built his planing mill at exactly the right time, just when a local building boom was beginning after the arrival of the Toronto and Nipissing Railway.[92] In the *Markham Economist* of February 5, 1874, a notice appeared in the local news column advertising the Unionville Planing Mill and the array of architectural components that the factory was capable of producing. Builders were implored to look no further for their construction materials:

> PLANING MILLS— Messrs. Eakin & Fenwick have on hand and are constantly making to order at their factory, Unionville, sash, doors and blinds of great variety. A good supply constantly on hand. They are prepared to do all kinds of matching, planing and ripping. Builders and contractors should see their work and obtain their price lists before selecting materials. See posters.[93]

Early on, William Eakin's partner in the business may have been James W. Fenwick, owner of the J.W. Fenwick & Co. General Store at 156 Main Street, or his brother Benjamin Fenwick. The small notice in the *Markham Economist* is the only mention of the Fenwick family's involvement in William Eakin's enterprise. If only one of posters advertising the planing mill had survived — what an interesting and valuable artefact that would be!

In the area to the south of the Union Mills a new commercial centre was emerging, drawn to the south due to the presence of the railway station. A formerly quiet residential area was being built up with fine new homes designed in the latest architectural styles. The planing mill supplied the dimensional lumber needed for all of this new construction, as well as siding, flooring, doors, windows, shutters, and the full range of decorative work to adorn the buildings of Unionville's "golden age." The products of the Unionville Planing Mill can still be seen throughout Markham in the many heritage buildings that still stand from that time period.

Once manufactured, standardized building components became available, the era of the hand-built house was over. Building components made in planing mills like this one increased the rate at which buildings could be erected, and therefore saved time and money. However, this more efficient means of production to some extent resulted in less variety in the style and detailing of new houses, and a less-skilled labour force. The Unionville

Planing Mill contained an array of woodworking machinery linked to a line shaft that distributed power throughout the building. Shapers, jointers, thickness planers, bandsaws, lathes, and a specialized machine for making shutters made short work out of what would have been hours of hand labour only a couple of generations before.

As Unionville's rush of growth of the 1870s began to wind down, William Eakin decided to sell his business to Robert Harrington, a carpenter and builder from the crossroads community of Armadale in northeast Scarborough Township, who had relocated to Unionville in 1874. An account book, preserved in the collection of the Markham Museum, records the names of Robert Harrington's many clients. Among them are James Robinson, reeve of Markham Township, who owned a tannery in Markham Village, James D. Harrington, a relative, and William Eakin, owner of the planing mill.

William Eakin had served as reeve of Markham Township in 1873, and again from 1879 to 1883. After his final election as reeve, and having sold his manufacturing business, he decided to turn his attention to the opportunities offered by the opening of Canada's west, and became a homesteader and politician in Saskatchewan.[94] He stepped down as reeve in that final year, and left his home township for greener pastures.

Robert Harrington moved into the fine brick house that overlooked the planing mill and, with his sons Delos and George, continued the operation of this important local business. The planing mill obtained the timber it turned into lumber and other wood products from Ontario's north, facilitated by the railway that ran south from Coboconk through Unionville. In addition to the production of building components, up until the early twentieth century the planing mill employed carpenters as house builders. The operation ran six days a week and employed many local men.[95]

Brothers Delos and George Harrington purchased the business from their father in 1896. Later, Delos bought his brother's share. When electricity came to Unionville in the early 1920s, the stationary steam engine that powered the mill's machinery was replaced by a large electric motor. In 1925 Arthur Harrington, one of George's sons, bought the planing mill from Delos Harrington and continued to operate in much the same way as things had been done since 1873. In 1960 the business was sold out of the Harrington family, to Alfred Giles. Tragedy struck in 1978. Just as Unionville's renaissance as a historic village was beginning to flower, the planing mill was badly damaged in a fire while undergoing restoration by a community group. It was left in restorable condition, but sat derelict for several years until another fire sealed its fate in 1982. After the second fire, nothing was saved.[96]

A new commercial development was built on the site in 1986, called the Unionville Planing Mill by name but somewhat different in character. The new building, like the old one, is clad in wood board-and-batten siding painted in barn red. Its orientation is similar to that of the historic planing mill, but its roof style and other details are different. Instead of a simple gable roof, the new planing mill has a monitor roof with a clerestory. A small millpond is located on the north side of the building, with a mill wheel that evokes the idea of an old water mill, but doesn't relate to the way the machinery of the actual planing mill was powered. It's more of a picturesque affectation, but still a popular backdrop for wedding photos.

Varley Art Gallery, 216 Main Street, 1997

The Frederick Horsman Varley Art Gallery of Markham, more commonly known as the Varley Art Gallery, occupies a prime location at the top of Unionville's commercial Main Street. On this site, circa 1840, Ira White built the Union Mills Mill Owner's House only a stone's throw from his sawmill and gristmill.[97] From his front door, he could look right down the winding lane that would eventually become Main Street, but when the house was first built there was not much to be seen. To the east Ira White could view the day-to-day operation of the gristmill. To the west he could see the adobe-brick cottage built by Frederick Eckardt in the 1820s. A little farther down the lane there was the two-storey wheelwright shop of Gottlieb Eckardt. In a few years, as Frederick Eckardt began to sell village lots on the east and west sides of the mill lane, the empty spaces gradually became filled with stores, workshops, and houses.[98]

At the time of the 1851 census, Ira White and his family lived in the long, low clapboarded house overlooking the gristmill. An archival photograph from the 1890s shows the front of the old house, with its odd placement of the main entrance at the west end of the facade.[99] This was a truly vernacular building, having elements of traditional Georgian and Neoclassical styling, but with an unconventional, asymmetrical arrangement of the main doorcase and windows. The main block of the Union Mills Mill Owner's House was one-and-a-half storeys, with a lean-to across the back. At the west end was a single-storey kitchen wing.

By 1861 Ira White had taken his mill-building ambitions to Elgin County in southwestern Ontario, leaving his son Benjamin White in charge of the Union Mills.[100] The Union Mills Mill Owner's House endured in its position at the top of Main Street through all the subsequent mill owners and operators. In 1922 it was purchased by Harold Parkinson, who converted Ira White's former residence into an automotive repair garage. The unique entryway, with its flanking windows, was cut out from the wall to create a large garage bay.[101] The formerly elegant dwelling became a busy workplace, a little rough around the edges, until it was replaced in the 1940s by the new home of the Pellatt family. The new house, built in the Cape Cod style favoured for suburban living after the Second World War, sat in the same place as the White residence built a century before. The white-painted, clapboarded Pellatt House became nestled in the trees as Unionville's mill era and the Parkinson garage became distant memories.

This key location in old Unionville was destined to remain important. A generous donation of Canadian art was gifted to Markham in 1988, under the condition that a proper gallery be built to house it.[102] The Pellatt property and the Toogood House next door were purchased in 1990 for the site of a future art gallery. By 1994 plans were being drawn up by architect Jerome Markson, of the Toronto firm Markson, Borooah, Hodgson Architects. The Unionville Heritage Conservation District had not been officially created at that time, but there was a strong desire in the community that the new gallery should be designed to suit the special, historic character of Unionville's Main Street. This point of view was at odds with the architectural thinking of the time, which espoused the idea that buildings should be products of their own time and not try to recreate the historical buildings of the past.

The final result of much deliberation between architect, political representatives, citizens, and municipal staff was a compromise. The completed art gallery of 1997 was indeed designed to be a product of the 1990s, rendered in the postmodern style, but its scale, red-brick finish, and angled rooflines were responsive to the historical context of its surroundings. A square clock tower with a cubic top is a dominant feature of the Varley Art Gallery, as is the public plaza that forms the building's foreground. An addition was made to enhance the gallery and office space of the Varley Art Gallery in 2010.

Kathleen Gormley McKay is a central part of the Varley Art Gallery story, as the donor of the core of the original collection and the provider of a substantial financial endowment to care for it.[103] Kathy McKay was born in Unionville, the daughter of George Gormley and Sarah Milne. The family had a farm on the east side of Main Street, north of the bridge over the Rouge River. She met Donald McKay at St. Philip's Anglican Church, where she sang in the choir. Kathy Gormley was a graduate of the Royal Conservatory of Music in Toronto. This experience provided a foundation of her lifelong interest in the arts. The couple married in 1927 and moved to the United States. When they returned to Canada they lived in Toronto, where in 1952 they met and befriended former Group of Seven artist Fred Varley. Varley lived as a boarder in the McKay household, and moved with the couple when they relocated to their original hometown of Unionville in 1957.

The McKays were dedicated art patrons. Not only did they provide lodging for Fred Varley in his later years within their home at 197 Main Street, they allowed him to have a studio in the basement.[104] The studio within the beautiful board-and-batten house, built for Salem Eckardt circa 1856, had a fine view of the McKay's back garden and the Rouge River valley because the basement was a walkout built into the natural slope.[105] Fred Varley lived there for his final twelve years before his death in 1969. During the McKays' long association with Varley, they amassed a fine collection of his work and the work of other Canadian artists who were Frederick Varley's contemporaries. Known in particular for his portraits, one of Varley's most significant and well-known works is the oil painting titled *Laughing Kathy*, a captivating portrait of Kathleen McKay painted in 1952 or 1953.

The Varley Art Gallery is a cultural focal point for Unionville and the region. Since the time of Kathleen Gormley McKay's donation, the collection has grown and the gallery has hosted many impressive exhibitions using its own collection as well as loaned works of art from other public galleries and private collections.

Afterword
A Word about Heritage Conservation

"One generation abandons the enterprises of another like stranded vessels."[1] So wrote the American philosopher Henry David Thoreau in his classic work *Walden*. I think that there is a lot of truth to that statement, particularly when it comes to our inheritance of old buildings. People seem to like new things: the latest phone, a new car with its new-car smell, or a new home with lots of square footage and a maintenance-free exterior. Old things are nowhere near as exciting to the average consumer. This state of things is nothing we haven't seen before. It's called progress — that forward movement toward the continuous improvement of the state of humanity that all of us are part of whether we like it or not.

Embracing progress is a basic part of human nature. Thanks to the ongoing process of change and advancements in science, technology, and social philosophy we have come a long way from a primitive condition of tenuous survival to the present state of civilization, where humanity is so successful that we threaten to overrun the finite boundaries of the Earth. Birth, growth, maturity, decline, and ultimately death are the elements of the natural cycle that governs most things in this world. This fact is very clearly observed in Canada, with the yearly pageant of the changing seasons. The same natural laws apply to the buildings that people constructed in the past, and continue to construct today.

Each building that is erected is a product of its time, reflecting the design preferences of the society that creates it, the types of materials available for construction and finishing, current building technology, and the economics that control the size, location, and quality of accommodation. Buildings are an indication of the values and aspirations of the people who commission and use them. All have their place in the stream of time, just like their builders.

Heritage conservation is a process that places value in the buildings, structures, and landscapes that belonged to past generations and have been carried forward to become today's cultural heritage resources. To preserve something that has reached the last days of the natural cycle of life, or even to think of it, runs contrary to human nature. There are many people who see absolutely no value at all in keeping anything old. They say, "Isn't it obvious that a new building is better than an old one? What about energy efficiency? What about having siding you don't have to paint? What about the highest and best use for my property?"

In contrast to this tendency to embrace the new and discard the old, there are those who see the world differently. While these people like to move forward and enjoy the benefits that progress brings, they value a sense of rootedness and continuity with the past to feel contented in their lives in the present. To appreciate the things that past generations have left behind as markers to say "we were here" has a certain appeal, helping us to place ourselves in the context of history, with the knowledge that what we have built will do the same for future generations.

Old houses, antique furniture, faded photographs in family albums, and museums displaying the fragments of past civilizations are reminders that we are involved in a continuing story, and that when we pass away our descendants will carry on. Maybe something that we created or accomplished will remain for people to pause to consider who we were and what we did. After all, when one walks through a building that has survived one hundred and fifty years of time and everything that

has happened in it and around it, isn't there a natural tendency to wonder about the people who once lived their lives within those walls?

What's strange is that heritage conservation is sometimes so difficult to accomplish when, through the important indicator of property values, we observe that the long-established neighbourhoods with old houses, mature trees, and a sense of the past are often the most expensive and desirable places to live. Why do these neighbourhoods have so much appeal when new developments are just around the corner, offering the latest in everything the builder's market research says we need?

A similar kind of paradox exists when we think of travel destinations. People love to visit places imbued with a sense of culture and history. Tourists marvel at European streets of well-preserved old houses, shops, and cafes, unmarred with garish plastic signs and architectural accidents, while at home they complain that old buildings are eyesores that stand in the way of property owners achieving the ultimate in resale value, or that heritage conservation districts are an impediment to an owner's property rights, akin to the edicts of a totalitarian regime.

One value that is especially difficult to get across to those who don't appreciate heritage conservation is that of authenticity. This is not meant in the same sense of maintaining buildings in present-day use in a museum-quality state, but rather it is about keeping enough of the original material of an old building to ensure the intangible spirit of continuity with the builders and past occupants of a place remains discernible.

The preservation of heritage buildings used to be limited to military fortifications and the residences of significant historical figures. Then, in the 1960s, as

Canada's centennial of Confederation approached, many communities, large and small, founded local historical museums to preserve their past. Often these museums were housed in an old building that was rescued from demolition and restored to represent a certain time period in the history of those communities.

With the establishment of the Heritage Canada Foundation in 1973 the idea of valuing and protecting entire streets, neighbourhoods, or even a complete community for its heritage significance was proposed. It has become clear that the preservation of selected buildings, and particularly buildings associated with elite families or historical events, is not enough to tell the whole story of Canada. The homes of ordinary people — tradesmen, farmers, and labourers — have their place in the fabric of our built heritage and deserve to be preserved along with the city mansions and county villas of the leading families.

This democratization of heritage conservation has shifted the responsibility of stewardship from governments and institutions to individual property owners. Many of those who live in heritage districts delight in coming up with an authentic paint colour scheme for their 1870s Gothic Revival home, and enjoy searching antique markets for the right period hardware for their front door. Others with no particular interest in heritage conservation simply find themselves living in a neighbourhood of older homes, and would prefer vinyl over board and batten and thermalpane over hand-blown window panes. The preservation of the homes of

ordinary people of the past has an impact on ordinary people of the present.

A story that made a strong impression upon me as a professional working in the field of heritage conservation relates to the designation of a heritage conservation district in a neighbouring community. The cultural heritage value of the neighbourhood under discussion was indisputable, however, one individual who opposed the designation while at the same time being an advocate for heritage conservation took the position that education, not legislation, was the most effective way to preserve old buildings and streetscapes in his town. Demonstrating the value of heritage buildings, offering practical reasoning for treating those resources with care, and teaching property owners the proper approach to maintaining and, where necessary, upgrading ageing structures does seem like a sound approach that has the potential to work for the old-house enthusiasts and reluctant old-house owners alike.

Unionville is a special place because of the history of collaboration between property owners, historical societies and preservation groups, and the municipal administration. Places like Unionville are few and far between. No place is secure forever, and conditions change as time goes on. It's important that education continues and the preservation ethic is carried forward so this old Ontario village remains a showpiece of heritage conservation in the midst of the tremendous changes that surround it.

Notes

Introduction

1. Unionville has acquired a significant cachet in real-estate terms and, as in the case of Toronto's highly desirable "Beach" neighbourhood, its unofficial boundaries continue to expand as an effective marketing strategy for expensive new houses.

2. The distinctive pattern of settlement in Ontario is wonderfully described in Thomas F. McIlwraith, *Looking for Old Ontario* (Toronto: University of Toronto Press, 1997), a study that reads clues in the landscape that reveal the past in the context of changes that have occurred since the first Europeans and Americans put down roots here.

3. Periods of economic stagnation and decline sometimes prove to be an effective agent for the preservation of older buildings, where there is little money or incentive for owners to undertake major renovations or rebuilding. In this way, historical buildings that would typically be drastically altered or destroyed remain long enough to be preserved as cultural heritage resources.

4. "Canadiana" is a term seldom heard today, but at one time it was commonly used to describe the uniquely Canadian artifacts being sold in antique shops across the country during the swelling of nationalistic pride around the time of Canada's centennial of Confederation. Stripped pine furniture, pressed glass, and butter moulds are just a few of the things that come to mind as typical pieces of Canadiana.

5. The old sugar maple and chestnut trees that once shaded Main Street, said to have been planted by Salem Eckardt in the late nineteenth century, were

removed to make way for a planned road widening that thankfully never occurred. Since that time, much of the remaining green space on the street has continued to disappear as buried utilities limit what can be planted in the boulevards and property owners favour the convenience of hard surfacing over landscaping.

6. Unionville was a destination featured in Harvey Currell's "Town and Country Trips," a weekly column in *The Toronto Telegram* newspaper in the 1960s and 1970s. This was just around the time when the heritage significance of the village was being "discovered" in the Greater Toronto Area.

7. The lengthy process that led to the designation of Unionville as a heritage conservation district is summarized in the *Unionville Heritage Conservation District Study, 1997*, produced by the Town of Markham. It is interesting to note that notwithstanding Unionville's well-known historical value, it was the third heritage district in the municipality to be protected. The first was old Thornhill in 1986.

8. In 2013 through 2014 Unionville was under study by a consultant team assembled by the firm of Torti Gallas and Partners Inc. to produce a thirty-year vision plan for the future of the village, with the goal of responding to economic and other changes that have occurred in Markham that have challenged the viability of the commercial heart of the heritage district. In summary, the vision is to preserve the heritage buildings that are important to maintaining the unique character of Unionville while allowing for residential intensification and enhanced infrastructure that will hopefully contribute to the vitality of the business district.

9. *Historic Unionville* looks at a selection of Unionville's historical buildings. For a complete overview of all of the cultural heritage resources in the area, see the *Unionville Heritage Conservation District Plan, 1997, Building Inventory.*

10. For a more detailed examination of historic building styles in Ontario, the books Marion MacRae and Anthony Adamson, *The Ancestral Roof* (Toronto: Clarke, Irwin & Company Limited, 1963), John Blumenson, *Ontario Architecture 1794 to the Present* (Toronto: Fitzhenry & Whiteside, 1990), and Robert Mikel, *Ontario House Styles* (Toronto: James Lorimer & Company Limited, 2004) are recommended.

Pre-Confederation Unionville

1. A concise history of First Nations populations in Markham Township prior to European settlement can be found in Isabel Champion, ed., *Markham 1793–1900* (Markham: Markham District Historical Society, second edition, revised, 1989), 3–6.

2. The story of the Berczy settlers in Markham Township appears in a number of local sources, including *Markham 1793–1900*, 11–16, and Lorne R. Smith, *A Story of the Markham Berczy Settlers — 200 Years in Markham, 1794–1994* (Markham: Markham Berczy Settlers Association, 1994).

3. Berczy's Settlement Report of 1798, which shows the lots upon which the original Berczy settler families first settled, is reproduced in *Markham 1793–1900*, 321.

4. Berczy's Census of Markham Settlers, 1803, is reproduced in *Markham 1793–1900*, 323–30.

5. The name "Settlers' Hill" was recently given to the height of land upon which Philip Eckardt and his family settled in 1808, and where the Lutheran church and cemetery that served the community were established. This unofficial place name was coined by the Markham Berczy Settlers Association to commemorate its special significance.

6. *A Story of the Markham Berczy Settlers — 200 Years in Markham*, 27.

7. Albert John Harrington Eckardt wrote a family history that was deposited in the cornerstone of Bethesda Lutheran Church, 20 Union Street, Unionville, in 1910. In this history, A.J.H. Eckardt provides a detailed and, at times, colourful view of the experiences of his ancestors in the United States and Upper Canada. He elaborated on this family history in A.J.H. Eckardt, "The Eckardt Pioneers of the Township of Markham, as told by A.J.H. Eckardt in the year 1932," *The Visitor — An Independent Paper Devoted to the Interests of Unionville and District* (Unionville: Excelsior Press, July 21, 1938). Some of the statements contained in those accounts have been questioned by local historians as to their accuracy, and more research is required to verify some of the information through sources other than A.J.H. Eckardt's writings.

8. "Fate of Historic House Proves Markham Poser," *Globe and Mail*, May 21, 1953.

9. Michael Bird and Terry Kobayashi, *A Splendid Harvest — German Folk and Decorative Arts in Canada* (Toronto: Van Nostrand Reindhold Ltd., 1981), 58, 59.

10. Extensive archaeological excavation work was done around the Philip Eckardt log house in 2012 by archaeological resource consultants This Land Archaeology Inc., under the direction of Dr. William D. Findlayson, in preparation for the residential development of the Beckett Farm. The author visited the site during the excavation of the area next to the building to observe the evidence of the southern extension of the building first-hand.

11. Lorne R. Smith, *Historic Cemeteries of Markham* (Markham: Town of Markham, 2004).

12. For a detailed historical account of Unionville's Lutherans, see Lorne R. Smith, "A History of Bethesda Lutheran Church," *Canadian German Folklore — More Pioneer Hamlets of York*, Volume 9, 1980, York Chapter, Pennsylvania German Folklore Society, 179–85.

13. *Holy Bible*, King James Version, John 5:2–9.

14. Bethesda Lutheran Church is today located at 20 Union Street.

15. A detailed description of adobe-brick construction in Ontario is found in John I. Rempel, *Building with Wood and Other Aspects of Nineteenth-Century Building in Central Canada* (Toronto: University of Toronto Press, Revised edition, 1980), 274–82.

16. *Markham 1793–1900*, 192.

17. Dr. Thomas Philip Eckardt's residency in the adobe-brick cottage is a local tradition that is difficult to substantiate using available primary source material. His association with this property may have originated with the Stiver family, longtime owners of this Unionville landmark. See Russell M. Stiver, *The Stiver Family in Canada 1794–1994* (Markham: Privately published, 1994), 20.

18. The ownership of the adobe-brick cottage by the Jenkins family, including the story of Reverend William Jenkins, and the later ownership by the Stiver family until recent times, is outlined in *The Stiver Family in Canada 1794–1994*, 20.

19. The historical and architectural significance of the Eckardt-Stiver cottage as the oldest standing house in the village is highlighted in *Markham 1793–1900*, 302.

20. *Markham 1793–1900*, 302, 309.

21. *Markham 1793–1900*, 192.

22. Mary B. Champion, ed., *Markham Remembered — A Photographic History of Old Markham Township* (Markham: Markham District Historical Society, 1988), 136.

23. Only a few historical buildings remain in the northern part of old Unionville. Many of the small frame houses and shops from the early days of the village were replaced by modern executive homes before they could be protected through the establishment of the heritage conservation district.

24. *Markham 1793–1900*, 301.

25. The name "Union Street" appears in the deed abstract for Lot 12, Concession 5 from 1845 to 1888, as part of the property descriptions of village lots being either on the east or west sides of Union Street. How long this name was in general use before being replaced by Main Street is at present not well documented. Advertisements for the Queen's Hotel in issues of the *Markham Economist* from the mid-1870s refer to its location on Main Street. To add to the confusion concerning the name Union Street appearing in the deed abstract for the village core, William Eckardt named one of the backstreets in his subdivision of 1856 Union Street, a name that endures to the present day.

26. A detailed documentation of plank-on-plank construction in old Ontario is found in *Building with Wood and Other Aspects of Nineteenth Century Building in Central Canada*, 178–80.

27. From 1798 until at about 1830, in order to receive the patent from the Crown for a land grant, the grantee was required to build and occupy a house with a minimum size of sixteen by twenty feet within one year, and within two years clear the road allowance in front of the lot and clear and plant a minimum of five acres. Verschoyle Benson Blake and Ralph Greenhill, *Rural Ontario* (Toronto: University of Toronto Press, 1969), 7.

28. Speculation about the date of construction of this house is found in an unpublished history of the property written by Tom Greenhough, whose family owned the house from 1949 to 1993.

29. A photo of the house prior to the application of the stucco treatment was given to the present property owner by the Greenhough family.

30. An archival photograph of the house showing all four brick chimneys is included in the Eckardt family file in the collection of the Markham Museum.

31. *Markham 1793–1900*, 80, 81.

32. Ibid., 81.

33. Ibid., 33.

34. Ibid., 126.

35. In a directory of antique shops in Ontario from the 1980s, the owner of the Jug and Basin gave the date of construction of the old house where the shop was located as 1846.

36. A summary of the early history of the Congregational Church in Markham Township, and specifically in Unionville, can be found in *Markham 1793–1900*, 146.

37. The later history of the original Congregational church building and its transformation into a residence after serving as a place of worship for a Presbyterian congregation appears in *Markham 1793–1900*, 144.

38. Members of the Eckardt family were locally known as strong supporters of the 1837 Rebellion, as noted in *Markham 1793–1900*, 192.

39. A detailed account of the Reverend Mayerhoffer is described in detail in *Markham 1793–1900*, 136, 138.

40. The expulsion of Revered Mayerhoffer is perhaps the most dramatic historical event in Unionville's history. An excellent account appears in Lorne R. Smith, "A History of Bethesda Lutheran Church," 181–82.

41. *St. Philip's Anglican Church in Unionville, 1829–1979*, commemorative program celebrating the congregation's 150th anniversary, Friday, October 12, 1979.

42. The most detailed published history of St. Philip's Anglican Church, and its association with other local Anglican congregations, is found in *Markham 1793–1900*, 138–39.

43. A.J.H. Eckardt, "The Eckardt Pioneers of the Township of Markham," *The Visitor — An Independent Paper Devoted to the Interests of Unionville and District*, July 21, 1938.

44. *Markham 1793–1900*, Appendix E, Post Offices in Markham, 337.

45. The history and contribution of the Eakin family in Markham is told in *Markham 1793–1900*, 303–04.

46. George Eakin's appointment as clerk of York County is documented in the history section of the *Historical Atlas of York County* (Toronto: Miles & Company, 1878), 19, and his position and location in Toronto is confirmed in the census of 1881. George Eakin served as clerk of York County until 1896.

47. A first-hand account of the Davison Store and Unionville Post Office is found in Grace Harrington's recollections of Unionville in the early twentieth century, written in 1982.

48. The Davison family's significant role in the life of Unionville is described in Mary B. Champion, *Markham Remembered — A Photographic History of Old Markham Township*, 138, 140, 151.

49. A remarkable and little-known account of the history of the Stamm family in Canada is provided in Hannah Reed's obituary "Death of a Centenarian," *Uxbridge Journal*, August 25, 1881.

50. Ibid.

51. Ibid.

52. A superb archival photograph of this building, while it was a butcher shop and residence, appears in *Markham, 1793–1900*, 304. It is remarkable how little the building has changed since the photograph was taken in the early 1920s.

53. Gottlieb Eckardt's 1852 will provides a valuable window into two of Unionville's earliest industries and helps date the construction of Hewlett Eckardt's house at 158 Main Street to c. 1853.

54. Brown's store is Unionville's best-documented and longest-lasting store, run by a series of members of the same family. A very detailed account of Brown's store is contained in *Markham 1793–1900*, 308, 310. Some longtime residents can still recall this landmark business.

55. The story of the McKinnon family and their experiences in early Canada is well documented in *History of Toronto and County of York, Ontario*, Volume II, Biographical Notices (Toronto: C. Blackett Robinson, 1885), 295, and also in *Markham, 1793–1900*, 72.

56. It is not certain how this house came to be associated with Neil McKinnon when primary source information contained in deed abstracts, census data, and family history clearly points to the Eakin family as the builders of the first frame house on the property. While the McKinnon family certainly were residing on the property at an early date, they lived in a log house, which was later replaced with the present frame dwelling on the property.

57. The early manufacturing enterprises of William and George Eakin in Unionville can be tracked in the 1861 and 1871 census data, Mitchell & Co.'s directory of 1866 and the *York Herald* newspaper of 1861 and 1862, which carries advertisements for the Unionville Carriage Factory. The quoted text comes from "Unionville Carriage Factory," *York Herald*, July 9, 1861.

58. A brief overview of the Eakin family history in Markham Township is found in *Markham, 1793–1900*, 303–04.

59. William Eakin's extraordinary life after he left Unionville for the Canadian West in the early 1880s is not well-known in existing published histories of Unionville. The Markham Museum family history collection includes a copy of a newspaper clipping titled "Prosperous Township of Markham Birthplace of Warden William Eakin." The clipping, unfortunately, does not include the name of the newspaper or date of publication, but appears to date from around the time of his death in 1918.

60. The early history of this little clapboarded cottage has proven difficult to pinpoint, even with a thorough examination of primary source data, which confirms ownership but leaves some unanswered questions about who actually resided there prior to the Brown family in the 1890s.

61. *Markham, 1793–1900*, 308.

62. The 1852 date of construction for this remarkable house appears to have originated in the recollections of A.J.H. Eckardt, "The Eckardt Pioneers of the Township of Markham…"

63. William Eckardt's 1856 plan of subdivision is Plan 190. Eckardt later modified his original plan of village lots in additional plans of subdivision, after the railway passed through his property.

64. *Markham, 1793–1900*, 306–07.

65. Howard Pain, *The Heritage of Upper Canadian Furniture* (Toronto: Van Nostrand Reinhold Ltd., 1978), is a definitive resource on early furniture in Ontario. A number of pieces of furniture illustrated in the book have Markham Township provenance and some were no doubt displayed in Pain's home when he resided in Unionville.

66. Most secondary sources state that Andrew Eckardt built the house at 197 Main Street and that

his brother Salem Eckardt later modified it. An examination of primary source records challenges that idea, particularly considering that Andrew Eckardt never owned the village lot where the house stands.

67. *Markham, 1793–1900*, 305.
68. A brief history of the Varley Art Gallery of Markham appears on the City of Markham website www.markham.ca. A contemporary account of Fred Varley in Unionville as a guest of the McKay family appears in Mrs. Claude Russell-Brown, "Unionville, 1961," *Canadian German Folklore, Pioneer Hamlets of York*, Volume 6, 1977, York Chapter, Pennsylvania German Folklore Society, 54.
69. Marion MacRae and Anthony Adamson, *The Ancestral Roof — Domestic Architecture of Upper Canada* (Toronto: Clarke, Irwin and Company, 1963), 214–16.
70. *Historical Sketch of Markham Township 1793 to 1950, Centennial Celebration of Municipal Government 1850 to 1950* (Markham: Historical Committee, 1950), 74.
71. The City of Markham's research file on the Crown Inn contains a list of innkeepers and the changing name of their establishments based on tavern licences, census data, and assessment data.
72. *Markham, 1793–1900*, 302.
73. *Markham Remembered — A Photographic History of Old Markham Township*, 235.
74. Interior renovations undertaken in 2014 exposed selected areas of the underlying structure of 249 Main Street, revealing the house was framed with a mixture of nineteenth- and early twentieth-century lumber. The older lumber was not necessarily

in its original configuration, based on nail holes and other markings, suggesting that when Hiram Powers undertook renovations to the Crown Inn c. 1904 he most likely demolished all or part of the old building and reused lumber salvaged from it.
75. *Markham, 1793–1900*, 303.
76. An excellent archival photograph of the Powers family residence, probably taken soon after the renovations of circa 1904, can be seen in *Markham, 1793–1900*, 354.
77. On Tremaine's map of 1860 the store is shown on the southeast corner of the crossroads of Kennedy Road and 16th Avenue, on the Braithwaite property. Some sources state that the store was on the northeast corner but this is likely an error since it makes more sense that the Braithwaite Store would be on the Braithwaite's own property.
78. *Mitchell & Co.'s General Directory for the City of Toronto and Gazetteer of the Counties of York and Peel for the Year 1866* (Toronto: Mitchell & Co., Publishers, 1866), 421.
79. *Markham 1793–1900*, 337. List of Unionville Postmasters.

Unionville's Golden Age

1. James W. Fenwick's life and career are summarized in an entry in *Commemorative Biographical Record of the County of York* (Toronto: J.H. Beers & Co., 1907), 570.
2. There is a local story that the store at 156 Main Street was moved to this location from Cashel. Current research indicates that it was the store's

proprietor rather than the building that relocated to Unionville.

3. Brown's Store is perhaps the best-documented and longest-lasting businesses on Unionville's Main Street. Isabel Champion, ed., *Markham 1793–1900* (Markham: Markham District Historical Society, Second edition, revised, 1989), 308–10, contains a detailed account of the general store through the generations of the Brown family.

4. The former site of the old Standard Bank building is now the beautifully landscaped front yard of 158 Main Street.

5. Michael Gonder Scherck, *Pen Pictures of Early Pioneer Life in Upper Canada* (Toronto: William Briggs, 1905), 154–56.

6. *Markham 1793–1900*, 28.

7. The story of how John N. Raymer learned the art of cheese making is told in *The Reesor Family in Canada — A Trail through the Centuries: Genealogical and Historical Records 1804–1980* (Markham: Privately published, 1980), 256.

8. The tragic circumstances of the death of John N. Raymer are described in *The Reesor Family in Canada*, 256.

9. John Noble Raymer's former home, a fine patterned brick L-plan farmhouse, was relocated to 6890 14th Avenue in 2005, a short distance west of its original site, where it now serves as a private school.

10. *Markham 1793–1900*, 274, 275.

11. Ibid., 306, and Rod Clarke, *Narrow Gauge Through the Bush — Ontario's Toronto & Grey Bruce and Toronto & Nipissing Railways* (Whitby: Rod Clarke and Ralph Beaumont, Publishers, 2007), 60.

12. The 1870 date of construction of the Unionville Train Station is confirmed in a newspaper article, "Toronto and Nipissing Railway Company," *Markham Economist*, November 24, 1870. Most other sources give a date of circa 1871.

13. Mrs. Claude Russell-Brown, "Unionville, 1961," *Canadian German Folklore – Pioneer Hamlets of York*, Volume 6, 1977, York Chapter, Pennsylvania German Folklore Society of Ontario, 48.

14. The history of narrow-gauge railways in Canada is described in detail in Rod Clarke, *Narrow Gauge Through the Bush, Ontario's Toronto, Grey & Bruce and Toronto & Nipissing Railways* (Whitby: Rod Clarke and Ralph Beaumont, Publishers, 2007) and Charles Cooper, *Narrow Gauge for Us* (Erin: Boston Mills Press, 1982).

15. The original design and layout of the Unionville Railway Station is illustrated in *Narrow Gauge Through the Bush*, 334–35. The original paint colour scheme of dark red trimmed with green is shown on page 353 of the same publication.

16. *Markham 1793–1900*, 179.

17. In his unpublished memoir, "Seventy Years Ago: The Quiet Life" (n.d.), Dr. Clarence A. Chant noted that after the Queen's Hotel opened, it was not long until the old frame hotels north of the Union Mills closed down.

18. *Markham 1793–1900*, 109–12 contains a detailed history of the Queen's Hotel and its role in the community. Much of the information on the hotel and the Webber and Hemingway families has been gleaned from this source.

19. Since no archival photographs of the interior of the Queen's Hotel are known, Grace

Harrington's reminiscences of its decor are particularly valuable in completing the impression of this village hotel in its heyday.

20. *Markham 1793–1900*, 111.

21. Ibid., 112.

22. Ibid., 112.

23. The later history of the Queen's Hotel is found in Mary B. Champion, ed., *Markham Remembered — A Photographic History of Old Markham Township* (Markham: Markham District Historical Society, 1989), 137.

24. *Quinquennial Catalogue of the Officers and Graduates of Harvard University 1630–1890* (Cambridge: Harvard University, 1890), 232.

25. *University of Toronto Calendar 1891–1892*, Appendix: Graduates in Medicine (Toronto: University of Toronto, 1891), 66.

26. Dr. Wesley Robinson, Abigail Robinson Eckardt's brother, lived at 152 Main Street North, Markham Village. The contribution of Dr. Robinson's son Edgar Bertram "Bert" Freel Robinson as one of the founders of the Canadian National Institute for the Blind is recorded on a plaque affixed to the facade of his former residence.

27. An account of Dr. T.P. Eckardt's residency in the mud-brick cottage at 206 Main Street is found in Russell M. Stiver, *Stiver Family in Canada 1794–1994* (Markham: Privately published, 1994), 20.

28. Memories of Jennie Harrington, the wife of Unionville Planing Mill owner Delos Harrington, as told to their daughter Grace Harrington.

29. Obituary notice for "Dr. Eckardt of Unionville, Ont." in *The Canadian Lancet*, September 1, 1880.

It is worth noting that in spite of Dr. Eckardt's standing in the community, his obituary in this publication, and also his death notice in the local newspaper, the *Markham Economist*, were scant in detail and provided no information on his life or medical career.

30. A detailed account of the circumstances of Dr. Eckardt's death, and the subsequent investigation by the Confederation Life Association of Toronto regarding a life insurance claim is found in Truth, "To Stephen English, Esq., Editor Insurance Times, New York City," *The Insurance Times*, December, 1882, 694. The insurance company refused to pay the claim to Dr. Eckardt's widow on the basis that they claimed that the doctor knew about a pre-existing medical condition when he took out the insurance policy the year prior to his death. Thanks to the intervention of Dr. Wesley Robinson of Markham Village, his body was exhumed and examined, and in the end the claim was paid by Confederation Life.

31. *Markham 1793–1900*, 23.

32. These house types are artfully illustrated and explained in A.J. Downing, *The Architecture of Country Houses* (New York: D. Appleton & Co., 1850). This architectural pattern book was in wide circulation throughout North America during the mid to late nineteenth century and was a significant influence on vernacular architecture.

33. *Markham 1793–1900*, 68.

34. Robert Harrington served as postmaster at Armadale, Scarborough Township, for only one year, resigning in 1870, presumably to pursue a career as a carpenter and builder.

35. *Markham 1793–1900*, 126, 303.

36. Markham Township assessment records list Robert Harrington, carpenter, on a one-quarter-acre property on Lot 13, Concession 6, rented from John Gormley, in 1881. His location is confirmed by the census of 1881. The Harringtons must have moved to 141 Main Street that same year, after their purchase of the house and planing mill from William Eakin.

37. In the 1881 census William Eakin's occupation is listed as "sash and door maker."

38. William Eakin's life after leaving Unionville for the Canadian West is outlined in his obituary "William Eakin Dies at Saltcoats, Sask., Old Resident of Markham Who Became Speaker of Northwest Assembly," *Markham Economist & Sun*, April 4, 1918.

39. *Markham 1793–1900*, 126–28.

40. Ibid., 306, 307.

41. Previously published accounts attribute the house at 14 Eureka Street to Philip D. Eckardt, William Eckardt's brother. Current research points to Job McDowell as the original owner.

42. Research by Susan Casella, a former resident of Buttonville, provides the history of weaver William Sutton.

43. *Markham 1793–1900*, 126.

44. A contemporary account of the life and career of Reuben A. Stiver is found in *History of Toronto and York County, Ontario*, Vol. II: Biographical Notices (Toronto: C. Blackett Robinson, 1885), 308, 309.

45. *Markham Remembered*, 137.

46. Ibid., 137, 138.

47. *Biographical Dictionary of Architects in Canada 1800–1950*, "Josiah Hall," dictionaryofarchitectsincanada.org.

48. Ibid.

49. *Markham 1793–1900*, 156.

50. Ibid., 273.

51. Ibid., 261.

52. Information about Joseph Havelock Chant from Dr. Clarence A. Chant's unpublished memoir, "Seventy Years Ago: The Quiet Life" (n.d.).

53. The restoration of the George Pingle House is a good example of how heritage district designation and the Unionville Heritage Conservation District Plan have contributed to the restoration of an altered heritage building through the development application process, where conditions of approval can be applied, with the co-operation of property owners.

54. *Markham 1793–1900*, 233.

55. Ibid., 305.

56. The John Stephenson that operated the Union Mills beginning in the late 1800s is a different John Stephenson than the blacksmith of the same name, younger by some twenty-nine years. In *Markham Remembered*, 137, it is noted that John Stephenson managed the flour mill from about 1885, followed by his brother Herbert in the early 1900s.

57. In *Markham 1793–1900*, 307, the contribution of local builder George Robinson to the variety of architectural styles for houses in Unionville in the 1870s through the 1880s is noted.

58. A cheque with the name "J. Stephenson & Co., Bankers," dated 1897, is illustrated in *Markham 1793–1900*, 307.

59. John Stephenson's career was summarized in the entry for his son, George Henry Stephenson, in William Cochrane et al, *The Canadian Album: Men*

of Canada, or Success by Example in Religion, Patriotism, Business, Law, Medicine, Education and Agriculture (Brantford: Bradley, Garretson & Co., 1893).

60. Grace Harrington recalled the Sovereign Bank on Main Street from her childhood reminiscences of the early 1900s. The building, now demolished, was located at 186 Main Street, the current location of a restaurant housed within the renovated post office of the 1960s.

61. *Markham 1793–1900*, 192.

62. The Eckardt sawmill, in the shallow valley of the Rouge River, a short distance from the northeast corner of Main Street and Highway 7, is described in A.J.H. Eckardt, "The Eckardt Pioneers of the Township of Markham," *The Visitor — An Independent Paper Dedicated to the Interests of Unionville and District*, July 24, 1938.

63. *Markham 1793–1900*, 307.

64. Previous accounts say that James Eckardt built the fine brick house at 137 Main Street for his second wife, Agnes, in 1875, however, at that time he was married to Sarah Jane Size. Sarah Jane died sometime between the 1881 census and the 1891 census, when James Eckardt was listed as a widower. He remarried in 1893, long after the house at 137 Main Street was constructed.

65. The author has observed shoes found hidden in wall cavities and under floorboards in over thirty years of examining old houses under renovation or demolition. Colleagues in the heritage conservation field have also made note of this curious custom.

66. *Walking Tours of Unionville* (Unionville: Unionville Historical Society, 1988), 26.

67. Reminiscences of Grace Harrington.

68. Before coming to Unionville, the Findlay brothers were associated with the Thornhill Hotel on the east side of Yonge Street, north of Colborne Street. The old hotel, a landmark on Yonge Street, was destroyed by fire in 1950. See Doris FitzGerald, *Thornhill 1793–1963* (Privately published, 1964), 59, 62, 63.

69. *Markham 1793–1900*, 111, and *Markham Remembered*, 137.

70. The history of the Chant family is summarized in *Markham 1793–1900*, 64. This history is based in large part on an entry in *History of Toronto and York County, Ontario*, Volume II, Biographical Notices (Toronto: C. Blackett Robinson, 1885)

71. *Markham 1793–1900*, 64.

72. *Walking Tours of Unionville*, 28.

73. Mrs. Claude Russell-Brown, "Unionville 1961," *Canadian-German Folklore: Pioneer Hamlets of York*, Volume 6, 1977, York Chapter, Pennsylvania German Folklore Society, 52.

74. Dr. Chant's distinguished career in the field of astronomy and astrophysics is noted in *Markham 1793–1900*, 64. Additional source material comes from information compiled by Gloria Boxen and Karen Cilevitz, who are part of a group of concerned citizens involved with efforts to preserve the David Dunlap Observatory at Richmond Hill as a significant site of scientific discovery.

75. An interpretive plaque has been installed in front of 147 Main Street to commemorate the history of the house, and in particular to highlight the contributions to science by Clarence A. Chant, who lived here in his youth.

76. *Walking Tours of Unionville*, 29.

77. George Robinson's birthplace, mentioned in *Markham 1793–1900,* is given as Whitchurch; however, census data consistently gives his birthplace as England.

78. Census data through the period 1851 to 1881 was essential in tracing the early history of George Robinson's career and family connections.

79. *Markham 1793–1900,* 307.

80. A pattern book popular at the time, with illustrations of houses and decorative details similar to those used by George Robinson is *Bicknell's Village Builder and Supplement* (New York: A. J. Bicknell and Company, 1878.).

81. *Markham 1793–1900,* 307.

82. One of the most important principles of heritage conservation is to retain historical buildings on their original sites to preserve their integrity as cultural heritage resources. Once a building is moved from its original location it loses its connection to the place where the history happened, and its value is thereby diminished. Sometimes relocation cannot be avoided, and notwithstanding principles, heritage buildings have to be relocated to preserve them, if they are deemed valuable enough to take that step.

83. *Walking Tours of Unionville,* 46.

84. The Pingle family were among the Berczy settler group. See *Markham 1793–1900,* 20–21.

85. Dr. Pingle's move to London, Ontario, was determined by searching the 1891 census. Strangely, he seems to have given the census-taker an age eleven years younger than his true age.

86. *Walking Tours of Unionville,* 46.

87. *Stiver Family in Canada, 1794–1994,* 17.

88. An excellent history of the early life and career of Reuben A. Stiver appears in *History of Toronto and York County, Ontario,* Volume II, Biographical Notices, 308, 309, which also contains this interesting story of his father's participation in the Upper Canada Rebellion of 1837.

89. This photograph is in *Markham Remembered,* 61.

90. *Stiver Family in Canada, 1794–1994,* 17, 18.

91. Ibid., 16.

92. Ibid., 17 and *Walking Tours of Unionville,* 6, 26.

93. This wonderful description of a general store interior of the early 1900s is found in the reminiscences of Grace Harrington. It seems natural that a childhood memory of the contents of a store would begin with the candy counter.

94. *Markham 1793–1900,* 288, 302.

95. Reminiscences of Grace Harrington.

96. *Markham 1793–1900,* 193.

97. *Walking Tours of Unionville,* 44.

98. *Markham 1793–1900,* 306-307.

99. *Walking Tours of Unionville,* 38.

100. Builders from the Unionville Planing Mill constructed a frame house for George and Hannah Weatherill circa 1890, now addressed 77 Main Street.

101. *Walking Tours of Unionville,* 38.

102. The unique character of Victoria Avenue has recently begun to be compromised by the construction of additions out of scale with the humble workers' cottages on the street, notwithstanding the policies and guidelines of the Unionville Heritage Conservation District Plan.

103. *Markham Remembered,* 138.

104. *Markham 1793–1900*, 111.
105. The history of Unionville's Lutherans is outlined in *Markham 1793–1900*, 134–38. However, the parsonage and its history are not mentioned in the text.
106. The small frame cottage that housed the Reverend Fishburn, locally known as the "Cobbler's Cottage," was moved a short distance from its original site on the west side of Woodbine Avenue in the 1980s, and later became an addition to another historical building in the historic hamlet of Buttonville at 10 Buttonville Crescent West, the William Morrison House.
107. The 1867 date of construction appears in *Walking Tours of Unionville*, 42, and some municipal reports supporting the designation of the property under the Ontario Heritage Act.
108. A list of the pastors of Bethesda Lutheran Church is found in Lorne R. Smith, "A History of Bethesda Lutheran Church," *Canadian-German Folklore — More Pioneer Hamlets of York*, Volume 7, 1985, York Chapter, Pennsylvania German Folklore Society of Ontario, 185.
109. Agreement attached to a mortgage between Joram Eckardt et al, Trustees of the Parsonage, and James Ferguson, Instrument No. 3611, July 28, 1879.
110. No pastor for the period 1880 to 1887 is noted in the list referred to in Note 108.
111. Lorne R. Smith, "A History of Bethesda Lutheran Church," 183.
112. The history of the Summerfeldt or Sommerfeldt family, who were among the Berczy settler group, is noted in *Markham 1793–1900*, 22, 23.
113. *Markham 1793–1900*, 307.
114. *Walking Tours of Unionville*, 47.
115. The history of Central United Church and the Primitive Methodist and Wesleyan Methodist congregations of Unionville that are its roots are summarized in *Markham 1793–1900*, 156, 157.
116. *Markham 1793–1900*, 157.
117. *Biographical Dictionary of Architects in Canada 1800–1950*.
118. *Walking Tours of Unionville*, 48.
119. The original Congregational Church from circa 1847 has served as a restaurant for many years.
120. *Dictionary of Architects in Canada 1800–1950*.
121. *Markham 1793–1900*, 146.
122. "Unionville — Laying the Foundation Stone of a New Congregationalist Church," *The Canadian Independent*, Spring 1879, 5.
123. "Unionville," *The Canadian Independent*, February 19, 1880, 5.
124. "The Canadian Congregational Yearbook," 1880–81, 157.
125. This remarkable reference to a well-known person from Canadian history comes from the memories of Jennie Harrington of Unionville in the late nineteenth and early twentieth centuries, as told to her daughter Grace Harrington.
126. "Unionville," *The Canadian Independent*, January 27, 1881.
127. "Unionville," *The Canadian Independent*, February 24, 1881, 6; and April 7, 1881, 6.
128. "The Canadian Congregational Yearbook," 1883–84, 163.
129. *Markham 1793–1900*, 144.
130. Ibid., 307.

131. An excellent overview of barn design and development in Ontario, including the emergence of the gambrel or hipped roof on barns, is found in Thomas F. McIlwraith, *Looking for Old Ontario* (Toronto: University of Toronto Press, 1997), 172–90.

132. *Markham 1793–1900*, 308, 310.

133. Lionel Dawson, *Hands Across the Waters: The Life and Times of Our Dawson Family* (Markham: Lionel Dawson, 2008), 162.

134. In *Markham Remembered*, 136, it is noted that Charles E. Stiver was a carpenter. He constructed a number of houses in the neighbourhood where he lived. Numbers 15 and 17 Euclid Street and 14 Pavilion Street are among them. Perhaps he assisted Reuben A. Stiver, a Unionville merchant and real estate investor, in constructing houses on some of his properties, but at this point this idea is speculative based on the fact that Charles E. Stiver purchased the house and property at 17 Euclid Street from his relative.

135. *Markham 1793–1900*, 156–57, and *Markham Remembered*, 136.

136. Edward Eckardt lived in the brick farmhouse built by his father, now addressed 60 Meadowbrook Lane.

137. According to the memories of Jennie Harrington from the late nineteenth and early twentieth centuries, as told to her daughter Grace Harrington, George Weatherill lived in a house at the south end of the village called the "Old Homestead." This was the circa 1840 home of William and Caroline Pingle. George Weatherill must have lived here before he built his own house at 77 Main Street. The "Old Homestead," for years an abandoned building, was demolished in the 1980s. It stood on the west side of Main Street, at 84 Main Street.

138. *Walking Tours of Unionville*, 45.

139. John N. Raymer and his brother Martin Raymer established a cheese factory at the property now addressed 233 Main Street circa 1870, as a branch of their Box Grove cheese-making business. The Raymer brothers died from smallpox in 1874, but the family carried on with the business until about 1877.

140. *Walking Tours of Unionville*, 41.

141. *Markham 1793–1900*, 111.

142. In early twentieth-century Ontario, communities that were not large enough to become incorporated villages could, by municipal by-law, become a police village to obtain a degree of autonomy over local affairs. A police village was administered by a board of trustees who oversaw public services and public works, such as fire protection, street lighting, and sidewalk construction, while other administrative matters continued to be the responsibility of the township council. The Police Village of Unionville existed as an administrative body from 1907 to 1969.

143. *Markham Remembered*, 140, 141.

Unionville's Second Century

1. The early history of the Crosby family is outlined in Isabel Champion, ed. *Markham 1793–1900* (Markham: Markham District Historical Society, Second edition, revised, 1989), 64, 65.

2. *Markham 1793–1900*, 64.

3. Ibid., 270.

4. Ibid., 217.

5. H.P. Crosby's political career is summarized in *Markham 1793–1900*, 195, 196.

6. The involvement of H.P. Crosby in the decision to alter the route of the Toronto and Nipissing Railway to pass through Unionville is described in *Markham 1793–1900*, 306. On the same page is a fine photographic portrait of Mr. Crosby as a young man.

7. The location of H.P. Crosby in the Lutheran parsonage was confirmed in the Markham Township Assessment Rolls of the 1890s.

8. *Walking Tours of Unionville* (Unionville: Unionville Historical Society, 1988), 42.

9. In an archival photograph in the collection of the Markham Museum taken not long after the house was built, the entrance tower is in the same state as it is in now, suggesting that it is likely that nothing has been removed from it since the date of construction.

10. *Markham 1793–1900*, 157.

11. The remarkable career of W.H. Crosby is told in a newspaper article concerning the construction of the Crosby Memorial Arena in the village: "Unionville Boy, Now U.S.A. Millionaire, Makes Fine Gift," *The Evening Telegram*, November 5, 1927.

12. The article, "Unionville Boy, Now U.S.A. Millionaire, Makes Fine Gift," provides the only known written description of the Crosby House that once stood on the site of the arena.

13. Grain elevators are among the distinctive aspects of the Canadian prairies described by Bernard Flaman at the Heritage Canada Foundation's Annual Conference 2005 in Regina, Saskatchewan. The sloped-shouldered, cribbed grain elevator appeared in the west in the early 1900s.

14. The leases for the land upon which the grain elevators stood were kept in the station master's safe in the Unionville Train Station. In 2013 some copies of these leases were donated to the Markham Museum by the son of Risto Puhakka, the last station master.

15. The history of the Stiver Brothers is compiled from two sources: Russell M. Stiver, ed., *Stiver Family in Canada, 1794–1994* (Markham: Privately published, 1994), 16, and a two-page history by Bob Stiver, "The Stiver Mill," unpublished, 2010. Bob Stiver worked in the mill as a youth and was one of the dedicated volunteers who were instrumental in seeing the building preserved and adapted to a viable new use.

16. The property adjoining the Canadian National Railway line was declared surplus to the needs of the railway and sold to the municipality in 1993. The land and the structures upon it were purchased for future municipal purposes relating to the preservation of this historical landmark.

17. An official opening of the newly restored Stiver Mill was held on June 29, 2014, with many members of the Stiver family in attendance.

18. The change in colour for the metal cladding was a controversial aspect of the project, with effective arguments presented to city council from both points of view. The change from silver to red, while not historically accurate for this structure, was shown to have been used on similar buildings in the area.

19. John I. Rempel, *Building with Wood and Other Aspects of Nineteenth Century Building in Central Canada* (Toronto: University of Toronto Press, revised edition, 1980), 178–80.

20. The machinery is not currently in working order. At present there are no plans to bring the machinery back into an operable state; rather, the remaining elements have been left in place as artifacts from the original function of the building as an industrial complex.

21. Reminiscences of Grace Harrington, daughter of Delos and Jennie Harrington, from the early twentieth century.

22. *Markham 1793–1900*, 126–28.

23. Reminiscences of Grace Harrington.

24. At a time when most people in the country used outhouses and chamber pots, to have an indoor bathroom must have been quite a luxury. The water supply would have been from a tank in the attic of the house, operated by gravity.

25. Sawn balusters, delicate in design, were primarily used for porch and balcony railings. Their use for fences was not as common. It is remarkable that the examples in Unionville survived for over a century.

26. *Markham 1793–1900*, 81.

27. Unionville does not seem to have many tales of haunted places. A few ghost stories are told by locals, but most have not been written down. The reference to the possible haunting of the C.H. Stiver House is found in *Stiver Family in Canada 1794–1994*, 14.

28. *Stiver Family in Canada, 1794–1994*, 17.

29. Ibid., 15.

30. Ibid., 15, 16.

31. Mary B. Champion, ed., *Markham Remembered — A Photographic History of Old Markham Township* (Markham: Markham District Historical Society, 1988), 136.

32. The Richardson Romanesque style was used for public buildings as well as private homes. The Ontario Legislature and Toronto's Old City Hall are the best-known local examples of this robust, masculine style popular in the late nineteenth century.

33. As rural areas are transformed from farmland to suburbs, the buildings and other features of old settlements gradually disappear until sometimes only a cemetery remains to provide physical evidence of a vanished community.

34. Markham Heritage Estates is a unique community of restored, relocated heritage houses that would have otherwise been lost to demolition. Established by the Town of Markham in the mid-1980s, Markham Heritage Estates is a showcase of restoration and historic vernacular architecture.

35. Grace Harrington fortunately recalled Ed Dixon's taxidermist studio, filling in some details of a story of Unionville that is otherwise not well documented.

36. Lionel Dawson, *Hands Across the Waters: The Life and Times of Our Dawson Family* (Markham: Lionel Dawson, 2008), 156.

37. *Markham Remembered*, 136.

38. Reminiscences of Grace Harrington.

39. Reminiscences of Grace Harrington.

40. Fire insurance maps, which show the outline of buildings, their building materials, and their number of storeys, were updated from time to

41. *Markham Remembered*, 138.

42. Many of the buildings within Unionville's commercial section were historically constructed as houses, and in recent years they have been converted to commercial uses. In most cases their original residential character has been maintained.

43. *Markham 1793–1900*, 303.

44. Ibid., 303; *Markham Remembered*, 138.

45. Mrs. Claude Russell-Brown, "Unionville, 1961," *Canadian-German Folklore, Pioneer Hamlets of York*, Volume 6, 1977, Pennsylvania German Folklore Society of Ontario, 51.

46. The history of the Maynard family in Canada is recorded in detail in this well-researched genealogical record: Judith Irene Leckie, ed., *A Genealogical Record of the Descendants of William Sr. Maynard and Salome Sarah Harbour* (Fenelon Falls: Privately published, 2005).

47. The former Don Valley Brickworks is now the Evergreen Brickworks, an innovative community facility that has transformed this former industrial site into a showcase of sustainable living. The historic structures have been repurposed to serve a variety of uses. The brick smokestack remains as a prominent landmark, visible daily to thousands of commuters travelling the Don Valley Parkway.

48. *Markham Remembered*, 138.

49. *A Genealogical Record of the Descendants of William Sr. Maynard and Salome Sarah Harbour*, 2.

50. *A Genealogical Record of the Descendants of William Sr. Maynard and Salome Sarah Harbour*, 2.

51. The Reverend Petersen was the first full-time pastor to serve St. Philip's Lutheran Church. When the Berczy settlers first came to Upper Canada, they were accompanied by Reverend George Sigmund Liebrich, who unfortunately died only a year or two after arriving in Markham Township. Lorne R. Smith, "A History of Bethesda Lutheran Church," *Canadian-German Folklore, More Pioneer Hamlets of York*, Volume 9, 1985, Pennsylvania German Folklore Society of Ontario, 180, 181.

52. The fascinating story of Reverend V.P. Mayerhoffer and how he came to minister to the Lutherans of Unionville is told in *Markham 1793–1900*, 136–38.

53. Without a doubt the most dramatic period of Unionville's history took place at the time of the Upper Canada Rebellion of 1837. St. Philip's Lutheran Church was a focus for the local manifestation of the conflicting political positions between the people of Unionville and vicinity. See *Markham 1793–1900*, 136, 138, 192.

54. *Markham 1793–1900*, 136.

55. A photograph of the 1862 church is found in *Markham 1793–1900*, 135. The architecture of this church building is Victorian in character, typical of its period of construction. The rebuilt church at 20 Union Street, although said to incorporate materials from the earlier church, is designed in what would have been an up-to-date version of the Gothic Revival style in 1910.

56. "He [Francis Stiver] is proud of being the owner of the first horseless carriage in Markham Township (a Tudhope)." *Stiver Family in Canada, 1794–1994*, 29.

57. *Markham 1793–1900*, 310.

58. *Markham Remembered*, 138.
59. Years of renovations concealed the architectural details of the building until a fire in 2007 resulted in the gutting of the damaged building, bringing to light the original siding, interior finish, and some surviving old windows for the first time in decades. The underlying structure indicated an early twentieth-century date of construction for the building.
60. *Markham Remembered*, 140.
61. Ibid.
62. *Hands Across the Waters: The Life and Times of Our Dawson Family*, 154, 155.
63. The fire-damaged building was largely demolished during its post-fire reconstruction. Only the facade remains from the pre-fire state of the structure.
64. "St. Philip's Unionville to Celebrate 100th Birthday," *The Evening Telegram*, October 12, 1929. See also *Markham 1793–1900*, 136, 138.
65. *Markham 1793–1900*, 138.
66. As in the case of Bethesda Lutheran Church, the dismantled and rebuilt St. Philip's Anglican Church was designed in the current mode of 1913, markedly different from the early Gothic Revival style of the building of 1839.
67. It is fortunate that the history of John Snowball and his brickworks was recorded in detail in his biographical notice in *History of Toronto and York County, Ontario*, Volume II, Biographical Notices (Toronto: C. Blackett Robinson, 1885), 308.
68. Published histories of Markham Township say that the Snowball brickworks was established circa 1860 on Lot 9, Concession 7, which is today the western part of Milne Park on McCowan Road. According to census records and township directories, John Snowball relocated from Buttonville to the area between Unionville and Markham Village between 1851 and 1861. If William Eckardt's house at 124 Main Street, built circa 1856, was one of the first in the area to have been constructed of Snowball brick, this would indicate that John Snowball made the move to the east in the mid-1850s.
69. By 1860 John Snowball expanded his business when he began to specialize in the manufacture of tile, using machinery imported from England. *History of Toronto and York County, Ontario*, 308.
70. The Snowball brickworks operated until 1923. *Markham Remembered*, 260.
71. The American Foursquare was more of a house form than an architectural style. In Robert Mikel, *Ontario House Styles* (Toronto: James Lorimer and Company Limited, 2004), 115, 116, the foursquare is described as an "Ontario standard."
72. *Markham Remembered*, 136.
73. Ibid., 136.
74. Ibid., 141. The village lamplighter's job was to keep the lamps filled with fuel, maintain the wicks, and manually light them at dusk.
75. Historically, the route of Highway 7, a short distance to the east of the Powers property, detoured to the south to avoid a part of the Rouge River valley, a low, wet area. Today, modern road engineering has effectively dealt with this topographical interruption of the surveyed road allowance, but a local street aptly named "Deviation Road" is a remnant of the former detour.

76. *Markham Remembered*, 142.

77. *Hands Across the Waters: The Life and Times of Our Dawson Family*, 159.

78. *Markham Remembered*, 142. Additional information on the history of Unionville's Old Fire Hall was provided to the author by Markham Fire Chief Bill Snowball, January 2015.

79. *Markham Remembered*, 138, and *A Genealogical Record of the Descendants of William Sr. Maynard and Salome Sarah Harbour*, 2.

80. *Markham Remembered*, 138.

81. *Walking Tours of Unionville*, 55.

82. Kit houses, or precut houses, were a type of prefabricated housing popular in the United States and Canada during the first half of the twentieth century. The T. Eaton Company Limited of Toronto and the Canadian Aladdin Company Limited were the principal kit house suppliers in Canada. More research is required to determine if the Maynard houses were constructed from precut kits.

83. *Walking Tours of Unionville*, 55.

84. *Markham 1793–1900*, 183.

85. The story of the earliest school in Unionville being near Bethesda Lutheran Cemetery is found in *Markham, 1793–1900*, 173. In Lorne R. Smith's "A History of Bethesda Lutheran Church," 180, the writer notes that "The Reverend S. Liebrich was pastor, teacher and doctor for his flock." This suggests that the Reverend Liebrich may have taught school to the children of the Berczy settlers in the mid-1790s, before his untimely death in a building accident.

86. "Unionville, 1961," 50.

87. *Markham 1793–1900*, 170, 171.

88. "Unionville, 1961," 50.

89. *Markham 1793–1900*, 173.

90. Ibid., 173.

91. The history of the Unionville Planing Mill, one of the best-documented and longest-lasting businesses in Markham, is contained in *Markham 1793–1900*, 126–28.

92. The tremendous impact the arrival of the Toronto and Nipissing Railway had on Unionville's development and the building boom of the 1870s are described in *Markham 1793–1900*, 306–08.

93. "Planing Mills," *Markham Economist*, February 5, 1874.

94. William Eakin's "second life" as a pioneer in the Canadian West is described in two newspaper clippings, "William Eakin Dies at Saltcoats, Sask., Old Resident of Markham Who Became Speaker of the Northwest Assembly," *Markham Economist & Sun*, April 4, 1918, and "Prosperous Township of Markham Birthplace of Warden William Eakin," source not noted on clipping. The second clipping, in the collection of the Markham Museum, is most likely from a newspaper in western Canada and probably dates from around the time of William Eakin's death.

95. The most detailed description of the Unionville Planing Mill, its machinery and its products, is found in Lionel Dawson's account of his apprenticeship there from 1947 to 1951, described in *Hands Across the Waters: The Life and Times of Our Dawson Family*, 192, 193. Mr. Dawson worked for Art Harrington, the grandson of Robert Harrington, who purchased the Planing Mill

from William Eakin in 1881. His account reveals that the planing mill was in many ways a nineteenth-century industry that somehow continued, little changed, into the modern era.

96. The later history of the Unionville Planing Mill is outlined in two sources: *Markham 1793–1900*, 126, 128; and *Markham Remembered*, 156, 238. In the second source there are photographs of the planing mill before and after the first fire.

97. A former house at 209 Main Street, now converted to commercial use, is commonly confused with Ira White's old residence, which stood on the site of the Varley Gallery. The house at 209 Main Street was the home of the Parkinson family, while the Parkinson automotive repair shop was in Ira White's former home, altered to serve as a garage.

98. In a brief description of the village of Unionville in Mitchell & Co.'s directory of 1866, Frederick Eckardt is correctly credited with laying out the village.

99. *Markham 1793–1900*, 303.

100. Ibid., 81.

101. *Markham Remembered*, 162, 163.

102. "Kathy and Her Dream," a brief history of the Varley Art Gallery, Town of Markham, 1997.

103. The story of Kathleen Gormley McKay and the origins of the Varley Art Gallery are largely drawn from Town of Markham publications "Kathy and Her Dream," and a brochure titled "The Frederick Horsman Varley Art Gallery of Markham," 1996.

104. "Unionville, 1961," 54.

105. Today Varley's former studio is not readily apparent to visitors to the McKay Art Centre, as it is simply a corner of the original basement kitchen of the Salem Eckardt House at 197 Main Street and is not set up to look like the artist's studio as depicted in an archival photograph. This space is programmed for art classes and provides studio space for new generations of aspiring artists.

A Word about Heritage Conservation

1. Henry David Thoreau, *Walden; or, Life in the Woods* (Boston: Ticknor and Fields, 1854), 13.

Bibliography and Recommended Reading

Biographical Dictionary of Architects in Canada, 1800–1950. dictionaryofarchitectsincanada.org. s.v. "Hill, Robert G., Architect."

Bird, Michael and Terry Kobayashi. *A Splendid Harvest, Germanic Folk and Decorative Arts in Canada.* Toronto: Van Nostrand Reinhold Ltd., 1981.

Blumenson, John. *Ontario Architecture 1794 to the Present.* Toronto: Fitzhenry and Whiteside, 1990.

Bradstreet's Reports of the Dominion of Canada, September 1, 1871. New York: Bradstreet Press, 1871.

Brown, George. *Directory of Toronto City and Home District for the Year 1846–47.* Toronto: George Brown, 1847.

Carley, Rachel. *The Visual Dictionary of American Domestic Architecture.* New York: Henry Holt & Co., 1994.

Champion, Isabel, ed. *Markham 1793–1900.* 2nd ed. Revised. Markham: Markham Historical Society, 1989.

Champion, Mary B., ed. *Markham Remembered — A Photographic History of Old Markham Township.* Markham: Markham Historical Society, 1988.

Clarke, Rod. *Narrow Gauge Through the Bush, Ontario's Toronto, Grey & Bruce and Toronto & Nipissing Railways.* Whitby: Rod Clarke and Ralph Beaumont, Publishers, 2007.

Cochrane, William. *The Canadian Album: Men of Canada or Success By Example in Religion, Patriotism, Business, Law, Medicine, Education and Agriculture.* Brantford: Bradley, Garretson & Co., 1893.

Commemorative Biographical Record of the County of York, Ontario. Toronto: J.H. Beers & Co., 1907.

Cooper, Charles. *Narrow Gauge for Us: The Story of the Toronto and Nipissing Railway.* Erin: Boston Mills Press, 1982.

Currell, Harvey. "Town and Country Trips — A Living Pioneer Village." *The Toronto Telegram,* April 11, 1970.

Dawson, Lionel. *Hands Across the Waters: The Life and Times of Our Dawson Family.* Markham: Lionel Dawson, publisher, 2008.

"Death of a Centenarian – Mrs. Hunter, of Markham, Called to Her Rest at the Age of 100 Years — A Pioneer's Life's Work Concluded." *Uxbridge Journal,* August 25, 1881.

Eckardt, A.J.H. "The Eckardt Pioneers of the Township of Markham, as Told By A.J.H. Eckardt in the Year 1932." *The Visitor — An Independent Paper Devoted to the Interests of Unionville and District.* Unionville: Excelsior Press, July 21, 1938.

"Fate of Historic House Proves Markham Poser." *Globe and Mail,* May 21, 1953.

Fisher & Taylor's County of York Townships Directory 1876. Toronto: Fisher & Taylor, Publishers, 1876.

FitzGerald, Doris M. *Thornhill 1793–1963.* Thornhill: Privately published, 1964.

The Frederick Horsman Varley Art Gallery of Markham. Markham: Town of Markham, 1996.

Historical Sketch of Markham Township 1793–1950, Centennial Celebration of Municipal Government 1850–1950. Markham: Historical Committee, 1950.

History of Toronto and County of York, Ontario. Vol. II. Biographical Notices. Toronto: C. Blackett Robinson, publisher, 1885.

Humphreys, Barbara A. and Meredith Sykes. *The Buildings of Canada, A Guide to Pre-20th Century Styles in Houses, Churches and Other Structures.* Montreal: The Reader's Digest Association (Canada) Limited, 1980.

Illustrated Historical Atlas of the County of York. Toronto: Miles and Co., 1878.

"Kathy and Her Dream." Markham: Town of Markham, 1997.

Leckie, Judith Irene, Viola Annie Margaret Durant, Alma May Walker. *A Genealogical Record of the Descendents of William Sr. Maynard and Salome Sarah Harbour.* Fenelon Falls: Judith I. Leckie, 2005.

MacRae, Marion and Anthony Adamson. *The Ancestral Roof — Domestic Architecture of Upper Canada.* Toronto: Clarke, Irwin and Company Limited, 1963.

McIlwraith, Thomas F. *Looking for Old Ontario, Two Centuries of Landscape Change.* Toronto: University of Toronto Press, 1997.

McKelvey, Marilyn. "Unionville Vets' Hall." *Markham Economist and Sun,* March 2, 1978.

Mikel, Robert. *Ontario House Styles: The Distinctive Architecture of the Province's 18th and 19th Century Homes.* Toronto: James Lorimer & Company Limited, 2004.

Mitchell & Co.'s General Directory for the City of Toronto and Gazetteer of the Counties of York and Peel for 1866. Toronto: Mitchell & Co. Publishers, 1866.

Nason, James Randle. *Nason's East and West Ridings of the County of York or Townships of Etobicoke, Markham, Scarboro', Vaughan and York Directory.* Toronto: Compiled and Published by James Randle Nason, Dudley & Burns Printers, 1871.

"New Brick Yard." *Markham Economist,* July 26, 1875.

"Planing Mills." *Markham Economist,* February 5, 1874.

Pollock, Michael. "The Unionville Festival — Trying to Preserve a Town." *Toronto Week,* n.d.

Quinquennial Catalogue of the Officers and Graduates of Harvard University 1630–1890. Cambridge: Harvard University, 1890.

The Reesor Family in Canada — A Trail through the Centuries: Genealogical and Historical Records 1804–1980. Markham: Privately published, 1980.

Rempel, John I. *Building with Wood and Other Aspects of Nineteenth-Century Building in Central Canada.* Revised edition. Toronto: University of Toronto Press, 1980.

Rowsell, Henry. *Rowsell's Directory of Toronto and County of York for Year 1850–51.* Toronto: Henry Rowsell, 1851.

Russell-Brown, Mrs. Claude. "Unionville 1961." *Canadian-German Folklore — Pioneer Hamlets of York.* Volume 6, 1977. York Chapter, Pennsylvania German Folklore Society of Ontario.

St. Philip's Anglican Church Unionville 1829–1879, 150th Anniversary Celebration, 1979. Unionville: St. Philip's Anglican Church, 1979.

Scherck, Michael Gonder. *Pen Pictures of Early Pioneer Life in Upper Canada.* Toronto: William Briggs, 1905.

Smith, Lorne R. "A History of Bethesda Lutheran Church." *Canadian German Folklore — More Pioneer Hamlets of York.* Volume 9, 1980. York Chapter, Pennsylvania German Folklore Society.

———. *A Story of the Markham Berczy Settlers — 200 Years in Markham 1794–1994.* Markham: Markham Berczy Settlers Association, 1994.

———. *Historic Cemeteries of Markham.* Markham: Town of Markham, 2004.

Stiver, Russell M., ed. *The Stiver Family in Canada 1794–1994.* Markham: Privately published in association with the Berczy Settlers' Centennial Celebration, 1994.

"Toronto and Nipissing Railway Company." *Markham Economist,* November 24, 1870.

Truth. "To Stephen English, Esq., Editor Insurance Times, New York City." *The Insurance Times.* Vol. 15 (December 1882).

"Unionville." *The Canadian Congregational Yearbook,* 1880–81 and 1883–84.

"Unionville." *The Canadian Independent,* February 13, 1879, February 19, 1880, January 27, 1881, February 24, 1881, April 7, 1881.

"Unionville Anglican Church Marks Centenary on Sunday." *The Toronto Evening Telegram,* October 18, 1927.

"Unionville Boy, Now U.S.A. Millionaire, Makes a Fine Gift — Descendent of York County Pioneers Donor of Skating Rink and Athletic Grounds in Memory of Parents." *The Toronto Evening Telegram,* November 2, 1927.

"Unionville Carriage Factory." Advertisement in the *York Herald,* July 19, 1861.

Unionville Heritage Conservation District Plan. Appendix A, Study Area: Building Inventory. Markham: Town of Markham Planning and Urban Design Department, Heritage Section, 1997.

University of Toronto Calendar 1891–1892. Appendix: Graduates in Medicine. Toronto: University of Toronto, 1892.

"The Veterans' Hall." *The Unionville Villager,* March 2008.

Walking Tours of Unionville. Unionville: Unionville Historical Society, 1988.

Walton, George. *Commercial Directory and Register for the City of Toronto and the Home District for the Year 1837.* Toronto: George Walton, 1837.

"William Eakin Dies at Saltcoats, Sask., Old Resident of Markham Who Became Speaker of Northwest Assembly." *Markham Economist and Sun,* April 4, 1918.

Primary Source Material and Other Unpublished Sources

Abstract Index of Deeds, focusing on Lots 10 through 17, Concession 5, and Lots 10 through 17, Concession 6, Markham Township. Ontario Land Registry Office, Aurora.

Assessment and Collector's Rolls for Markham Township, beginning with the earliest available Assessment Roll volume, 1852. Markham Museum Archival Collection.

Census of Canada. Canada West 1851, 1861; Ontario 1871, 1881, 1891, 1901, and 1911. Library and Archives Canada.

Chant, Dr. C.A. "Seventy Years Ago: The Quiet Life." Markham Museum Archival Collection, circa 1950.

Eckardt, Albert John Harrington. Typescript of a family history placed in the cornerstone of Bethesda Lutheran Church, 20 Union Street, Unionville, in 1910. A J.H. Eckardt was a son of William Eckardt and his second wife, Sarah Harrington. He stated in his history that the events he recounted were directly told to him by his great-uncles. Also included with the typescript were a list of local businesses in 1910 and letterhead or blank invoices from many of those businesses.

Harrington, Grace. Typescript of personal reminiscences of Unionville in the early 1900s, as recalled by Miss Grace Harrington, at eighty-five years old, May 4, 1982. Markham Museum Archival Collection.

Harrington, Jennie. "Memories of My Mother, Mrs. Jennie Harrington, January 5, 1877 of Hagerman's Corners and Unionville." Typescript by Grace Harrington, 15 Hubbard Blvd., Toronto, November 20, 1966. Markham Museum Archival Collection.

Latimer, Wilbur. Notes on the history of numerous properties in Unionville dated September 8, 1982.

McPhillips, George. Map of Markham Township, 1853–54.

Stephenson, Aubrey. Notes on the history of numerous properties in Unionville dated August 31, 1982.

Stiver, Bob. "Historic Stiver Mill." A two page history to assist in community efforts to restore the Stiver Mill, 2010.

Tremaine, George. *Map of York County, 1860.*

Tweedsmuir History of Unionville. Unionville Women's Institute, bound volumes from 1914 an 1957. Much of the historical information on old Unionville and its people that appears in secondary sources appears to have been gleaned from these volumes.

Index

Of Related Interest

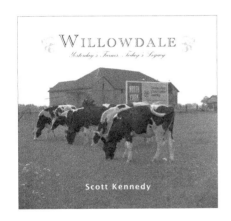

Willowdale
Yesterday's Farms, Today's Legacy
Scott Kennedy

In 1855, Willowdale's post office opened in Jacob Cummer's store on Yonge Street. Today, streets in Toronto's community of Willowdale are peppered with the names of the early farm families of North York, such as the Shepards, Finches, and Kennedys.

Author Scott Kennedy's intriguing stories embrace the evolution of Willowdale from the earliest acquisition of land to today's urban environment. You will read about combat training for the ill-fated Rebellion of 1837 that took place in the community fields; about Mazo de la Roche's estate, Windrush Hills, which stood at Bayview and Steeles, and is a Zorastrian temple today; about the Kingsdale Jersey Farm, which was located on Bayview until 1972; and about Green Meadows, the estate of "Bud" McDougald, which was the last operating farm in North York.

Available at your favourite bookseller

VISIT US AT

Dundurn.com
@dundurnpress
Facebook.com/dundurnpress
Pinterest.com/dundurnpress